Innovative Theory and Empirical Research on Employee Turnover

A volume in
Research in Human Resource Management
Series Editor: Rodger Griffeth, *Department of Management,*
University of New Orleans

Innovative Theory and Empirical Research on Employee Turnover

Edited by

Rodger Griffeth
Department of Management
University of New Orleans

and

Peter Hom
Department of Management
Arizona State University

INFORMATION AGE
PUBLISHING

80 Mason Street • Greenwich, Connecticut 06830 • www.infoagepub.com

Library of Congress Cataloging-in-Publication Data

Innovative theory and empirical research on employee turnover / edited
by Rodger Griffeth and Peter Hom.
    p. cm. – (Research in human resource management)
Includes bibliographical references.
  ISBN 1-59311-096-0 (pbk.) – ISBN 1-59311-097-9 (hardcover)
  1. Labor turnover. 2. Labor turnover–Research. I. Griffeth, Rodger
W., 1946- II. Hom, Peter W., 1951- III. Series.
  HD5717.I56 2004
  331.12'6'01–dc22

                                                    2003024770

Printed in the United States of America

LIST OF CONTRIBUTORS

David D. Allen — Fogelman College of Business and Economics, University of Memphis

James P. Burton — School of Business, University of Washington

Stefan Gaertner — Consultant, Mercer Human Resource Consulting

Rodger Griffeth — Department of Management, University of New Orleans

Reldar Hagtvedt — Terry College of Business, University of Georgia

Roderick D. Iverson — Faculty of Business Administration, Simon Fraser University

Gregory Todd Jones — College of Law, Georgia State University

Meni Koslowsky — Bar-Ilan University

Thomas W. Lee — School of Business, University of Wasington

Carl P. Maertz, Jr. — Department of Management and Information Science, Mississippi State University

Meyrav Merom — Bar-Ilan University

Terence R. Mitchell — School of Business, University of Washington

Charles W. Mueller — Department of Sociology, University of Iowa

James L. Price — Department of Sociology, University of Iowa

Loriann Roberson — Arizona State University

Chris J. Sablynski — School of Business, University of Washington

Robert P. Steel — School of Management, University of Michigan–Dearborn

Mindy S. West — San Diego State University

Xin Yao — School of Business, University of Washington

CONTENTS

part III
Innovative New Ways of Thinking About Turnover

part IV
Generalizing Turnover Theory and Research to Neglected Populations

FOREWORD

This book includes contributions from a variety of different perspectives on employee turnover. We categorize these myriad papers in terms of history, scope, theory development, and population generalization. Part I thus begins with an article by James Price, a pioneering thinker in the turnover field. Initiating the most systematic turnover research ever undertaken, Dr. Price describes his persistent quest to develop and refine a comprehensive theory of turnover. His 30-year intellectual journey offers valuable insight into theoretical and methodological challenges that continue to confront all turnover researchers.

Chapters in Part II identify explanatory constructs and processes neglected by current turnover frameworks. The first two chapters consider individual differences overlooked by conventional perspectives. Specifically, Dr. David Allen's paper focuses on moderators, such as risk propensity, self-monitoring, and locus of control, which may moderate relationships between quit intentions and turnover. His theoretical analysis explains why some people who form withdrawal cognitions do not actually quit. By comparison, Iverson, Mueller and Price elucidate how the familiar cosmopolitan-local construct affects resignations among professionals. Despite popular beliefs about conflicting dual allegiances to firm and profession, research studies have not conclusively shown that people who are strongly attached to a profession necessarily develop weaker job loyalty. Rather than a single dimension, they reconceptualize this construct into two dimensions defined by professional and organizational commitment and identify four distinct commitment profiles when dichotomizing these commitment forms. Their survival analysis demonstrated that school teach-

Innovative Theory and Empirical Research on Employee Turnover, pages ix–xi
Copyright © 2004 by Information Age Publishing
All rights of reproduction in any form reserved.

ers who are cosmopolitans (high professional commitment but weak company commitment) are more prone to quit than locals (weak professional commitment but high organizational commitment) or cosmopolitan/locals (dual attachments to both profession and employer). These intriguing findings suggest that organizations should not presume that professionals who bond with their occupation are necessarily disloyal but can commit to firms given appropriate inducements from firms.

The final two papers in Part II consider still other neglected constructs and processes. Going beyond past tests, Meni Koslowsky and Meyrav Merom more comprehensively examine various types of stress: critical life events (rare but powerful events that have major impact on individuals, such as a divorce); hassles (benign events that occur at specific times, such as waiting on a link in a bank); and chronic stressors (continuous taxing demands, such as caring for aging parents or working excessive hours). Surveying Israeli nurses, they found that all stress forms can materially affect the termination process. Their findings imply that turnover researchers must expand their narrow conceptualizations (which emphasize work role stress, including the burnout syndrome) to include stressful events that happen outside the workplace.

Complimenting this empirical piece, Robert Steel's theoretical essay criticizes dominant conceptualizations of the "labor market" as too broad and simplistic. Instead, Dr. Steel contends that prospective leavers actually attend to *relevant* segments of the job market that offers them the greatest chances of replacement employment. For nurses, the occupational market is more germane than local or regional employment conditions. By contrast, fast food restaurant workers would focus on the labor market in their community, ignoring occupational or national labor markets. Besides more precise job-market operationalizations, Dr. Steel suggests replacing traditional depictions of the job search as a passive collection of job market data with descriptions reflecting a more interactive process between job seekers and the marketplace.

Part III comprises comprehensive theory-building efforts. First, Carl Maertz introduces a theory that elegantly summarizes the "proximal" motives of turnover into seven categories, such as affective forces (such as job satisfaction and company commitment), behavioral forces (representing the costs of quitting), and normative forces (expectations of family and friends to stay or leave). Using this parsimonious framework, he then specifies how five sets of relatively unexplored antecedents–namely, the Big Five personality traits, culture (company and national), corporate performance, occupational attachments, and location attachments–impact turnover. Thus, his framework offers persuasive logic that will stimulate future inquiry into the role these new determinants play in the withdrawal process.

Next, Xin Yao, Thomas Lee, Terence Mitchell, James Burton, and Chris Sablynski propose their new model of job embeddedness, which summarizes an array of forces that keep incumbents from severing their employment ties. Their theory captures nonwork and nonattitudinal determinants that are neglected or underappreciated by current conceptual formulations. Their paper specifies the various components of this construct and differentiates them from existing turnover causes. Moreover, Xin and colleagues describe preliminary investigations into the psychometric soundness of their measurement operations and concurrent and predictive validity of this new construct. Lastly, they suggest future research avenues for investigating job embeddedness.

Finally, Reidar Haftvedt, Gregory Jones, Stefan Gaertner, and Rodger Griffeth introduce a radically different perspective on turnover. Because traditional, linear models explain less than 20% of the turnover variance, they prescribe chaos theory as a superior theoretical alternative. Chaos theory is especially suitable for the turnover phenomenon as nonlinear effects and feedback loops are posited by several turnover theories. Reidar and his colleagues also suggest methods for validating a chaos description of the resignation process.

Part IV includes contributions that generalize turnover theory and work to underrepresented populations. On the basis of her review of available research on racial differences in quit rates, Loriann Roberson disputes widespread claims that racial minorities exit firms at higher rates than do majority employees. To clarify conflicting findings on racial differences, she introduces a theoretical framework that posits five potential moderators of race-turnover linkages: job level; work group demographic composition; tenure and career stage; ethnicity and racial identity attitudes; and organizational climate for diversity. Roberson's creative thinking may inspire more rigorous research on this topic and correct prevailing stereotypes of job-hopping minority employees that the business press fosters.

The final chapter by Mindy West extends turnover perspectives cross-culturally to Mexico. As she points out, domestic findings undergird most turnover theories, casting doubt on their validity for different cultures. To better explain turnover in a different culture, Dr. West designs a special model to explain turnover among Mexican workers in maquiladora factories. Based on a review of cross-cultural management research and descriptive studies of maquiladora turnover, she selectively draws relevant constructs (including reconceptualizes them) from prevailing (US) turnover models to develop her framework. Beyond this, her own qualitative studies furnish additional justification for the explanatory constructs in this country-specific theory of turnover. Given that the workforces of many corporations are becoming globalized, interest in understanding and controlling turnover in different cultural milieus will surely increase. Future investigators may follow Mindy West's lead for how to tailor and adapt general (domestic) models to optimally explain organizational withdrawal in different countries or cultures.

part I

THE EVOLUTION OF A PIONEERING TURNOVER THEORY

CHAPTER 1

THE DEVELOPMENT
OF A CAUSAL MODEL
OF VOLUNTARY TURNOVER

James L. Price

ABSTRACT

This chapter's focus is on strategies for the construction of causal models. The paper has two parts. First, a description is offered of research conduct by Price/Mueller and their colleagues at the University of Iowa regarding the development of a causal model of voluntary turnover. Five research projects are described. Second, Price and Mueller's research is then used as basis for discussion of strategies for the construction of causal models. It is suggested that more papers regarding strategies should be written.

INTRODUCTION

The purpose of this paper is to describe the development of a causal model of voluntary turnover. Voluntary and involuntary turnover are usually distinguished. Employees who leave an organization at their own discretion are examples of voluntary turnover (Price, 1977). "Quits" is a common des-

Innovative Theory and Empirical Research on Employee Turnover, pages 3–32
Copyright © 2004 by Information Age Publishing

ignation for these employees. Dismissals, exits due to serious illness, and deaths are examples of involuntary turnover. Retirements may be either voluntary or involuntary turnover.

The model of turnover, whose development is described, is often referred to as the "Price-Mueller" model. This model is one of the three major explanations of turnover in the literature (Hom & Griffeth, 1995). The other two models are those proposed by Mowday and his colleagues (Mowday, Porter, & Steers, 1982) and Mobley (1982).[1]

The model's development will be described historically. Five phases of development will be indicated. After the development is described, reflections will be offered regarding the process. The focus of the reflections will be on strategies of causal model construction in the field of turnover research. Throughout the description "variables" and "determinants" will be used interchangeably.

PHASE 1: DEVELOPMENT OF A PRELIMINARY CAUSAL MODEL

In the Spring of 1972, Price and a small number of sociology graduate students at the University of Iowa reviewed literature which offered explanations of voluntary turnover. The purpose of this review was to develop a preliminary causal model of voluntary turnover. Models proposed by economists dominated the literature review (some examples are Burton & Parker, 1969; March & Simon, 1958; Pencavel, 1970; and Stoikov & Raimon, 1968). The work of psychologists, however, was also prominent (Farris, 1971 and Lyons, 1968 are illustrations).

The question arises as to why a preliminary model was sought. It would have been possible, for instance, to have estimated one of the economic models. However, based on his acquaintance with the turnover literature, Price was of the opinion that the economic models, which dominated the literature, focused on too narrow a range of determinants to explain turnover adequately. The monetary variables emphasized by the economists, for instance, seemed to be important, but needed to be supplemented by non-monetary determinants. Economic explanations also ignored the process whereby turnover was generated. The economists, for example, suggested the amount of monetary income as a determinant: the more money received, the less the likelihood of turnover. However, they did not indicate how monetary income impacted on turnover. Increased money received may, for instance, decrease turnover by increasing the employees' job satisfaction. It seemed necessary, therefore, to attempt to develop a more inclusive model of turnover than those proposed by economists— thus the 1972 review.

The review resulted in a series of summaries and critiques of the literature. There was a summary and critique for each piece of literature reviewed. These summaries and critiques posed a vexing set of problems. Different terminologies were used to describe the various determinants; some of the proposed determinants were overlapping; a causal order was not proposed for the determinants; a beginning for the causal sequence was not specified; and some of the determinants were not empirically well supported. A sizeable amount of work thus remained to be done to develop a preliminary model. The summaries and critiques, by themselves, were clearly not sufficient.

During the 1972–1973 academic year, Price was on leave from the University of Iowa as a research professor at Bradford University in Bradford, England. During this time he transformed the summaries and critiques into a preliminary model. The model will now be described (Price, 1975). Figure 1.1 constitutes a diagram of the model.

The model had four exogenous variables: pay, primary group, communication, and centralization. Pay was monetary income and is the type of variable commonly emphasized by economists. Two moderation conditions were proposed for pay.[2] Pay will not be a significant determinant unless it is important to the employees and is perceived to be high. The use of "moderating conditions" illustrates the contingency approach to the study of organizations (Woodward, 1965). The second determinant was not assigned a label but was simply referred to as "participation in a primary group." Kinship-type systems are examples of primary groups whose organizational importance, though not under this label, was emphasized by the Western Electric Research (Roethlisberger & Dickson, 1939). The primary group label came from scholars at Columbia University (Merton, 1968). Communication was the transmission of information among the members of an organization and centralization was the distribution of power within an organization. Turnover from an organization, it was hypothesized, was likely to be low if pay, primary group participation, and communication

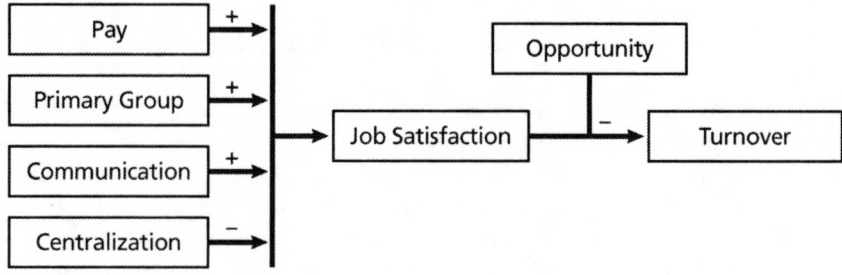

Figure 1.1.   Preliminary causal model of turnover.

were high. Pay, however, must be important to the employees and be perceived as high. High centralization was hypothesized to increase turnover.

The model had two intervening, or process, variables, job satisfaction and opportunity. Job satisfaction was defined as a positive affective orientation toward the organization and opportunity as the number of jobs in the environment. The two intervening variables, however, impacted on turnover quite differently. Job satisfaction was believed to mediate the impact of the exogenous variables, whereas opportunity was a moderating variable. If, for instance, the exogenous variables produce more dissatisfaction than satisfaction, and if there are jobs in the environment, then turnover is likely to occur. This, of course, assumes that pay is important and is perceived to be low. The model stressed the necessity of examining the balance of satisfactions and dissatisfactions. This balance was referred to as "costs and benefits." More dissatisfactions than satisfactions, for instance, means a situation that is costly to the employees. It is assumed that employees will attempt to leave a costly situation.[3] Opportunity was accompanied by two conditions. If there were many jobs in the environment, the employees must know about these jobs and be free to leave before turnover will occur.

Two of the six variables in the model—pay and opportunity—are those commonly proposed by economists. However, the economists do not accompany pay and opportunity with any conditions and they do not specify the intervening process between their determinants and turnover.

Five variables were excluded from the model because of insufficient evidence: role clarity, programmed coordination, inequity, industrial concentration, and size. Role clarity was precise definition of the work that was to be done, programmed coordination was central management of work, inequality was the lack of fairness in the distribution of rewards, industrial concentration was the extent to which the output of an industry was produced by a small number of organizations, and size was scale of operation.[4] Turnover decreases with more role clarity, greater industrial concentration, and more programmed coordination. Inequity, however, increases turnover. No proposition was advanced for size.

PHASE 2: PILOT STUDY

The next phase of the research was to estimate the preliminary model. Price decided to estimate the model with a sample of registered nurses employed in a voluntary, short-term, general hospital. Registered nurses were a good sample because their turnover rate was comparatively high in the Fall of 1973, often reaching 50% a year. Hospitals were a good site because Price could perform the research under the auspices of the College of Medicine, where he had a joint academic appointment. Voluntary, short-term, general hospitals were a good site because they were the most common type of hospital in the United States. Price obtained permission, in the Fall of 1973, to study the Department of Nursing in a hospital in Iowa City, the location of the University of Iowa.

A pilot study was necessary because Price knew very little about nurses or hospitals. It was decided that most of the data to estimate the model would be collected by a questionnaire. Before the questionnaire could be constructed, Price had to observe and interview in the Nursing Department for several months. He spent so much time observing and interviewing that he was designed by the Nursing Director as "an honorary nurse." The pilot study also provided the opportunity to develop a questionnaire. The plan was to use the questionnaire in a later, large-scale study of nurses.

There were continuities and changes in the pilot study from the preliminary model. Figure 1.2 provides a diagram of the model estimated (Price & Bluedorn, 1980).

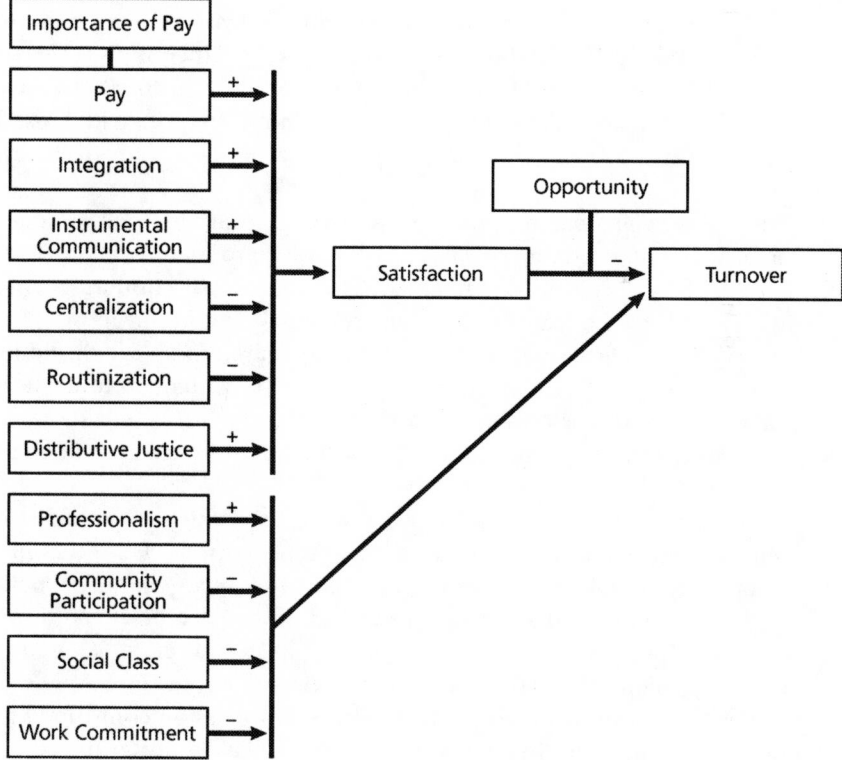

Figure 1.2.   Causal model of turnover for the pilot study.

Six variables from the preliminary model were included in the estimation: pay, primary group, communication, centralization, satisfaction, and opportunity. Pay was again defined as monetary income and its importance was again a condition. However, no mention was made about the perception of pay's level. Based on the work of Blau (1959–1960), primary group was termed "integration." This variable previously had no label. Communication was narrowed to the transmission of job-related information and was designated as "instrumental communication." Pay, integration, instrumental communication, and centralization continued as exogenous variables; satisfaction and opportunity were again viewed as intervening variables. Satisfaction and opportunity continued as mediating and moderating variables, respectively.

Routinization and distributive justice were added to the model as the result of another review of the literature conducted for a book on turnover (Price, 1977). Repetitive work was defined as routinization and distributive justice was conformity to organizational norms followed by positive sanctions. Distributive justice was previously excluded from this preliminary model developed in England due to insufficient data. "Inequity"—the earlier term—was not widely used as a label in the literature as distributive justice. The idea was to standardize labels as much as possible. Widely-used labels, it seemed, would result in greater standardization than narrowly-used labels.

Changes were also made in the pilot study regarding the four variables excluded from the preliminary model: role clarity, programmed coordination, industrial concentration, and size. The conceptual content of role clarity seemed to be captured by instrumental communication; programmed coordination's conceptual content appeared to be caught up by centralization; industrial concentration looked like a demographic variable, a term to be discussed shortly; and size still lacked sufficient supporting data. Role clarity and programmed coordination were thus included in the pilot study but under different labels.[5]

The nurses were professional employees, a fact which prompted an examination of the sociological literature about professions. This literature seemed to suggest that highly professionalized employees generally experienced greater turnover than less professionalized employees. It was more difficult, for instance, for the employer to meet the high standards required by highly professionalized employees. Professionalism was defined as the extent to which the members of a profession conformed to its norms. The nurses in the pilot study appeared likely to differ in professionalism, since their training was quite varied. Some nurses were university graduates (12%), a few were graduates of community colleges (10%), and most were trained in hospitals (78%).

During the pilot study it became apparent to Price that there were two distinct categories of nurses employed by the hospital. The first category consisted of nurses who had been born in the community, were members of a local Roman Catholic church, were trained in the nursing school run by the hospital, and were married to local men, when they were married. The hospital studied was affiliated with the Roman Catholic church and all the nurses were women. This first category of nurses might be termed "locals." The second category consisted of nurses whose husbands were obtaining education or training at the University of Iowa, were also usually born outside the community, less likely to be Roman Catholics, were not trained in the hospital's nursing school, and were not married to local men, when they were married. This second category of nurses might be termed "non-locals." The last three variables of the model—community participation, social class, and work commitment—were an attempt to capture conceptually the key variables which seemed to distinguish the local and non-local nurses.

Community participation was involvement in the life of the non-hospital environment, social class was the community's prestige structure, and work commitment was the extent to which work was the central life interest of the employee. Local nurses were expected to score higher than non-local nurses on community participation, social class, and work commitment. Work commitment was expected to be lower for the non-local nurses, since they had the reputation of quitting their jobs to go with their husbands when their spouses had completed their university education or training, thus indicating greater commitment to a kinship role (wife) than an occupational role (nurse).

Demographic variables, such as age and seniority, were distinguished and excluded from the model. "Correlates" was the label for the demographic variables in the reported research. Demographic variable was a more widely used label than correlates. The demographic variables were included in the analysis to check the explanatory power of the model (Price, 1995; Price & Kim, 1993).

As previously indicated, this site for the pilot study was a voluntary, short-term, general hospital. The hospital was of medium size (about 250 beds). No attempt was made to generalize the results of the research to government or specialty hospitals. Only non-supervisory, registered nurses were included in the sample. All administrative employees in the Nursing Department—managers and clerks—were excluded from the sample. The N for the nurses was 130. Systematic data to estimate the model were collected by a mailed questionnaire administered to the nurses by Price in February 1974 and returned to the University of Iowa. Turnover data were collected from the hospital in February 1975. The sample was divided into "leavers" and "stayers." Since none of the nurses left because of death, retirement, or dismissal, it was likely that most of the nurses voluntarily left the hospital. The sample consisted of 98 stayers and 32 leavers, a 75/25 split. Data were analyzed by regression and path analytic techniques.

The most important determinants, in terms of total effects, were the following: satisfaction (.30), professionalism (.26), integration (–.24), pay (–.29), distributive justice (–.23), and routinization (.15). Turnover was increased by professionalism and decreased by integration, pay, distributive justice, and routinization. All of these results were expected. It was not anticipated, however, that satisfaction would increase turnover. This unanticipated result may have been due to the local and non-local types of nurses in the sample. Many of the non-local nurses would ordinarily have been stayers. However, when their husbands finished their university training or education, the non-local nurses quit their jobs to go with their spouses to a new location. The adjusted explained variance, with the demographic variables included, was 33%.

As previously indicated, demographic variables were included in the analysis to check the explanatory power of the model. With a sophisticated model and psychometrically sound measures, the demographic variables should not be important. The conceptual content indicated by demographic variables should be captured by the theoretical variables of the model. However, two demographic variables—length of service (–.37) and age (–.24)—had substantial total effects. The effects for length of service (seniority) and age were in agreement with the literature. Time worked, whether full time or part time, had a relatively small total effect (–.12). The adjusted explained variance, without the demographic variables, was not specified but it was probably fairly high, to judge from the total effects of length of service and age. The size of the demographic variables in the pilot study did not auger well for the model's power.

PHASE 3: THE IOWA-ILLINOIS STUDY
OF NON-SUPERVISORY, REGISTERED NURSES

The plan was to expand the pilot study after it was completed. When the pilot study was finished, nursing turnover was still high and voluntary, short-term, general hospitals remained the dominant type of patient-care facility in the United States. Price continued to hold his joint appointment with the Medical College, so it was possible to perform another study with official health sponsorship. The completion of the pilot study also provided a track record which facilitated obtaining research grants from the Division of Nursing of the Bureau of Health Manpower and the American Nurses' Foundation. The assistance of Dr. Myrtle Aydelotte, who agreed to serve as the Principal Investigator for the Iowa-Illinois study, was the major factor in obtaining the research grants. Dr. Aydelotte had previously been Dean of the College of Nursing at the University of Iowa and Director of the Nursing Department of the University of Iowa Hospitals and Clinics. Before the research could begin, Dr. Aydelotte relinquished her involvement with the research to become Executive Director of the American Nurses' Association. Price then became the Principal Investigator of the project. Dr. Charles Mueller joined the research project. Dr. Mueller was in the Sociology Department at the University of Iowa and specialized in statistical analysis. Early in 1976, Price obtained permission to study non-supervisory registered nurses in seven hospitals located in Iowa and Illinois. Five of the hospitals were located in Iowa and two were in Illinois. The hospitals were all voluntary, short-term, general units.

There were continuities and changes in the new model to be estimated (Price & Mueller, 1981). Figure 1.3 contains a diagram of the model.

The following seven exogenous variables were the same in the pilot study and the Iowa-Illinois Study: routinization, centralization, instrumental communication, integration, pay, distributive justice, and professionalism. "Participation" was substituted for centralization to make the label consistent with the definition of centralization. Centralization was defined as the power exercised by an employee in his or her job—an individual focus—and the new label had an individual rather than an organizational reference. Art Brief, a faculty member in the College of Business at the University of Iowa, suggested the use of the participation label. Brief (1976) had conducted research on nursing turnover. The possibility that pay's importance may vary was discussed but not estimated. No mention was made of the perception of pay's magnitude.

There were four substantial changes in the Iowa-Illinois Study, compared to the pilot study. First, opportunity was changed from a moderating variable to an exogenous variable. This change was suggested by Allen Bluedorn (1976) as the result of his turnover research. Bluedorn had also worked with Price in the analysis of the data from the pilot study and had participated in the Spring 1972 review of turnover models. No mediating variables were suggested between opportunity and turnover. Second, promotional opportunity—the chance to advance in the organization—was added as an exogenous variable. The literature on "internal labor markets" suggested promotional opportunity as a determinant (Osterman, 1984). Satisfaction was hypothesized to mediate the relationship between promotional opportunity and turnover. Promotions bring increased pay, power, and prestige and this should result in more satisfaction. The third change in the exogenous variables was the addition of general training, that is, the ability of increase productivity in different organizations. General training comes from the human capital tradition of research in economics (Becker, 1964). The impact of general training on turnover was hypothesized to be

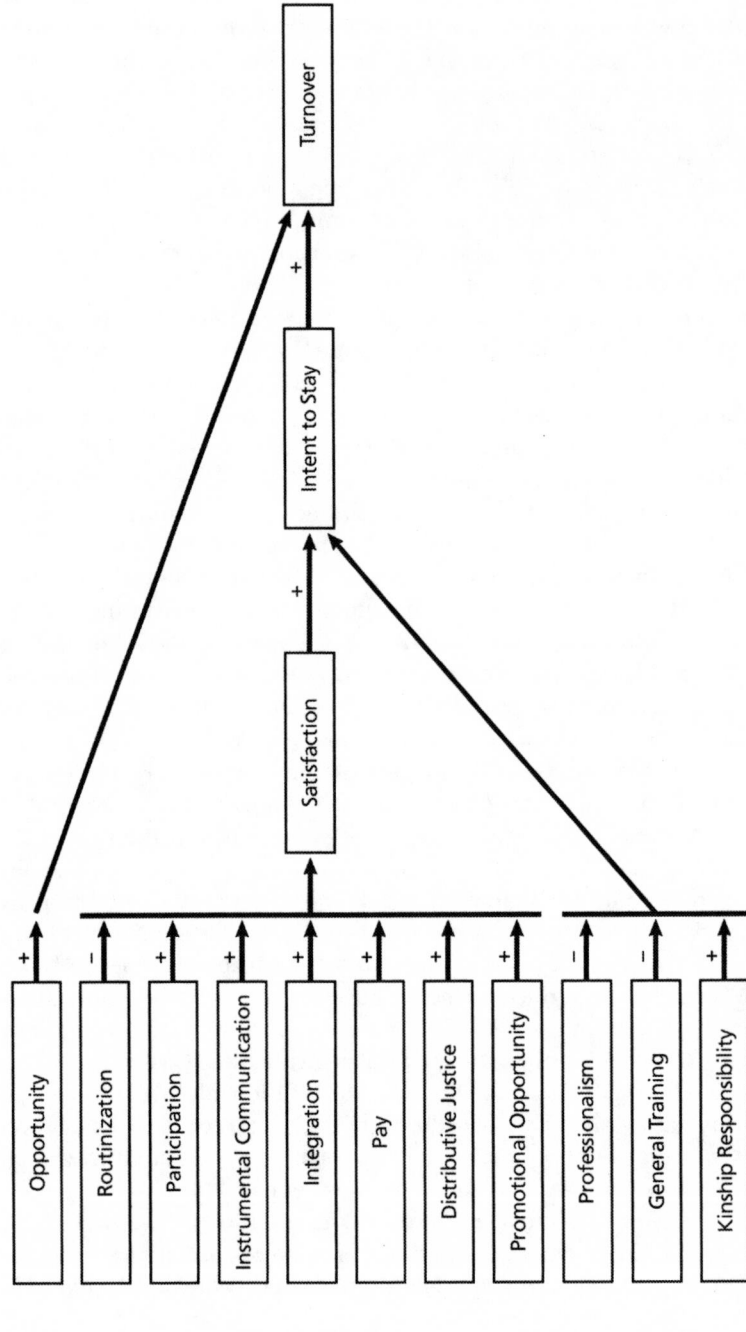

Figure 1.3. Causal model for Iowa-Illinois study of nonsupervisory, registered nurses.

through intent to stay, a concept to be discussed shortly. Kinship responsibility was the fourth new exogenous variable. The pilot study suggested that local and non-local nurses appeared to differ by community participation, social class, and work commitment. However, in the empirical data, none of these variables turned out to be a statistically significant determinant of turnover. Kinship responsibility was proposed as another variable to capture an apparent conceptual difference between the local and non-local nurses. Price's fieldwork had already indicated that the local and non-local nurses appeared to be quite different and he wanted conceptually to capture this difference. Kinship responsibility was defined as obligations to relatives living in the community. The local nurses, it was hypothesized, should have more kinship responsibility than the non-local nurses. Kinship variables were not commonly studied by the economists and psychologists who did most of the research on turnover. However, scholars interested in migration, who were often sociologists, stressed the importance of kinship variables in migration. Since migration is conceptually similar to turnover (both concepts involve movement out of social systems), kinship responsibility seemed to be an interesting determinant to explore. Kinship responsibility was hypothesized to impact on turnover through intent to stay. No specification was made as to how kinship responsibility would increase intent to stay.

Satisfaction continued as mediating variables. Intent to stay, however, was added as a variable that mediated the relationship between satisfaction and turnover. Intent to stay has an interesting history in the development of the model.

Graduate sociology students who planned to do their dissertations on turnover at the University of Iowa did not relish the idea of waiting for turnover to occur in the organizations they were studying. The practice was first to ask the employees to describe, by questionnaire, their work situations and then wait for the employees to quit. The content of these descriptions was indicated by the variables of the model estimated. The period of waiting was usually about a year. A speeding up of the process was needed by the students. Price discovered a major study of turnover of priests by Greeley (1972) who measured not turnover but intent to turnover. Greeley provided no data to support a link between intent and turnover. Intent to turnover became intent to stay in the Iowa-Illinois Study. Intent to stay was given scholarly legitimacy when Mobley (1982) used it as intervening variable in his model. Mobley hypothesized that intent was the variable immediately preceding turnover.

During the course of the Iowa-Illinois Study, Price became aware of substantial data supporting commitment as a possible determinant of turnover. Mowday and his colleagues (Mowday et al., 1982) proposed commitment as an intervening process and suggested that it was more important than satisfaction. Intent to stay seemed, to Price, to be a dimension of commitment and thus provided a means to link the Iowa-Illinois Study to the research conducted by Mowday and his colleagues. Mowday et al.'s research was part of the expectancy tradition which had its contemporary origins in the work of Vroom (1964).

As with the pilot study, demographic variables were excluded from the model. The demographic variables, termed "correlates" in the Iowa-Illinois Study, were used as controls in the analysis. Three demographic variables were used as controls: length of service, age, and amount of time worked (whether full time or part time).

The sample and site of the Iowa-Illinois Study were the same as the pilot study. As intended, however, the Iowa-Illinois Study was larger than the pilot study. Eleven hundred and one nurses returned questionnaires in the Iowa-Illinois Study; these nurses, as previously indicated, were distributed among seven hospitals. As before, most of the data were collected by questionnaires mailed to the homes of the nurses and returned to the University of Iowa.[6] Questionnaires were mailed to the nurses' homes in August 1976 and turnover data were collected from the hospitals in October 1977. Interviews with hospital personnel were used to eliminate from the sample all nurses who had left involuntarily. The final sample consisted of 880 stayers and 221 voluntary leavers, an 80–20 split. Factor analysis was used to construct the measures and to assess validity. Reliability was evaluated with coefficient alpha.[7] The resulting measures possessed adequate psychometric properties. As with the pilot study, analysis was conducted with regression and path analytic techniques.

The five most important determinants, in terms of total effects for the entire sample, were intent to stay (–.37), opportunity (.16), general training (.13), satisfaction (–.10), and kinship responsibility (–.07). Turnover was increased by opportunity and general training but decreased by intent to stay, satisfaction, and kinship responsibility. All of these results were consistent with the model. The results for satisfaction were especially encouraging, since its outcome had been inconsistent with the model in the pilot study. The adjusted explained variance for turnover, including the demographic variables, was 18%.[8]

Total effects were given for amount of time worked but not for age and length of service. The total effects for amount of time worked was not comparatively large (.01). The three demographic variables only added 1% to the adjusted explained variance, the type of result that augers well for the explanatory power of this model.

PHASE 4: THE DENVER STUDY OF HOSPITALS

Reflections suggested three features of the Iowa-Illinois Study that should be modified. First, too much time has elapsed—fourteen months— between the collection of data about the nurses' situation at time one and the collection of the turnover data. Since the data at time one were used to explain turnover, the situations of the nurses might have changed substantially by the time the turnover data were collected. There was a problem here, however. If the time elapsed was to be substantially shortened, a situation must be found with very high turnover if one was going to obtain an adequate split between the leavers and stayers. The Iowa-Illinois Study had an 80–20 split between the leavers and stayers and future research, it was thought, should not go much below this, to a 90–10 split, for instance. A 50–50 split is, of course, the preferred ratio. It took fourteen months to get the 80–20 split in the Iowa-Illinois Study.[9] Second, the focus on non-supervisory nurses was helpful in that occupation and supervisory position were controlled. Since these two variables commonly produce many differences in the employees, it was helpful that they were controlled. However, the focus on non-supervisory registered nurses probably created too homogenous a sample to detect variations in the determinants of turnover. Pay, for example, despite its massive support in the literature, was not a significant determinant in the Iowa-Illinois Study. The lack of significance for pay may have been due to the fact that there was little variance in pay in this sample. Third, since all the nurses in the Iowa-Illinois Study were female, this raised questions about kinship responsibility as a determinant. Females were the traditional providers of kinship services, so perhaps kinship responsibility was a determinant due to the female composition of the sample. More males were needed in the next study. Price and Mueller arranged to study five hospitals in the area of Denver, Colorado to make the changes which needed to be made.

Professor Sam Levey, Chair of the Graduate Program in Hospital and Health Administration at the University of Iowa, joined the Denver project. Professor Levey was especially interested in hospital administration and was a major reason why Federal funds were obtained from the National Center for Health Services Research. Professor Levey also provided a site for Price and Mueller to do their research at the Medical School.

The expectations for the Denver Study were not fully realized. A recession was experienced shortly after the Denver Study was begun in the Summer of 1980. What had been a booming economy in the Denver area was transformed into a recession and turnover rates were depressed throughout the region. More variance, however, was obtained in the determinants, since all employees in the hospitals were sampled and the sample became somewhat less dominated by females. The new sample, however, was still predominantly female, since 88% of the employees in the five Denver hospitals were female. A plus for the Denver study was that three of the hospitals were small (under 100 beds) and two were of medium size (between 100 and 500 beds), thereby making it easy to include size as a possible determinant. Size had previously been excluded because it supporting evidence was mixed.

Most of the variables and propositions used in the Denver Study (Price & Mueller, 1986) were the same as those used in the Iowa-Illinois Study: opportunity, routinization, centralization, instrumental communication, integration, pay, distributive justice, promotional opportunity, professionalism, general training, satisfaction, and intent to leave. "Participation" was changed to "centralization," integration became close friends in the immediate work unit rather than close friends somewhere in the hospital, and "intent to leave" replaced previous "intent to stay." Figure 1.4 is a diagram of the model used in the Denver Study.

Three changes were made in the model used in the Denver Study. First, role overload—excessive work demands—was added as an exogenous variable. Role overload was included because hospital personnel emphasized its importance during the field work Price conducted prior to the administration of the first questionnaire. There was also data in the literature supporting role overload, conceptualized as a dimension of job stress, as a determinant of turnover (House, 1981). Second, commitment was added as a variable that intervened between satisfaction and intent to leave. Following the work of Mowday and his colleagues (Mowday et al., 1982), commitment was viewed as employee loyalty to the organization. Increased commitment was hypothesized to decrease turnover. Third, as previously indicated, size was also added as an exogenous variable. Hospital and work unit size were examined, but no propositions were proposed.[10]

The number of checks for moderating variables were increased in the Denver Study.[11] Moderating checks were made for all the exogenous variables. It is possible, it was hypothesized, that the importance of all the exogenous variables could vary for the employees. The previous focus had only been on the importance of pay for the employees.

Like the Iowa-Illinois Study, the Denver Study used the demographic variables as controls and not as components of the model. Fifteen demographic variables are used as controls—the most ever.

All of the employees in the five hospitals were included in the sample. Physicians working in the hospitals were not considered employees. The sample consisted of 2,152 employees. One hundred and twenty-nine work units were also analyzed, because work unit results can differ from individual results. The five hospitals were all voluntary, short-term, general units. The Denver Study included two questionnaire administrations, in November 1980 and June 1981. Turnover data were collected by mail from each

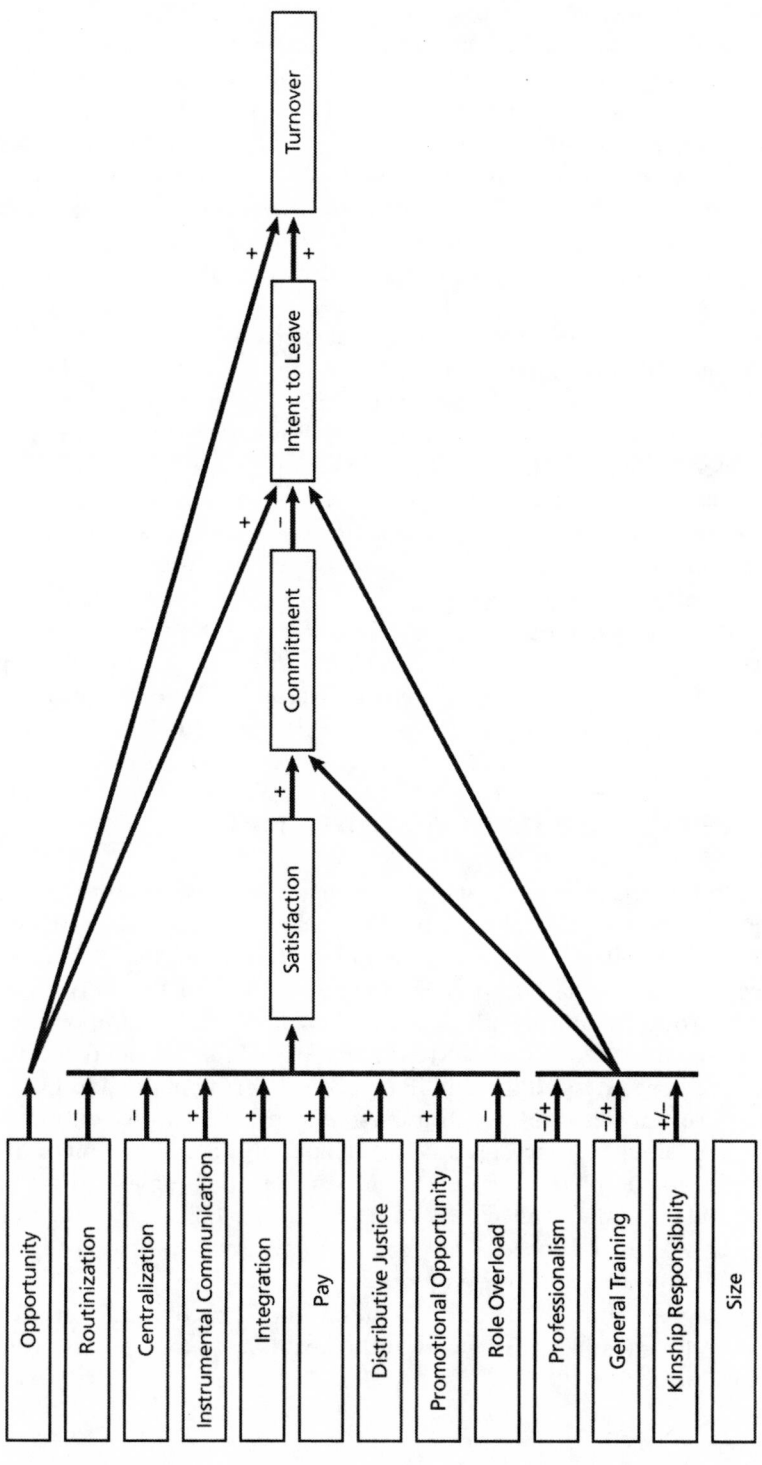

Figure 1.4. Causal model of turnover for the Denver study.

hospital. During the field work, discussions were held with each hospital to help them distinguish voluntary and involuntary leavers. The sample analyzed had the following distribution: 1,748 stayers (80%), 404 voluntary leavers (18%), and 40 voluntary leavers (2%). An unsuccessful effort was also made to collect data about each of the employees who left. Preceding the first questionnaire administration, Price conducted field work in the five hospitals from June 1980 to November 1980. Factor analysis was again used to construct the measurements. As before, the measures used had acceptable psychometric properties. Regression and path analytic techniques were again used to analyze the data.

Seven determinants had substantial total effects on turnover: intent to leave (.32), satisfaction (–.11), pay (–.09), kinship responsibility (–.08), opportunity (.07), and integration (–.07).[12] All of the effects were in agreement with the model. Turnover was increased by intent to leave and more opportunity and decreased by high satisfaction, pay, kinship responsibility, commitment, and integration. Pay referred to individual and not family income. The adjusted explained variance for turnover, without the demographic variables, was 12%. None of the moderating variables were statistically significant.

Total effects were not computed for the demographic variables. However, the fifteen demographic variables increased the adjusted explained variance by 1%, the type of result which indicates that the model is capturing most of the conceptual content indicated by the demographic variables, the type of situation anticipated by Price and Mueller.

PHASE 5: THE TEXAS STUDY OF A MILITARY HOSPITAL

The finding that kinship responsibility again decreased turnover emphasized the need for a sample with more males, especially males delivering healthcare services. An opportunity to obtain such a sample came when Price obtained a U.S. Air Force Summer Fellowship in 1990. Price worked at Armstrong Laboratory, which was near Wilford Hall, an important military hospital located at Lackland Air Force Base. Price obtained permission from the hospital to study its military medical personnel. In addition to its large core of males employed as nurses, doctors, and dentists, the Air Force also made available demographic data about all the military medical personnel who completed the questionnaires. This demographic data eased the problem of data collection. All the military medical personnel in the hospital worked full time. The three pervious samples had consisted of both full time and part time employees.

There were continuities and changes in the Texas Study. Figure 1.5 is a diagram for the model estimated in the Texas Study (Kim, Price, Mueller, & Watson, 1996).

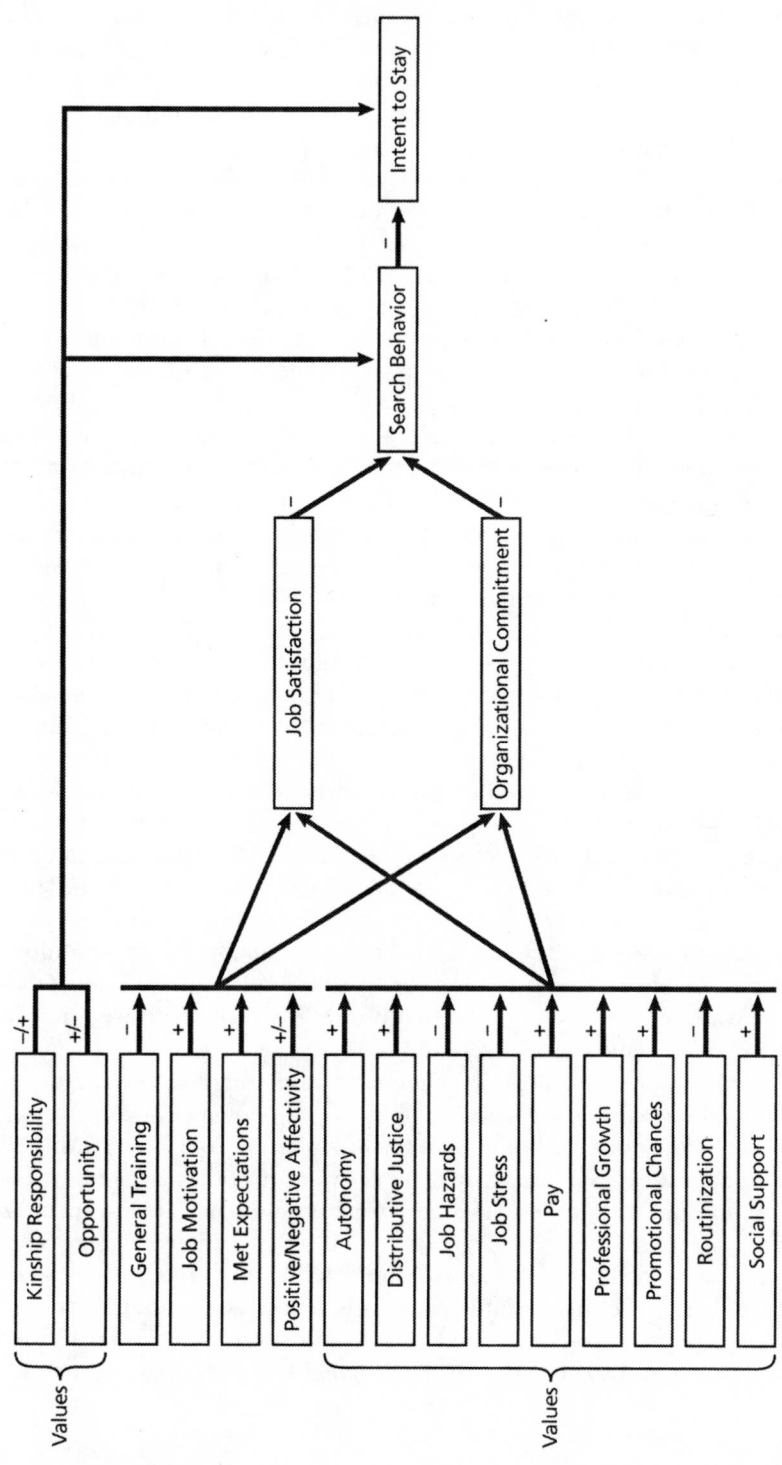

Figure 1.5. Causal model of intent to stay for the Texas study of a military hospital.

Eleven determinants and propositions were basically the same from the Denver Study: kinship responsibility, opportunity, general training, autonomy, distributive justice, pay, promotional chances, routinization, satisfaction, commitment, and intent to stay. There were two minor changes in labels: "centralization" became "autonomy" and "intent to leave" became "intent to stay." Autonomy was a widely used label and more accurately described the variable previously investigated as centralization in the Denver Study. All subsequent research used the label of autonomy for this concept. It is not clear why intent to stay—rather than intent to leave—became the label for the dependent variable. Since the Denver Study had started, new data indicated that intent to stay was moderately correlated (about .50) with turnover (Steel & Ovalle, 1984). Another reason for using intent to stay rather than turnover was the fact that the military medical personnel in the sample had signed contracts to remain in the Air Force to repay the government for their medical education. It was not unusual for these contracts to last for six years, a long time to wait for turnover data.

There were nine major changes in the model to be estimated. First, job motivation became a determinant. Price became convinced that the concept that had been investigated as "professionalism" was more accurately designated as "job motivation." Work commitment had been investigated in the pilot study but it was not statistically significant. However, a new measure was available (Kanungo, 1982), so work commitment was reintroduced as job motivation. The label of professionalism was dropped. Motivation was also a label widely used in the psychological literature. Job motivation was viewed as willingness to exert effort at work and was hypothesized to impact on intent to stay through satisfaction and commitment. No links were specified between job motivation and satisfaction/commitment. Second, met expectations was added from the work of Mowday and his colleagues (Mowday et al., 1982). For a long time, Price believed that expectations, a critical concept in the Parsonian-Mertonian tradition in which Price was trained, was identical to norms. One of the Iowa students (Jean Wallace), however, argued that two different concepts were involved and her arguments were accepted for the Texas Study.

Third, positive and negative affectivity were added as exogenous variables. These were dispositional—that is, psychological—concepts that referred, respectively, to the tendency to experience pleasant/unpleasant emotional states. The affectivity variables were hypothesized to impact on intent to stay through satisfaction and commitment. The hypothesized impact on satisfaction was suggested by Brief and his colleagues (Brief, Burke, George, Robinson, & Webster, 1988). No links were specified between the affectivity variables and satisfaction/commitment. Brief and his colleagues (1988) also argued that the affectivity variables must be controlled in the investigation of satisfaction, because they might contaminate the exogenous variables. Watson and Clark (1987) were the major scholars working with the affectivity variables.

Fourth, job hazards were added as an exogenous variable. Job hazards came from the research by Viscusi (1979) which indicated that turnover was increased by physically dangerous work. Factory work had historically been viewed as often hazardous but current research on hospitals had indicated that its work was often quite hazardous. An interesting feature of Viscusi's research was that its controls were almost exclusively demographic variables. Price and Mueller's research mostly used theoretical variables as controls and the Texas Study provided an opportunity to check Viscusi's analysis. With many theoretical controls, job hazards may not be a significant determinant. Fifth, role overload from the Denver Study was expanded to "job stress" and included three variables in addition to role overload: role inadequacy, role ambiguity, and role conflict. Job stress was viewed as the extent to which job duties cannot be fulfilled and was hypothesized to impact negativity on intent to stay through satisfaction and commitment. The previous emphasis on instrumental communication seemed to be conceptually captured by role ambiguity. Instrumental communication was thus no longer used as a label. The job stress label came from research done at the Survey Research Center of the University of Michigan (House, 1981).

Sixth, Mangelsdorff's (1989) work emphasized the importance of professional growth in a military setting. Since most of the Texas sample were professional employees, and since research on professionals stressed the importance of knowing the literature, this seemed to be an important determinant to explore. Mangelsdorff emphasized the importance of this variable in a discussion with Price in Texas. Professional growth was the degree to which the Air Force provided the chance to increase job-related knowledge and skills. With a good chance for professional growth should come increased intent to stay through satisfaction and commitment. The empirical data supporting professional growth, however, was not as extensive as the evidence for job hazards. Seventh, integration became a dimension of social support. Social support was viewed as assistance with job-related problems and could come from the family, supervisor, and peers. Peer support was previously termed "integration." Increased social support was hypothesized to increase intent to stay by its positive impact on satisfaction and commitment. The social support label also came from research performed at the Survey Research Center (House, 1981) and was a widely used label in the literature.

Eighth, search behavior was the extent to which an employee was looking for another job. The proposition was that the greater the search behavior, the greater the likelihood of decreased intent to stay. Search behavior was a variable emphasized by economists and, when combined with intent to stay, partially captures the conceptual content of Hom and Griffeth's (1995) "thoughts of quitting." Ninth, the Denver Study had intensively investigated the moderating variables of values without formally incorporating them into the model. The early research, for example, did not support values' hypothesized moderating effects. However, most of the turnover literature emphasized the importance of values' moderating effects, especially the research of Mowday and his colleagues, so they were finally incorporated into the model in the Texas Study, as Figure 1.5 indicates. It was also hypothesized that autonomy and social support would moderate the impact of job stress on satisfaction (Karasek & Thorell, 1990). Job stress, for example, it was hypothesized, will not decrease satisfaction if autonomy and social support are high. The moderating effect of autonomy and support was not formally incorporated into this model, however. There was more evidence for the moderating effect of values, it seemed, than for the moderating effect of autonomy and social support.

The Texas Study also divided the determinants into four classes: endogenous, environmental, individual, and structural. Satisfaction, commitment, search, and intent were endogenous variables, whereas kinship responsibility and opportunity were environmental variables. General training, job motivation, met expectations, and the affectivity determinants were individual variables. The remaining thirteen variables were classified as structural.

As in previous research, demographic variables were included in the analysis as controls but were not incorporated into the model. Four demographic variables were included in the analysis: education, rank, age, and length of military service obligations.

The model was estimated for a sample of male physicians to see how well it would explain intent to stay for a non-female sample (Kim et al., 1996). As previously indicated, all the previous estimates of the model had been made for females. The results for kinship responsibility were of special concern. There were 244 male physicians in the sample. The hospital at Lackland Air Force Base—Wilford Hall—was a tertiary care center with 806 beds, a large hospital. Data were collected by questionnaires and records. The questionnaires were mailed in July 1990 and returned in August and September to Armstrong Laboratory, where Price worked. Demographic data about the sample were obtained from military records. Price conducted intensive field work in the hospital for two months before the questionnaires were administered. Factor analysis was used to construct the measures, which turned out to have adequate psychometric properties. The data were analyzed with regression analysis and path analytical techniques.

Six determinants had substantial total effects: commitment (.42), satisfaction (.23), search behavior (−.23), opportunity (−.19), met expectations (.16), and positive affectivity (.12). There were no total effects for kinship responsibility. So with a male sample, kinship responsibility was not a significant determinant. Nor was job hazards a significant determinant. All of the significant effects were in agreement with the model. None of the moderating variables was statistically significant. The adjusted explained variance, with the demographic variables included, was 41%.

Total effects were not computed for the four demographic variables used in the analysis. Data also were not given regarding the amount of explained variances added by the demographic variables. The demographic variables were important early in the development of the model, but by this phase of the research, they did not yield much information, a result that was anticipated. Significant results for the demographic variables would indicate that the model was not working well.

REFLECTIONS ON THE DEVELOPMENT
OF THE CAUSAL MODEL

Strengths and weaknesses of the developmental process will now be presented. The focus will be on strategies of model construction in the context of turnover research. Three strengths and seven weaknesses are apparent. Consider first the strengths.

First, reviews of the literature were helpful. A review of models, as was previously indicated, was first conducted in the Spring of 1972. When Price returned to Iowa in 1973, after his research professorship in England, he began a review of the entire field of turnover research—definitions, measures, models, empirical generalization, and extent of turnover (Price, 1977). Reviews are, of course, traditional in research, so there is nothing unusual here. What was a bit different about these reviews, from the perspective of turnover research, is that they were not bound by the confines of any single discipline or applied area. Everything pertinent to turnover was examined. Many turnover researchers, especially economists, stay very close to their disciplines or applied areas. As the descriptions indicated, smaller reviews continued during the entire process of model development.

Second, contact with other researchers working on turnover was basic to the process. The results of this contact are apparent throughout the descriptions of the developmental process. The importance of the research community—the famous "invisible college"—is, of course, traditional so there is nothing extraordinary here. What is somewhat different, again in the context of turnover research, is the range of contacts. Price sought to discuss turnover with everyone he could find who did research on the topic. He described the research at meetings, especially professional gatherings; he eagerly spoke to classes of students about the research; he commented, by letter and telephone, on publications and asked for additional material cited in the publications; he sent his publications to others to stimulate discussion; he sent large amounts of material about the Iowa research to individuals just beginning their study; to open discussions with managers, he spoke at meetings devoted to the reduction of absenteeism and turnover; and he served as a paid consultant on numerous turnover projects, especially projects studying nursing turnover. Foreign and domestic meetings, where material about turnover were presented, were regularly attended. These contacts began in the Spring of 1972 and continued to the present time.

Third, repeated estimations of the model were integral to the developmental process. Models must, of course, be estimated to be pronounced as empirically sound. What was somewhat different in this process were the repeated estimations. And the description in this paper has not examined the thirty-three theses and dissertations which Price and Mueller directed. The theses and dissertations continually improved the measures and confirmed the different components of the model. Every estimation was a learning process and sought to improve on preceding studies.

Mistakes were, of course, made in the developmental process. Seven mistakes are noteworthy.

First, the process was too often ignored in the development of the model. The intervening process between the determinants and turnover has been a component of the model from the beginning. Satisfaction and opportunity, for instance, were in the preliminary model developed when Price was on leave in England in 1972–1973. Satisfaction and opportunity were, respectively, mediating and moderating variables in the preliminary model. The focus on process was an explicit attempt to remedy the lack of a process emphasis in the economic research on models examined in the Spring of 1972. However, in many instances determinants were proposed without specification of how the variable impacted on turnover. When opportunity, for example, was made an exogenous variable in the Denver Study, no mediating variables were proposed. Again, when kinship responsibility was included in the Iowa-Illinois Study, in an attempt to conceptualize the apparent differences between local and non-local nurses observed in the pilot study, no mediating variables were proposed. Still again, when positive and negative affectivity were used as exogenous variables in the Texas Study, a process was not hypothesized between these variables and satisfaction/commitment. However, when the Texas Study, focusing on physicians, was published in 1996, some of the neglected processes were suggested. The most recent statement of the model (Price, 2000) attempts to specify all of the intervening processes.[13] However, for far too long, many intervening processes were ignored.

Journal reviewers forcefully noted the lack of a process for many determinants. Price then became aware of the fact that those processes were often in his mind but had not been specified. Mueller was especially discouraged by the journal reviews and the fact that sociologists were not much interested in turnover.[14] An effort was then made to specify the processes for the propositions, such as the 1996 article on physicians. Of major importance is the fact that Prices's training never stressed the need for process to make propositions complete. Price was aware of the need for some processes—his criticism of economic research illustrates this awareness—but his conception of theory never included an explicit directive about specifying processes for propositions, when such processes were needed.

Second, scope conditions for the models were never specified. Consider the situation of full-time and part-time employees. The hospitals in the first three studies employed both full-time and part-time employees. This employment pattern was viewed as an asset, since the research was able to examine a growing segment of the labor force, the part-time employee. Controls were, of course, always used for amount of time worked, whether full time or part time. In the Iowa-Illinois Study, amount of time worked and age were even used to classify the nurses for subgroup analysis. Never did it occur to Price and his colleagues to consider the possibility that the model might apply most readily to the full-time employees. During most of the time that research has been done on turnover—from the early 1900s—nearly all of the employees had worked full time, so the models developed would naturally be constructed to explain the turnover of full-time employees.

Price never thought of the possibility of specifying the universe to which the model would apply until he was introduced to the idea of "scope conditions" by the Stanford-trained researchers in the Sociology Department at Iowa (Cohen, 1991), especially by Barry Markovsky.[15] Price then realized that the model seemed to work best for full-time employees and he began to use amount of time worked as a scope condition.[16]

Third, some of the samples and sites were designed too narrowly. The pilot study and the Iowa-Illinois Study were probably all right, since the research was just beginning and it is difficult to avoid narrowness at the beginning. However, the Denver Study was probably a mistake, since it was not very different from the first two studies. Due to the recession in the early 1980s, the rate of turnover in the Denver area was also greatly depressed, thereby nullifying the major reason for this sample and site. Too much attention was devoted to obtaining a high rate of turnover in a brief period of time. The sample and site for the Texas Study was good, since it was very different from the first three studies. The problem with the Texas Study was that during this time Mueller decided to end most of his participation in the developmental process. Price continued the Texas Study with a graduate student (Sang-Wook Kim) but the range of the research was considerably reduced.

The narrowness of the sample and site raises questions about the generality of the model. Kinship responsibility, for instance, was significant as long as females were studied, but when male physicians were examined, it was no longer significant. The narrowness of the sample may also account for the fact that none of the moderating variables were statistically significant. All of the samples were mostly composed of middle-class employees, for example, and these individuals may be too homogenous in what they value. Rather than the Denver sample and site, a large, public hospital in a major metropolitan area, such as Chicago, would have obtained more lower-class employees. It was probably a good idea to keep doing research in the healthcare area, despite the problem of generality, because of official health sponsorship—the Medical School at the University of Iowa—and the opportunity to develop a track record in the area, which facilitated funding. There is a great variety in the American healthcare delivery system, but this variety was not explored.

Fourth, analysis was somewhat slighted in the studies. This neglect characterizes all the studies. The pilot study should have, but never did, conduct a systematic analysis of the local and non-local nurses. The Iowa-Illinois Study found that the classification of the nurses by age and amount of time worked did not very well explain the differences observed, but other subdivisions—by theoretical variables, for instance—was not attempted. The Denver Study was very concerned to get more men into the sample, and succeeded in doing so, but never did a matched subgroup analysis of males and females. Nor did the Denver Study, with its longitudinal data, wrestle with the causal orders of the exogenous/intervening variables and within the endogenous variables. Two points in time may not be ideal for longitudinal analysis, but two points are better than the one point of a cross-sectional analysis. When the Texas Study was written up, there was an awareness of the controversy concerning the causal order of search behavior and intent to stay (Sager, Griffeth, & Hom, 1998), but this topic was not even considered, and the Texas Study had longitudinal data—though for two points in time—available for the analysis. An immense amount of analysis was conducted in the development of the model. However, at critical points, analysis was not thoroughly explored. There was too much of a rush through analysis in the development process.

Fifth, a systematic procedure to access the empirical validity of the different components of the model was never developed. The procedure was to evaluate the studies on a case-by-case basis. The rule was that each study should improve on the preceding study, theoretically and methodically. When a study was done, if a determinant was statistically significant, the determinant was retained in the next study. If, however, a better measurement instrument was found, the next study would incorporate the new measurement. If a determinant was not statistically significant, an effort was made to see what went wrong. A variable would not be estimated unless it was supported by some empirical data, so if the variable was not statistically significant, something should be wrong. Usually what was wrong was an inferior measure. Many variables were estimated which had not been subjected to the extensive controls that were used in the research, so it was anticipated that quite a few of these variables would not be statistically significant. The bias of the research was to retain determinants for the next study.

A major result of this case-by-case approach was that knowledge was not available regarding the explanatory power of the different variables. An example illustrates this lack of knowledge. In the Spring Semester of the 1987–1988 academic year, Price was on leave at Birkbeck College of the University of London (England). While at Birkbeck, he was asked to describe the turnover research to the faculty and students. The description focused mostly on the model developed and the studies performed to estimate the model. When his oral presentation was finished, Price was asked to describe the major results of the research. Price could cite no major results: there was only a series of different studies, each one, supposedly, better than the preceding one. The studies had not been "added up," had not been cumulated.

Meta-analysis (Hunter, Schmidt, & Jackson, 1982) is a systematic way to assess, quantitatively, the results of a series of studies. One of the graduate students in Sociology (Roderick Iverson) started a meta-analysis of the Iowa Research in the early 1990s, but returned to Australia before the research was finished. The meta-analysis was dropped because Iverson began a series of new empirical studies of turnover in Australia which fully occupied his time. A graduate student in the College of Business (Chris Quinn-Trank) worked several years in the mid–1990s on a meta-analysis of the Iowa research, but was unable to use the results of her work for a Ph.D., so she did not complete the project. Frank Schmidt, a major scholar of meta-analysis in the College of Business, would not approve Quinn-Trank's dissertation because the Iowa research did not use a standard set of determinants. Finally, one of Rodger Griffeth's graduate students in the College of Business at Georgia State University (Stefan Gaertner) did a meta-analysis, with a standard set of determinants, on part of the Iowa research (Gaertner, 1990). Meta-analysis should have been done throughout the development of the model. Too much time had elapsed before such an analysis was done.

Sixth, longitudinal analysis was not fully used in the research. All of the studies which focused on turnover made sure that it was measured after the exogenous and intervening variables were assessed. There was, therefore, a longitudinal element in all these studies. The Denver Study also collected data at two points in time and had a longitudinal dimension in its analysis.

Data were collected for a longitudinal analysis in the Texas Study, but the data were never analyzed. None of the studies, however, collected data at three points in time and built the entire analysis around the longitudinal data. In the Denver data, the longitudinal analysis is quickly inserted after a long series of cross-sectional analyses. Three data-collection points seem to be necessary for a complete longitudinal analysis.

Seventh, none of the studies used event history analysis as a statistical technique (Allison, 1984). The samples were always divided into leavers and stayers, thereby ignoring the different lengths of time that the sample's member had been employed. Important data were thus lost with the leaver/stayer dichotomy. Two of the graduate students working with Price and Mueller designed a study of the Chicago Public Schools to make use of event history analysis. The students obtained their dissertations (Currivan in 1998 and Iverson in 1992) from the Chicago research, but never used event history analysis in a published study. Event history analysis requires a large entering cohort—thus the selection of an entering cohort of teachers from the Chicago Public Schools—but it is clear that there are genuine advantages in this technique.

Three final comments should be made before concluding this paper. The comments deal with largely misplaced criticisms of the model.

First, the model is often criticized for having too many variables. The Texas Study had, for instance, twenty-four variables. This is certainly too many variables. Simpler models are, of course, favored over complex ones. However, there are many explanations of turnover in the literature and these explanations, at least the major ones, must be estimated at some time. The explanations must also be estimated against each other, which means including a substantial number of the variables in the same research. An effort can be made to eliminate variables with little support, but this will still, if past experience is a guide, leave too many variables. The models will eventually be simplified, but this will take time. Meta-analysis should facilitate the simplification.

Second, the model is often criticized for a large percentage of insignificant variables. Twenty-four variables may be proposed, for instance, but only 50% may be statistically significant. Three comments are pertinent to this criticism. (1) Some of the determinants have been proposed without many theoretical controls. Viscusi's (1979) study is an example of such research. With extensive theoretical controls, these determinants often do not become significant. (2) Statistical significance is strongly influenced by sample size. Statistical significance is easier to obtain with a large sample. And few studies of turnover have samples of a thousand or more. The samples must, of course, be even larger with many variables in the model. (3) Explained variance is an important criterion by which to evaluate the explanatory power of a model. But so also is the extent to which the results conform to predictions of the model. Price is partial to the use of confirmed predictions, but both criteria should be used for evaluation.

Third, the model contains two paths between the exogenous variables and turnover (see Figure 1.5). One path goes from kinship responsibility and opportunity to turnover, the second path goes from the remaining exogenous variables to turnover through satisfaction and commitment. All of the exogenous variables are not hypothesized to impact on turnover through satisfaction and commitment.

CONCLUSION

An effort has been made in this paper to describe the development of the Price/Mueller causal model of voluntary turnover by analyzing select studies conducted by these researchers. An effort has been made to select studies which illustrate critical features of the model's development. A sizeable amount of research has, of course, been excluded, since the Iowa research has been conducted for more than twenty-five years. The most serious exclusion has been the thirty-three dissertations and theses directed by Price and Mueller. These theses and dissertations have contributed substantially to the research that Price and Mueller have conducted. It has also been a distinct pleasure working with the students who did the research; we found these students to be marvelous colleagues. What has been outstanding is the fact that five of the dissertations have been performed in South Korea. These South Korean dissertations are an attempt to extend the generality of a model developed in the west. However, the four studies described seem to represent the development process quite accurately. Critical features of the model's development are covered by the four studies. Descriptions, such as the one presented in this paper, are rare and it is hoped that other turnover researchers will benefit from this description of model development and will provide descriptions of the development of other models.

NOTES

1. An excellent review of the field of turnover research is Hom and Griffeth (1995). The Hom and Griffeth review comments on the major models of turnover.

2. The two moderating conditions are not in Figure 1.1, because they were not in the original text.

3. The motivational approach of Homans (1961) is basically accepted, though often with different terminology, by all of the research by Price and Mueller.

4. Scale of operations was not the definition in the original text.

5.   It was a mistake to equate programmed coordination with centralization. Programmed coordination, for example, decreases whereas centralization increases turnover.

6.   The questionnaires for one of the hospitals were distributed to the nurses when they picked up their pay checks.

7.   Factor analysis and alpha were used in all of the studies described in this historical review.

8.   Results for the work units and subgroups are not presented mostly due to space considerations.

9.   Extreme splits can, of course, but analyzed with logistic regression. There was too much emphasis on avoiding extreme splits in the Denver Study.

10.   Absenteeism was also added as a dependent variable in the Denver Study. However, absenteeism is excluded from consideration in this paper to simplify the presentation.

11.   The focus on more moderators was made, because of the work of Mowday and his colleagues (Mowday et al., 1982).

12.   The emphasis is on individual and cross-sectional data, because these results were confirmed by the work unit and time-series data.

13.   The most recent statement of the model also indicates the model's connection to the exchange approach (Blau, 1964). An exchange of benefits between the employers and the employees is assumed by this model. The employers distribute benefits—the structural variables can be viewed as benefits—to the employees in return for the employees' service to the organization.

14.   Sociologists may also have not been interested in the Price/Mueller model. This lack of interest may be because turnover and absenteeism have a connection with cost consideration in business, a topic in which sociologists are not too interested.

15.   The Stanford sociologists also did not favor the use of demographic variables, like amount of time worked, as scope conditions. They preferred theoretical variables as scope conditions. Price is not aware, at this time, of the theoretical variable(s) indicated by amount of time worked.

16.   It was previously noted that the Iowa-Illinois Study used age and amount of time worked to conduct a subgroup analysis of the nurses. This analysis demonstrated to Price that demographic variables should not be used to construct subgroups for analysis. The differences which were observed for the subgroups of nurses could not be accounted for by age and amount of time worked. Demographic variables, by their very nature, do not indicate what are producing effects. Subgroups should not be created with theoretical variables (Price, 1995; Price & Kim, 1993).

REFERENCES

Allison, P.D. (1984). *Event history analysis.* Beverly Hills, CA: Sage.

Becker, G.S. (1964). *Human capital.* New York: Columbia University Press.

Blau, P.M. (1959–1960). Social integration, social rank, and process of interaction. *Human Organization, 18,* 152–157.

Blau, P.M. (1964). *Exchange and power in social life.* New York: Wiley.

Bluedorn, A.C. (1976). *A causal model of turnover in organizations.* Unpublished Ph.D. dissertation, University of Iowa.

Brief, A.P. (1976). Turnover among hospital nurses: A suggested model. *Journal of Nursing Administration, 6*, 55–58.

Brief, A.P., Burke, M.J., George, J.M., Robinson, B.S., & Webster, J. (1988). Should negative affectivity remain an unmeasured variable in the study of job stress? *Journal of Applied Psychology, 73*, 193–198.

Burton, J.F., & Parker, J.E. (1969). Interindustry variations in voluntary labor mobility. *Industrial and Labor Relations, 22*, 199–216.

Cohen, B.P. (1991). *Developing sociological knowledge.* Chicago: Nelson-Hall.

Currivan, D.B. (1998). *An analysis of causal relationships in a model of organizational commitment.* Unpublished dissertation, University of Iowa.

Farris, G.F. (1971). A predictive study of turnover. *Personnel Psychology, 24*, 311–328.

Gaertner, S. (1999). Structural determinants of job satisfaction and organizational commitment in turnover models. *Human Resource Management Review, 9*, 479–493.

Greeley, A.M. (1972). *Priests in the United States.* Garden City, NY: Doubleday.

Hom, P.W., & Griffeth, R. (1995). *Employee turnover.* Cincinnati, OH: Southwestern College Publishing.

Homans, G.C. (1961). *Social behavior.* New York: Harcourt, Brace.

House, J.S. (1981). *Work stress and social support.* Reading, MA: Addison-Wesley.

Hunter, J.E., Schmidt, F.L., & Jackson, G.B. (1982). *Meta-analysis: Cumulating research findings across studies.* Beverly Hills, CA: Sage.

Iverson, R.D. (1992). *Employee intent to stay: An empirical test of a revision of the Price and Mueller model.* Unpublished dissertation, University of Iowa.

Kanungo, R.N. (1982). *Work alienation.* New York: Praeger.

Karasek, R., & Thorell, T. (1990). *Healthy work.* New York: Basic Books.

Kim, S.W., Price, J.L., Mueller, C.W., & Watson, T.W. (1996). The determinants of career intent among physicians at a U.S. Air Force hospital. *Human Relations, 49*, 947–975.

Lyons, T.F. (1968). *Nursing attitudes of turnover.* Ames: Iowa State University, Industrial Relations Center.

Mangelsdorff, A.D. (1989). A cross-validation study of factors affecting military psychologists' decision to remain in the service: the 1984 active duty psychologists survey. *Military Psychology, 4*, 241–251.

March, J.G., & Simon, H.A. (1958). *Organizations.* New York: Wiley.

Merton, R.K. (1968). *Social theory and social structure.* Glencoe, IL: The Free Press.

Mobley, W.H. (1982). *Employee turnover.* Reading, MA: Addison-Wesley.

Mowday, R.T., Porter, L.W., & Steers, R.M. (1982). *Employee-organization linkages.* New York: Academic Press.

Osteman, P. (Ed.). (1984). *Internal labor markets.* Cambridge, MA: MIT Press.

Pencavel, J.H. (1970). *An analysis of the quit rate in American manufacturing industry.* Princeton, NJ: Princeton University Industrial Relations Section.

Price, J.L. (1975). A theory of turnover. In B.O. Pettman (Ed.), *Labor turnover and retention* (pp. 51–75). Epping: Gower Press.

Price, J.L. (1977). *The study of turnover.* Ames: Iowa State University Press.

Price, J.L. (1995). A role for demographic variables in the study of absenteeism and turnover. *The International Journal of Career Management, 7*, 26–32.

Price, J.L. (2000). Reflections on the determinants of turnover. *International Journal of Manpower, 22*, 600–624.

Price, J.L., & Bluedorn, A.C. (1980). In D. Dunkerley & G. Salaman (Eds.), *The international yearbook of organizational studies 1979* (pp. 217–236). London: Routledge & Kegan Paul Ltd.

Price, J.L., & Mueller, C.W. (1981). *Professional turnover: The case of nurses.* Bridgeport, CT: Luce.

Price, J.L., & Mueller, C.W. (1986). *Absenteeism and turnover of hospital employees.* Greenwich, CT: JAI Press.

Price, J.L., & Kim, S.W. (1993). The relationship between demographic variables and intent to stay in the military: Medical personnel in a U.S. Air Force hospital. *Armed Forces and Society, 20*, 125–144.

Roethlisberger, F., & Dickson, W. (1939). *Management and the worker.* Cambridge, MA: Harvard University Press.

Sager, J.K., Griffeth, R.W., & Hom, P.W. (1998). A comparison of structural models representing turnover cognitions. *Journal of Vocational Behavior, 53*, 254–273.

Steel, R.P., & Ovalle, N.K. (1984). A review and meta-analysis of research on the relationship between behavioral intentions and employee turnover. *Journal of Applied Psychology, 69*, 673–686.

Stoikov, V., & Raimon, R.L. (1968). Determinants of differences in the quit rate among industries. *American Economic Review, 58*, 1283–1298.

Viscusi, W.K. (1979). *Employment hazards.* Cambiridge, MA: Harvard University Press.

Vroom, V.H. (1964). *Work and motivation.* New York: Wiley.

Watson, D., & Clark, L.A. (1984). Negative affectivity: The disposition to experience aversive emotional states. *Psychological Bulletin, 96*, 465–490.

Woodward, J. (1965). *Industrial organization.* London: Oxford University Press.

part II

**IDENTIFYING CONSTRUCTS AND PROCESSES MISSING
FROM PREVAILING TURNOVER FORMULATIONS**

CHAPTER 2

EXPLAINING THE LINK BETWEEN TURNOVER INTENTIONS AND TURNOVER

The Roles of Risk, Personality, and Intentions-Behavior Linkages

David G. Allen

ABSTRACT

Attitudes typically only explain around 5% of turnover variance, while intentions to quit rarely exceed 10–15% (Griffeth et al., 2000; Hom & Griffeth, 1995), and the relationship between intentions to quit and turnover varies widely (Vandenberg & Barnes-Nelson, 1999). The purpose of this chapter is to explore possible mechanisms explaining why individuals do or do not follow through on expressed desire and even intentions to leave the organization, and offer directions for future research. I focus on three areas of research that can inform our understanding of why individuals who have decided they want to quit sometimes do and sometimes do not. One is a consideration of the risks involved in quitting a job. Turnover decisions inherently involve elements of risk and uncertainty, and there is an extensive literature on risky decision mak-

Innovative Theory and Empirical Research on Employee Turnover, pages 35–53
Copyright © 2004 by Information Age Publishing

ing that could be applied to turnover. Two is a consideration of personality as it affects the relationship between turnover intentions and turnover. Although personality variables have in some cases been related to turnover, only limited research has investigated personality as a potential moderator of the intentions-turnover relationship. Three is a consideration of research on how attitudes and intentions are translated into behavior in terms of behavioral control and consistency, and emotional arousal.

INTRODUCTION

What makes individuals, who express dissatisfaction with their jobs and organizations, desire to quit their jobs, and even fully intend to quit in the near future more or less likely to actually quit? Although considerable research shows that job dissatisfaction, low organizational commitment, and especially withdrawal cognitions such as intentions to quit are consistent predictors of turnover, the mechanisms translating desire to quit into turnover behavior remain ambiguous and require greater attention (Hom & Kinicki, 2001). We know a good deal about the factors that push employees to voluntarily leave organizations (e.g., job dissatisfaction), factors that pull employees away from organizations (e.g., alternative job opportunities), and the processes by which individuals make turnover decisions. However, our ability to explain and predict individual voluntary turnover decisions remains limited. Some employees who are satisfied with their jobs leave, while many who are dissatisfied stay. Alternative opportunities sometimes lead employees to quit, but often do not. Even the majority of employees who report intending to quit their jobs do not actually do so. Attitudes typically only explain around 5% of turnover variance, while intentions to quit rarely exceed 10–15% (Griffeth et al., 2000; Hom & Griffeth, 1995), and the relationship between intentions to quit and turnover varies widely (Vandenberg & Barnes-Nelson, 1999).

The purpose of this chapter is to explore possible mechanisms explaining why individuals do or do not follow through on expressed desire and even intentions to leave the organization, and offer directions for future research. In doing so, I will make no attempt to add to the already voluminous literature on why and how individuals become dissatisfied or begin thinking about quitting, the possible methodological and measurement issues that may account for variance and attenuation in observed relationships between turnover intentions and turnover (e.g., Steel, Shane, & Griffeth, 1990), or process models aimed at understanding how individuals decide to search, compare alternatives, and finally decide they intend to quit. Instead, the focus is on three areas of research that can inform our understanding of why individuals who have decided they want to quit sometimes do and sometimes do not.

One is a consideration of the risks involved in quitting a job. Turnover decisions inherently involve elements of risk and uncertainty, and although some elements of uncertainty and risk have received limited attention, there is an extensive literature on risky decision making that could be applied to turnover. Two is a consideration of personality as it affects the relationship between turnover intentions and turnover. Although personality variables have, in some cases, been related to turnover, only limited research has investigated personality as a potential moderator of the intentions-turnover relationship. Three is a consideration of research on how attitudes and intentions are translated into behavior. Although turnover research has drawn from models of attitudes, intentions, and behavior linkages, several important elements of these relationships have been largely neglected.

THE ROLE OF RISK IN TURNOVER DECISIONS

One aspect of turnover decision making that has not been systematically and comprehensively attended to is the risk involved in deciding to quit one's job. Turnover decisions are inherently risky in that they involve significant consequences coupled with uncertainty regarding probabilities and outcomes. In fact, behavioral measures of individual propensity to take risks sometimes include job quits as an indicator of willingness to engage in risky behavior (e.g., MacCrimmon & Wehring, 1985). The most obvious case is deciding to quit a current job without a concrete alternative job or role in hand. This decision involves risk and uncertainty about a number of factors including the likelihood of finding another role, the relative desirability of alternatives, and the time frame for obtaining an acceptable alternative. Even if quitting for a specific alternative, there is risk and uncertainty involved. A new job, for example, may have some known attributes, such as pay and benefits, but will also consist of numerous uncertain aspects, such as relationships with supervisors and co- workers, evolving job responsibilities and advancement, and the day-to-day work environment. Even more uncertainties would accompany a new job involving geographic relocation. Quitting for nonwork alternatives, such as to become a student or to assume greater child rearing duties, would also involve uncertainty, for example, whether the new role will be as satisfying or fulfilling as expected.

What makes a decision more or less risky? Researchers on risky decision making have focused on the possibilities of loss and gain, and the variance of probability distributions of outcomes (Highhouse & Yuce, 1996; Singh,

1986). Sitkin and Pablo (1992) characterized risk in decisions as the extent to which there is uncertainty about whether potentially significant or disappointing outcomes of decisions will be reached, and stressed three aspects of this definition. The first is outcome uncertainty. Decisions are riskier to the extent there is variability in potential outcomes, uncertainty about expectancies of potential outcomes, and uncontrollability of outcome attainment (Sitkin & Pablo, 1992). These characteristics would apply to many turnover decisions. Those considering leaving their jobs may or may not find an alternative, and alternatives vary in their desirability. Moreover, the odds of attaining desired outcomes are difficult to calculate with certainty, and there are certainly elements outside the individual's control that determine whether potential outcomes are attained.

The second element of risky decisions concerns the expectations associated with outcomes. Decision making risk is relevant for both potentially positive and negative expected outcomes, since both involve uncertainty. However, there is evidence that there are fundamental differences in how decision makers approach positive versus negative expected outcomes (Bazerman, 1998; Khaneman & Tversky, 1979). Turnover decisions involve both potentially positive expected outcomes (e.g., new experiences, better pay) and potentially negative expected outcomes (e.g., loss of valued relationships at work, loss of benefits associated with seniority). The extent to which positive or negative expected outcomes are more salient should influence turnover decision making.

The third element is the significance of potential outcomes, which must be perceived as of sufficient magnitude to influence decision-making. Turnover decisions would certainly seem to involve sufficiently significant outcomes. Outcomes such as job satisfaction, life satisfaction, financial situation, and family situations are all potentially influenced by turnover decisions. Thus, turnover decisions generally contain all the elements of risky decisions.

Previous Turnover Theory Incorporating Risk

Of course, a number of turnover theories implicitly acknowledge the role of risk and uncertainty in quit decisions in three different ways. One is the recognition of the importance of the uncertainty associated with alternatives. March and Simon (1958) argued that the decision to quit, even if dissatisfied, depends on an evaluation of the expected utility of perceived alternatives, requiring estimates of the probabilities of attaining alternatives. Mobley's (1977) process model of turnover also incorporated the probabilities of obtaining alternatives as a key component, while Mobley, Griffeth, Hand, and Meglino (1979) stressed the comparison of the expected utilities of the present job with the expected utilities of alternatives. Thus, turnover theory does implicitly consider risk by incorporating uncertainty associated with the availability, attainability, and attractiveness of alternatives. To the extent the labor market or perceived alternatives are less favorable for the individual, quitting should be seen as a riskier decision, and so be less likely. However, this role of perceived risk is typically assumed, as only the labor market or the quantity and quality of perceived alternatives are measured, whereas actual risk perceptions are not. Further, there is evidence that both situational and dispositional factors may influence individual responses to perceptions of risk. Thus, risk may not always be negatively associated with turnover behavior.

A second way prior turnover theory has dealt with risk is the recognition that frames of reference play an important role in how individuals interpret turnover decisions. Turnover researchers have noted that quit decisions take place within a context of personal experience. Hulin, Roznowski, and Hachiya (1985) argued that individual frames of reference affect evaluations of the current job. Past experience with job change decisions and perceptions of relevant economic conditions affect the way employees view their current job and alternatives. More recently, Lee and Mitchell's (1994) unfolding model also stressed the importance of individual frames of reference, particularly in terms of turnover history, for interpreting events and making turnover decisions. This is consistent with research on risky decision making showing that previous outcome history affects responses to risky situations. The unfolding model also implicitly addresses issues of framing. Research on risky decision making indicates that whether decisions are framed positively or negatively influences how decision makers respond. Lee and Mitchell (1994) suggest that events that stimulate turnover decisions can be positive, neutral, or negative, but that different types of precipitating events might result in different decision processes. Thus, turnover theory has begun to recognize the importance of turnover history, frames of reference, and framing on turnover. However, there are important processes associated with framing that have not been explicitly incorporated in the turnover literature. For example, research on prospect theory (Khaneman & Tversky, 1979) shows that individuals are risk averse in responding to issues framed in terms of gains while risk seeking when issues are framed in terms of losses. Further, empirical tests in the turnover literature have rarely assessed outcome history or framing.

Finally, a third way prior turnover theory has dealt with risk is the recognition that leaving a job requires sacrifices that must be taken into consideration. Becker's (1960) side-bet theory suggests that employees continuously make investments in organizations, such as job effort, friendships, skill development, and political deals that are only repaid over time. Since leaving may mean sacrificing return on these investments, the greater the employee investments the less likely they are to quit. This idea is consistent with Mobley's (1977) cost of quitting, Farrell and Rusbelt's (1981) job investments, and Allen and Meyer's (1990) continuance commitment. More recently, Mitchell, Holtom, Lee, Sablynski, and Erez (2001) stressed the importance of considering the sacrifices involved in quitting, including material and psychological benefits associated with the job, organization, and community forfeited by leaving. These approaches do not explicitly incorporate risk, but they imply that greater perceived sacrifices would make turnover decisions appear riskier. Researchers have not, though, measured these perceptions of risk or taken into account the research on how decision makers respond to risky decisions.

Decision Making under Risk

Thus, I believe there may be value in applying research on decision making under conditions of uncertainty and risk to turnover decisions. Most of the research on risky decision making involves choices between hypothetical alternatives and focuses on departures from the normative theory of decision making. The normative theory suggests that rational decision makers ought to be indifferent between choices with equal expected values. However, there is substantial evidence that decision makers deviate from this approach for a number of reasons (see Bazerman, 1998, for a review). For example, respondents are much more likely to choose a certain $500 than a 50% chance for $1,000 and a 50% chance for nothing, despite the equal expected values of the choices (Khaneman & Tversky, 1979).

Prospect theory (Khaneman & Tversky, 1979) suggests a number of ways decision makers depart from the normative theory. One is the certainty effect illustrated above, suggesting that decision makers overweight certain outcomes such that certainty increases the attractiveness of gains and the aversiveness of losses. Another is that gains and losses are evaluated relative to a current reference point, and the utilities of changes from this reference point are more important than the utilities of final positions. Another is that losses loom larger than gains, such that the pain associated with losing an amount is greater than the pleasure associated with gaining that same amount. Perhaps the most important implication of prospect theory is the crucial role of issue framing. Decision makers faced with an issue framed in terms of potential gains tend to exhibit risk averse behavior, while those faced with the same issue framed in terms of potential losses tend to exhibit risk seeking behavior (Bazerman, 1998; Khaneman, & Tversky, 1979). Although most research on decision making under uncertainty has used scenarios with known probabilities and monetary outcomes,

Khaneman and Tversky (1979) argued that prospect theory is applicable to choices involving attributes other than money and when probabilities are not explicitly known.

These findings have also been applied to organizational decision-making contexts. For example, Sitkin and Pablo (1992) provided a review, integration, and model of decision making under risk in an organizational context. In this model, there are two key predictors of risky decision-making: risk propensity and risk perceptions. Risk propensity is a tendency to take or avoid risks in a current situation. It is determined primarily by risk preferences, inertia, and outcome history. Risk preferences are a stable disposition to be risk averse or risk seeking. Inertia refers to habitual routines of handling similar risky situations. Individuals develop a relatively stable pattern of responses and tend to respond in similar ways in future decisions. Outcome history refers to the success or failure of prior risky decisions in similar situations. Successes will lead to similar risk propensity in future decisions, while failures will lead to greater variability of risk propensity.

The second key predictor of risky decision making is risk perceptions, the assessment of how risky a situation is. These perceptions are a function of risk propensity, problem framing, social influences, and problem familiarity. Risk propensity is described above, and Sitkin and Pablo (1992) suggest that risk averse decision makers will perceive more risk while risk seekers will perceive less risk. Problem framing refers to whether alternatives are compared in the domain of gains or losses. Considerable evidence suggests decision makers are risk averse in the domain of gains and risk seeking in the domain of losses, which suggests that framing may have more direct effects on risk propensity. Social influences refer to the opinions and norms of salient others, which can influence decision-maker perceptions of risk. Problem domain familiarity refers to experience with similar problems or decisions. Sitkin and Pablo (1992) suggest that both low and high levels of familiarity can lead to underestimates of risk because of poor assessment and overconfidence. Subsequent empirical tests (e.g., Sitkin & Weingart, 1995) support several of the model's predictions.

Implications for Turnover

These risky decision making models have important implications for turnover decisions. As argued earlier, there is risk associated with any stay or leave decision. Perceptions of how much risk is involved (risk perceptions) as well as attitudes toward risk taking in this particular situation (risk propensity) should influence choice. Risk propensity is a function of risk preferences, inertia, and outcome history. Risk preferences refer to a stable disposition to be risk seeking or risk averse across situations, and there is evidence that individuals differ in this trait. Individuals who are more risk seeking in general should have a higher risk propensity when considering turnover decisions, while those who are more risk averse in general should have a lower risk propensity when considering quitting.

Risk inertia suggests that individuals develop habits with regard to how they respond in similar situations. This implies that individuals who have chosen to quit when faced with turnover decisions in the past should be more likely to quit when faced with turnover decisions subsequently. Similarly, those who have typically chosen to stay when faced with past turnover decisions should be more likely to stay in subsequent similar situations. Thus, there may be a sound basis for organizational hiring standards suggesting that applicants with a history of frequent job changes are more likely to quit any job. Inertia in conjunction with risk preferences might also help explain the hobo syndrome (Ghiselli, 1974) finding that some individuals seem to be more prone to job-hopping.

Of course, the perceived success or failure of past turnover decisions likely also plays a role. The outcome history of past turnover decisions should influence behavior in subsequent similar situations. Sitkin and Weingart (1995) proposed and found evidence for a straightforward relationship between outcome history and risk propensity such that success would lead to propensity to repeat the past decision and failure would lower that propensity. So, seeing the outcome history associated with previous turnover decisions as successful would lead to an increased likelihood of making the same decision in a similar situation.

Risk perceptions are a function of problem framing, social influences, problem domain familiarity, and risk propensity. Prospect theory argues that problem framing affects risk aversion and risk seeking such that positive framing leads to risk aversion and negative framing leads to risk seeking. This suggests that framing directly influences risk propensity. Also, Sitkin and Pablo (1992) suggest that framing directly influences risk perceptions. Framing a turnover decision in terms of gains may be positively related to turnover risk perceptions, negatively related to turnover risk propensity, or both.

Social influences may also influence risk perceptions such that the opinions of salient others play an important role. Sitkin and Pablo (1992) focused on organizational culture and leaders as social influences on organizational decisions. For individual turnover decisions, co-workers, supervisors, mentors, as well as family and friends might all influence perceptions about how risky a turnover decision.

Problem domain familiarity influences decisions such that individuals with little experience tend to underestimate risk because of poor assessment, while those with a lot of experience also tend to underestimate risk because of overconfidence (Sitkin & Pablo, 1992). Thus, individuals who have never faced a turnover decision before and those who have faced numerous turnover decisions are both likely to underestimate the risks associated with quitting and thus have lower risk perceptions.

Finally, risk propensity and risk perceptions in a given situation are the primary determinants of risk-related behavior. Turnover risk propensity should be positively related to turnover, while turnover risk perceptions should be negatively related to turnover. However, it may not be accurate to consider risk perceptions and risk propensity independently of each other. High turnover risk perceptions should indeed make it less likely that a risk averse decision maker will turnover, but might not hinder a risk seeking decision maker. Thus, risk propensity and risk preferences may interact in influencing turnover behavior.

THE ROLE OF PERSONALITY IN THE INTENTIONS–TURNOVER RELATIONSHIP

Individual differences may influence the extent to which individuals are likely to exhibit consistency between expressed intentions and behavior, and certain aspects of personality may predispose individuals to either actively attempt to accomplish their expressed intentions or not, and thus might moderate the relationship between intentions to quit and turnover behavior. Personality has a long history in turnover research. Ghiselli (1974), for example, suggested a Hobo hypothesis that some individuals are inherently more likely to quit jobs than others. Research has found a variety of personality traits to be related to turnover, such as conscientiousness, agreeableness, and openness to experience (Barrick & Mount, 1991). However, the results of research positing a direct relationship between personality and turnover have been characterized as disappointing and inconsistent (Hom & Griffeth, 1995).

Instead, perhaps personality moderates the way individuals respond to dissatisfaction, desire to quit, and intentions to quit. Research suggests that individual differences may moderate attitude-behavior links (Kim & Hunter, 1993). For example, there is research suggesting that negative affectivity interacts with satisfaction in influencing turnover (Judge, 1993). However, the focus here is on aspects of personality that are likely to influence how and whether individuals who express intentions to quit actually pursue and follow through on those intentions. Therefore, the role of three personality variables that affect consistency between expressed intentions and behavior and that predispose individuals to either actively attempt to accomplish their expressed intentions or not are explored: self-monitoring, locus of control, and proactive personality.

Self-Monitoring

High self-monitors' actions are sensitive to situational and interpersonal cues about what is appropriate, whereas low self-monitors lack the motivation and/or ability to regulate their behavior to match such cues. Thus, high self-monitors tend to respond to the people and situation surrounding them and often exhibit contradictions between appearances and reality; low self-monitors do not intentionally attempt to change their behavior to match the situation and exhibit greater behavioral consistency between what they say and what they do (Snyder, 1974, 1987). Research on self-monitoring in the context of relationships suggests that high self-monitors are more likely to focus on the immediate outcomes of relationships and to be less interested in maintaining long term relationships and to be more likely to end relationships when an alternative presents itself (Simpson & Gangestad, 1996; Snyder & Simpson, 1984). Low self-monitors, on the other hand, tend to develop greater commitment in relationships and to maintain relationships longer (Glick, 1985; Simpson & Gangestad, 1996). Thus, high self-monitors might be more likely to quit than low self-monitors.

More interesting, though, is the effect self-monitoring might have on relationships of attitudes and intentions with subsequent behavior. Research suggests that attitudes will be better predictors of behavior for low self-monitors than for high self-monitors (Gangestad & Snyder, 2000). Low self-monitors express what they think and feel and then act accordingly, while high self-monitors are more likely to respond and act in ways they see as appropriate to the situation. Thus, if low self-monitors report strong intentions to quit, they may be more likely to both actually hold such intentions and follow through with them then high self-monitors who may report intentions to quit for more varied reasons and might also make turnover decisions for more varied reasons. A meta-analysis of attitude-behavior links found that attitude-behavior consistency was indeed higher for low self-monitors than for high self-monitors, although relationships between turnover intentions and turnover were not examined (Kraus, 1995).

Jenkins (1993) suggested that self-monitoring would moderate the relationships of attitudes such as satisfaction and commitment with turnover intentions, as opposed to actual turnover. He found that such relationships were stronger for high self-monitors than low self-monitors. This is not surprising, given that high self-monitors might be expected to report similar attitudes and intentions because such consistency would be the expected response pattern, while low self-monitors would be expected to respond according to their actual attitudes and intentions. However, Jenkins (1993) did not examine actual turnover behavior. Theory and research on self-monitoring suggest that when examining links with actual turnover behavior, the relationship between turnover intentions and subsequent turnover behavior should be stronger for low self-monitors, whose behaviors are expected to be more consistent with their stated intentions, than for high self-monitors. Thus, self-monitoring may moderate the relationship between turnover intentions and turnover such that the relationship is stronger for low self-monitors than for high self-monitors.

Locus of Control

Research on locus of control suggests that individuals vary in their expectancies regarding their ability to control events affecting them and their tendency to attribute the causes of their successes or failures to either internal or external sources. Those with an internal locus of control, or internals, have high expectancies of their ability to control events and attribute success or failure to themselves. Those with an external locus, externals, have low expectancies of control and attribute success or failure to external sources such as the situation, other people, or fate (Rotter, 1966). Research suggests that internals are likely to exhibit greater intrinsic motivation, be more achievement oriented, be rated as having higher job performance, report greater job satisfaction, and report lower turnover intentions (Renn & Vandenberg, 1991; Spector, 1982).

Again, the more interesting question is how locus of control might influence the relationship between intentions to quit and subsequent turnover. Since internals are more likely to believe that they are able to master their environment and control their outcomes, they may be more likely to believe they will be successful in obtaining an attractive alternative and thus more likely to act on their turnover intentions than externals. For example, Spector (1982) suggested that externals would be more likely to remain on a job even if they were dissatisfied and wanted to quit, while internals in that situation would be more likely to quit. Spector and Michaels (1986) found that locus of control did not moderate the relationship between satisfaction and turnover, but Blau (1987) found that locus did moderate the relationship between withdrawal cognitions and turnover such that the relationship was stronger for internals. These conflicting results suggest that this possibility requires greater investigation.

Griffeth and Hom (1988) suggested that internals' turnover intentions and behavior would be more strongly affected by external alternatives, while externals' turnover intentions and behavior would be more strongly affected by job satisfaction. Their rationale was that internals are more likely to defer immediate rewards in order to gain larger rewards in the future, and they found that attraction of alternatives explained more variances in turnover intentions and behavior than satisfaction for internals, and the reverse for externals. They concluded that internals who perceive attractive alternatives are more likely to act on those perceptions. However, they did not address the possibility that locus of control could moderate the relationship between turnover intentions and turnover. Since internals are more likely to believe in their ability to control events and the environment, they should be more likely to act on their turnover intentions and exhibit turnover behavior. Thus, locus of control could moderate the relationship between turnover intentions and turnover such that the relationship is stronger for internals than for externals.

Proactive Personality

Research suggests that some individuals are more likely to take action to influence the situation and people around them. More proactive individuals are more likely to take initiative and act to manipulate the environment and accomplish their goals. Less proactive individuals are more likely to allow events to happen and then react to changes (Bateman & Crant, 1993). More proactive individuals should be more likely to make changes, act to solve problems, and actively pursue possibilities that could advance their interests and careers. Thus, we might suspect more proactive individuals to be more likely to turnover in general.

However, the more interesting question is how this aspect of personality influences the relationship between turnover intentions and turnover. Bateman and Crant (1993) suggest that proactive personality should be positively related to problem solving and coping. Thus, individuals encountering factors either pushing or pulling them from their jobs may be more likely to actively pursue options that may involve quitting. Since more proactive individuals are more likely to act on their turnover intentions, they would have a stronger relationship between turnover intentions and turnover than less proactive individuals who are less likely to act on their intentions. Thus, proactive personality should moderate the relationship between turnover intentions and turnover such that the relationship is stronger for more proactive individuals than for less proactive individuals.

TRANSLATING ATTITUDES AND INTENTIONS INTO BEHAVIOR

Turnover process models draw heavily from rational decision making models such as Fishbein and Ajzen's (1980) theory of reasoned action, which stresses the importance of behavioral intentions in predicting and understanding turnover. However, there is research on the manner on which attitudes and intentions get translated into behavior that can inform turnover theory and research. Examples include research on perceptions of behavioral control, behavior consistency, and the role of emotional arousal.

Perceived Behavioral Control

Many prominent models of the turnover process implicitly or explicitly use elements of Fishbein and Ajzen's (1980) theory of reasoned action. This theory and its evolution into the theory of planned behavior (Ajzen, 1991) suggest that intentions to perform a behavior are the most immediate precursors to actual behavior. Intentions are a function of attitudes toward performing the behavior, which are in turn a function of beliefs concerning the consequences and desirability of such consequences of performing the behavior, and subjective norms concerning the behavior, which are a function of beliefs concerning what important referents think about the behavior and one's motivation to comply with those referents. A good deal of empirical research has supported this model, especially the critical role of intentions (see Kim & Hunter, 1998, for a meta-analytic review).

Turnover process models consistently recognize the importance of turnover intentions in predicting turnover behavior, beginning with Mobley (1977). A few studies have also tested more complete versions of the planned behavior model (Hom, Katerberg, & Hulin, 1979; Hom & Hulin, 1981; Newman, 1974; Prestholdt, Lane, & Matthews, 1987), generally finding that this approach predicted turnover behavior better than job satisfaction or organizational commitment. Hom and Hulin (1981), in particular, tested a relatively complete version of the Fishbein and Ajzen model compared to other alternative models. Their results suggested turnover was strongly predicted by this model. However, there are several aspects of the model that subsequent research has tended to neglect. For example, turnover researchers frequently focus on attitudes toward the job and toward the organization as major predictors of turnover intentions and behavior; however, the theory of planned behavior suggests that attitudes toward the specific behavior of interest are most important. Thus, there may be an additional mediating mechanism between job and organizational attitudes and withdrawal. Turnover research also rarely includes the opinions and norms of important referent groups concerning turnover, such as those of the work group, organization, profession, family, and friends. These opinions and norms, along with the individual's motivation to comply with such norms, may be very important in turnover decisions. There is evidence that turnover of friends at work can have a snowball effect leading to turnover (Krackhardt & Porter, 1986), that the opinions of family members can play an important role in decision making, and that some organizations and job types (e.g., information technology workers) have developed a turnover culture with norms that expect turnover and devalue longevity with a single organization.

From the perspective of explaining why some individuals who desire to quit and even intend to quit do not, perhaps the most overlooked element of the theory of planned behavior in this context is the role of behavioral control. Ajzen (1991) defined control beliefs as the presence or absence of factors that may facilitate or impede the performance of a behavior. Perceived behavioral control is an individual's perceptions of their ability to perform a behavior based on control beliefs. Behavioral control is expected to reinforce behavioral intentions through increased perseverance and consideration of potential obstacles (Hom & Griffeth, 1995). In fact, Ajzen (1991) argues that behavior is a function of compatible intentions and perceptions of behavioral control. Perceived behavioral control should moderate the effect of intentions on behavior such that favorable intentions only produce behavior when behavioral control is positive. The construct of behavioral control is similar to yet distinct from that of locus of control. Locus of control is described as a relatively stable individual difference, whereas behavioral control focuses on situational circumstances and constraints that influence perceptions of the ability to take some course of action.

Thus, in a turnover context, turnover intentions may only lead to turnover when individuals perceive that they have control over the decision to quit. There are a number of reasons that individuals might perceive less control over this decision. Family or financial constraints could restrict mobility. Over time, individuals become increasingly invested in an organization, making it more difficult to leave (e.g., Becker, 1960). Perceptions of the availability and quality of alternatives may affect perceived control. There is some evidence perceptions of alternatives interact with job satisfaction in leading to withdrawal (e.g., Jacofsky, Ferris, & Breckenridge, 1986). Steel, Griffeth, Allen, and Bryan (in press) recently suggested that barriers to mobility are critical components of labor market cognitions. However, turnover researchers do not typically directly measure perceived behavioral control over turnover decisions and have not assessed control as a potential moderator of the relationship between turnover intentions and turnover. Behavioral control should moderate the intentions-turnover relationship such that the relationship is stronger when control is higher, and weaker when control is lower.

Behavior Consistency

Direct experience with the behavior under consideration also plays a role in consistency of attitudes and intentions with behavior. Conventional wisdom suggests that individuals who have quit jobs before may be more likely to do so in the future. Many organizations implicitly or explicitly are more hesitant to hire an applicant with a history of multiple job changes. However, there is little theory or research in the turnover literature explaining why this might be the case. Ghiselli's (1974) hobo hypothesis suggests that some individuals are simply more prone to frequent job change than others. Similarly, Hulin et al. (1985) suggested that some populations labeled as casual workers or drifters are not committed to long-term work and are only drawn into the labor market by surplus jobs. Thus, these individuals are more likely to exhibit more frequent turnover behavior.

Besides the possibility of a relatively stable turnover personality, however, there is research to suggest that previous turnover behavior can affect the translation of attitudes and intentions into behavior. Specifically, attitudes and intentions associated with direct experience with the object of those attitudes and intentions are more predictive of later behavior than those associated with only indirect experience (Fazio & Zauna, 1981; Wu & Schaffer, 1987). Therefore, the relationship between turnover intentions and turnover should be stronger for those with direct experience with quitting jobs than for those without such experiences.

Emotional Arousal

Finally, research suggests that emotional arousal levels may interact with affective and cognitive desires in influencing behavior. For example, some research shows that negative affect paired with emotional arousal leads to risk seeking behavior, whereas either negative affect or emotional arousal alone does not (Leith & Baumeister, 1996). We argued earlier that the decision to quit is inherently a decision involving uncertainty and risk. Thus, it may be the case that negative affect such as job dissatisfaction or desire to quit may be more likely to lead to action when paired with some kind of emotionally arousing stimulus. This is particularly likely to be true in the case of clearly risky behavior such as impulsive quitting without searching or without an alternative in hand. Some recent turnover theory and research suggest that turnover decisions are often initiated by jarring events or shocks to the system (Lee & Mitchell, 1994). It seems likely that these shocks will be associated with some emotional reaction and arousal. Taken together, these two streams of research suggest that it may be fruitful to consider shocks in conjunction with affective and cognitive responses to the organization in explaining turnover.

SUMMARY

The purpose of this chapter was to explore possible mechanisms explaining why individuals do or do not follow through on expressed intentions to leave the organization and offer directions for future research. I identified three types of underexplored mechanisms that might influence actual quit decisions among those considering leaving. The first was consideration of the role of risk in making quit decisions. This analysis suggests that risk-aversion, turnover habits, outcome history, framing, opinions of salient others, and familiarity with turnover decisions influence perceptions of the risk associated with quitting as well as the willingness to take risks in this particular situation. Perceptions of risk and willingness to take risks then interact to influence turnover decision-making. Research is needed to test these propositions and assess the role of risk perceptions and risk propensity in turnover models.

The second was consideration of personality as a potential moderator of intentions-turnover relationships. This analysis identified three personality variables that influence consistency between expressed intentions and behavior and that predispose individuals to actively attempt to accomplish their expressed intentions or not: self-monitoring, locus of control, and proactive personality. Individuals low on self-monitoring, those with a more internal locus of control, and those with more proactive personalities may be more likely to follow through on their intentions to quit. Research is needed to empirically assess the validity of these ideas, and recognize that there are other individual differences that could influence the intentions-turnover relationship.

The third was consideration of theory and research on how intentions are translated into behavior. Research on predicting behavior from intentions suggests that turnover explanation would benefit from paying closer attention to volitional behavioral control, attitudes toward specific quitting behaviors, and norms of important others regarding quitting along with the motivation to comply with such norms. Additionally, research on behavior consistency and emotional arousal may also help explain the intentions-turnover relationship, especially in terms of habitual quitters and those who quit impulsively.

Researchers and managers are calling for more targeted retention strategies to manage turnover levels, especially in critical jobs and among highly valued employees. One way to address this issue is to do a better job of explaining the links between intentions to quit and actual turnover behavior. Examining the roles of risk, personality, behavioral control and consistency, and emotional arousal may help develop a more comprehensive understanding of when and why people choose to quit their jobs.

REFERENCES

Allen, N.J. & Meyer, J.P. (1990). The measurement and antecedents of affective, continuance, and normative commitment to the organization. *Journal of Occupational Psychology, 63,* 1–18.

Ajzen, I. (1991). The theory of planned behavior. *Organizational Behavior and Human Decision Processes, 50,* 179–211.

Barrick, M.R., & Mount, M.K. (1991). The big five personality dimensions and job performance: A meta-analysis. *Personnel Psychology, 44,* 1–26.

Bateman, T.S., & Crant, J.M. (1993). The proactive component of organizational behavior: A measure and correlates. *Journal of Organizational Behavior, 14,* 103–118.

Bazerman, M. (1998). *Judgment in managerial decision making.* New York: Wiley.

Becker, H.S. (1960) Notes on the concept of commitment. *American Journal of Sociology, 66,* 32–42.

Blau, G.J. (1987). Locus of control as a potential moderator of the turnover process. *Journal of Occupational Psychology, 60,* 21–30.

Farrell, D., & Rusbult, C.E. (1981). Exchange variables as predictors of job satisfaction, job commitment, and turnover: The impact of rewards, costs, alternatives, and investments. *Organizational Behavior and Human Performance, 28,* 78–95.

Gangestad, S.W., & Snyder, M. (2000). Self-monitoring: Appraisal and reappraisal. *Psychological Bulletin, 126,* 530–555.

Ghiselli, E.E. (1974). Some perspectives for industrial psychology. *American Psychologist, 80,* 80–87.

Glick, P. (1985). Orientations toward relationships: Choosing a situation in which to begin a relationship. *Journal of Experimental Social Psychology, 21,* 544–562.

Griffeth, R.W., & Hom, P.W. (1988). Locus of control and delay of gratification as moderators of employee turnover. *Journal of Applied Social Psychology, 18,* 1318–1333.

Griffeth, R.W., Hom, P.W., & Gaertner, S. (2000). A meta-analysis of antecedents and correlates of employee turnover: Update, moderator tests, and research implications for the next millennium. *Journal of Management, 26,* 463–488.

Highhouse, S., & Yuce, P. (1996). Perspectives, perceptions, and risk-taking behavior. *Organizational Behavior and Human Decision Processes, 65,* 159–167.

Hom, P.W., & Griffeth R. (1995). *Employee turnover.* Cincinnati, OH: South-Western College Publishing.

Hom, P.W., & Hulin, C.L. (1981). A competitive test of the prediction of reenlistment by several models. *Journal of Applied Psychology, 66*(1), 23–39.

Hom, P.W., Katerberg, R., & Hulin, C.L. (1979). Comparative examination of three approaches to the prediction of turnover. *Journal of Applied Psychology, 64,* 280–290.

Hom, P.W., & Kinicki, A.J. (2001). Toward a greater understanding of how dissatisfaction drives employee turnover. *Academy of Management Journal, 44,* 975–987.

Hulin, C.L., Roznowski, M., & Hachiya, D. (1985). Alternative opportunities and withdrawal decisions: Empirical and theoretical discrepancies and an integration. *Psychological Bulletin, 97* (2), 233–250.

Jenkins, J.M. (1993). Self-monitoring and turnover: The impact of personality on intentions to leave. *Journal of Organizational Behavior, 36*, 364–396.

Judge, T.A. (1993). Does affective disposition moderate the relationship between job satisfaction and voluntary turnover. *Journal of Applied Psychology, 78*, 395–401.

Kahneman, D., & Tversky, A. (1979). Prospect theory: An analysis of decision under risk. *Econometrica, 2*, 263–291.

Kim, M., & Hunter, J.E. (1993). Relationships among attitudes, behavioral intentions, and behavior. *Communication Research, 20*, 331–364.

Kraus, S.J. (1995). Attitudes and the prediction of behavior: A meta-analysis of the empirical literature. *Personality and Social Psychology Bulletin, 21*, 58–75.

Lee, T.W., & Mitchell, T.R. (1994). An alternative approach: The unfolding model of voluntary employee turnover. *Academy of Management Review, 19*, 51–89.

Leith, K.P., & Baumeister, R.F. (1996). Why do bad moods increase self-defeating behavior? Emotion, risk taking, and self-regulation. *Journal of Personality and Social Psychology, 71*, 1250–1267.

MacCrimmon, K.R., & Wehrung, D.A. (1985). A portfolio of risk measures. *Theory and Decisions, 19*, 1–29.

March, J.G., & Simon, H.A. (1958). Motivational constraints: The decision to participate. In *Organizations* (pp. 83–111). New York: Wiley.

Mitchell, T.R., Holtom, B.C., Lee, T.W., Sablynski, C.J., & Erez, M. (2001). Why people stay: Using job embeddedness to predict voluntary turnover. *Academy of Management Journal, 44*, 1102–1121.

Mittal, V., & Ross Jr., W.T. (1998). The impact of positive and negative affect and issue framing on issue interpretation and risk taking. *Organizational Behavior and Human Decision Processes, 76*, 298–324.

Mobley, W.H. (1977). Intermediate linkages in the relationship between job satisfaction and employee turnover. *Journal of Applied Psychology, 62*, 237–240.

Mobley, W.H., Griffeth, R.W., Hand, H.H., & Meglino, B.M. (1979). Review and conceptual analysis of the employee turnover process. *Psychological Bulletin, 86*, 493–522.

Newman, J. (1974). Predicting absenteeism and turnover: A field comparison of Fishbein's model and traditional job attitude measures. *Journal of Applied Psychology, 59*, 610–615.

Renn, R.W., & Vandenberg, R.J. (1991). Differences in employee attitudes and behaviors based on Rotter's (1966) internal-external locus of control: Are they all valid? *Human Relations, 44*, 1161–1178.

Rotter, J.B. (1966). Generalized expectancies for internal versus external control of reinforcement. *Psychological Monographs, 80*, 1–28.

Singh, J.V. (1986). Performance, slack, and risk taking in organizational decision making. *Academy of Management Journal, 29*, 562–586.

Sitkin, S.B., & Pablo, A.L. (1992). Reconceptualizing the determinants of risk behavior. *Academy of Management Review, 17*, 9–38.

Sitkin, S.B., & Weingart, L.R. (1995). Determinants of risky decision-making behavior: A test of the mediating role of risk perceptions and propensity. *Academy of Management Journal, 38*, 1573–1592.

Snyder, M. (1974). Self-monitoring of expressive behavior. *Journal of Personality and Social Psychology, 30,* 526–537.

Snyder, M. (1987). *Public appearances/private realities: The psychology of self-monitoring.* New York: Freeman and Company.

Snyder, M., & Simpson, J.A. (1984). Orientations toward romantic relationships. In S. Duck & D. Perlman (Eds.), *Intimate relationships: Development, dynamics, and deterioration.* Beverly Hills, CA: Sage.

Spector, P.E. (1982). Behavior in organizations as a function of employee's locus of control. *Psychological Bulletin, 91,* 482–497.

Spector, P.E., & Michaels, C.E. (1986). Personality and employee withdrawal: Effects of locus of control on turnover. *Psychological Reports, 59,* 63–66.

Steel, R.P, Griffeth, R.W., Allen, D.G., & Bryan, N. (in press). Development of a multi-dimensional measure of labor market cognitions: The employment opportunity index. *Journal of Applied Psychology.*

Steel, R.P., Shane, G.S., & Griffeth, R.W. (1990). Correcting turnover statistics for comparative analysis. *Academy of Management Journal, 33,* 179–187.

Vandenberg, R.J., & Barnes-Nelson, J. (1999). Disaggregating the motives underlying turnover intentions: When do intentions predict turnover behavior? *Human Relations, 52,* 1313–1336.

CHAPTER 3

REVISITING THE COSMOPOLITAN–LOCAL CONSTRUCT

An Event History Analysis of Employee Turnover

Roderick D. Iverson, Charles W. Mueller, and James L. Price

ABSTRACT

This study examines Gouldner's (1957) original cosmopolitan-local construct. Using organizational and professional commitment, we extended the cosmopolitan-local construct by the two additional categories of cosmopolitan/local, and nether cosmopolitan/local (Blau & Scott 1962; Grimes & Berger, 1970). Three hypotheses were proposed. First, locals will display lower turnover than cosmopolitans. Second, individuals who are classified as cosmopolitan/local (i.e., dually committed) will display lower turnover than cosmopolitans. Third, and final, individuals who are classified neither cosmopolitan/local (i.e., dually uncommitted) will display higher turnover than cosmopolitans. These hypotheses were tested (controlling for demographic, job-related, environmental, and contextual variables) on a sample of 838

Innovative Theory and Empirical Research on Employee Turnover, pages 55–72
Copyright © 2004 by Information Age Publishing

public school teachers from 405 schools over a five-year period employing the statistical procedure of event history analysis. During this period, 104 teachers voluntarily left the school district, representing a corrected turnover rate of approximately16 percent. Hypotheses 1 and 2 were affirmed: Both locals and those teachers who were dually committed (cosmopolitan/local) were less likely to leave than their cosmopolitan counterparts. We failed to find support for Hypothesis 3. The theoretical and practical implications of these findings are discussed.

INTRODUCTION

Nearly 50 years ago, Merton (1957) and Gouldner (1957, 1958) introduced theories concerning latent identities and social roles in organizations. Emerging from this research was the cosmopolitan-local construct which was used as a taxonomy to classify attitudes, values, and behaviors of employees. Gouldner (1957, p. 290) hypothesized that cosmopolitans were those employees who were "...low on loyalty to the employing organization, high on commitment to specialized role skills, and likely to use an outer reference group orientation." Locals, in contrast, were those employees who were "...high on loyalty to the employing organization, low on commitment to specialized role skills, and likely to use an inner reference group orientation." It was posited that employees manifesting two such different combinations of attributes would have differing "...self-conceptions and identities, as well as being differently perceived and identified by others in their group" (Gouldner, 1957, p. 293).

Currently there is a resurgence of interest in the two latent roles of cosmopolitans and locals. This derives from researchers attempting to understand the motives of some employees to stay and others to voluntarily leave organizations. Cosmopolitans are characterized as careeists, and are primarily orientated externally to their career or profession via specialized skills. Gouldner (1958) argued that cosmopolitans display very little loyalty to the organization, have relatively little integration in the formal or informal structure of the organization, and "do not intend to remain with it permanently" (p. 449). Organizational citizenship is considered as a means to an end in securing better jobs elsewhere. Locals, in contrast, are primarily committed to the organization via the congruence of values that they deem as important. This commitment is stronger than that to the profession. Locals are well integrated in the formal and informal structure of the organization and are generally regarded as membership "pillars." That is, locals are "...'deployables,' who accept transfer from job to job or department to department" (Gouldner, 1958, p. 446) rather than leave the organization.

Debate regarding the dimensionalty of the cosmopolitan-local construct continues to plague the area. Rather than treat cosmopolitans and locals as distinct groups, researchers, such as Glaser (1963), considered the possibility of a dual orientation whereby individuals may be high on both dimensions. In this situation, it would be expected that this dual commitment would lead to positive organizational outcomes such as reduced turnover (Carson, Carson, Roe, Birkenmeier, & Phillips, 1999). Alternatively, individuals may also be low on both the cosmopolitan and local dimensions (Blau & Scott, 1962; Grimes & Berger, 1970) and engage in antisocial behavior such as increased turnover (Carson et al., 1999).

The aim of the present paper is fourfold. The first objective is to develop a taxonomy of the cosmopolitan-local construct using organizational and professional commitment.[1] The second objective is to operationalize this taxonomy using midpoints of the two commitment constructs to form the dimensions of local, cosmopolitan, cosmopolitan and local, and nether cosmopolitan nor local. The third objective is to examine the relationship between these dimensions and voluntary turnover (collected from personnel records). The fourth, and final objective is to estimate a turnover model using event history analysis on a sample of teachers across 405 schools.

MEASUREMENT ISSUES

Gouldner (1957) originally formulated a single cosmopolitan-local continuum. He considered the three variables of organizational commitment, professional commitment, and reference group orientation to be so highly correlated that they formed a single dimension. Subsequent testing of the dimensionality has produced mixed results. In a later study of teachers, researchers and administrative employees from a liberal arts college in 1958, Gouldner, using factor analysis, reported that the construct yielded six factors—extreme locals to extreme cosmopolitans. However, Gouldner's analysis has been criticized on a number of grounds. This stems from the low statistical power (i.e., type II error) from analyzing the 94-item questionnaire on 125 employees and from interpreting factor loadings as low as .25 as significant (Grimes & Berger, 1970).

Although some researchers (e.g., Abrahamson, 1965; Ritti, 1968) pursued the bipolar unidimensional construct as originally proposed by Gouldner (1957), most researchers considered that there were theoretical and empirical reasons to investigate the multi-dimensionality of the construct (e.g., Blau & Scott, 1962; Grimes & Berger, 1970; Larwood et al., 1998). Moreover, the role of reference group orientation in the construct has been questioned. Grimes and Berger (1970), in reviewing the literature, omitted the internal-external reference dichotomy as they observed that it is "not related to professional orientation in a simple way, but depends upon organizational variables" (p. 413). Blau and Scott (1962), studying a sample of social workers, failed to find a strong relationship between group orientation and the two forms of commitment. In a cross-tabulation analysis of employees high in professional commitment, 36 per cent had an internal orientation. This led the authors to conclude that the relationship is "far from pronounced" (p. 67). This conclusion was also affirmed in a later study by Tuma and Grimes (1981). The bivariate results on a sample of university academics and administrators indicated that the correlation between professional commitment and external orientation was a non-significant .09. Hence, because of the lack of support for the variable of reference group orientation, we focus on the dimensions of organizational and professional commitment in our taxonomy.

TAXONOMY OF THE COSMOPOLITAN-LOCAL CONSTRUCT

As shown in Figure 3.1, we employ the taxonomy as proposed by Blau and Scott (1962) and Grimes and Berger (1970). Given the lack of theoretical and empirical support for reference group orientation, our approach in focusing on organizational and professional commitment is consistent with current research (Carson et al., 1999; Somers & Birnbaum, 2001). Further, we propose four categories of the cosmopolitan-local construct. First, individuals high on organizational commitment and low on professional commitment are classified as local. Second, individuals high on professional

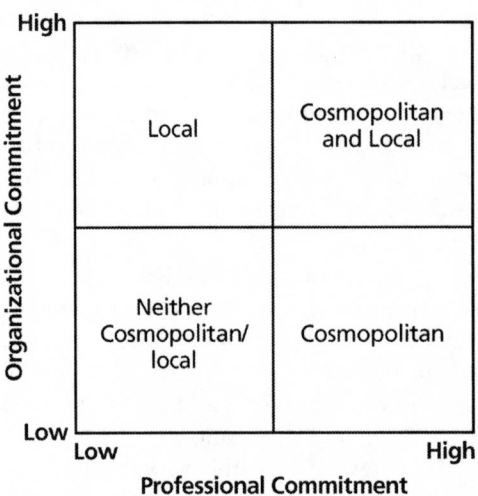

Figure 3.1. Taxonomy of the Cosmopolitan–Local construct.

commitment and low on organizational commitment are classified as cosmopolitan. Third, individuals high on both organizational and professional commitment are classified as cosmopolitan/local (i.e., dually committed). Fourth and finally, individuals low on organizational and professional commitment are classified as neither cosmopolitan/local (i.e., dually uncommitted). These profiles have important implications for understanding turnover.

HYPOTHESES

Although organizational and professional commitment are distinct constructs, several meta-analyses have reported correlations ranging between .438 and .452 (Lee, Carswell, & Allen, 2000; Matheu & Zajac, 1990; Wallace, 1988). Carson et al. (1999) note that the strength of association is contingent on the focal outcome. In our case this is employee turnover, defined as the movement across the membership boundary of an organization which is initiated by the employee (Price, 1977). Studies by Carson et al. (1999) and Somers and Birnbaum (2000) using ANOVA reported that locals displayed significantly lower levels of intention to leave than cosmopolitans.[2] This finding is consistent with Gouldner's (1957) notion that locals are more organizationally committed and inner referenced group focused. In addition, those individuals high on both organizational and professional commitment (i.e., dually commitment) found to have significantly lower levels of intention to leave than cosmopolitans. This result is explained by the fact that employees did not have to make an either/or choice between their organization and career. Further, it was found that those individuals low on both organizational and professional commitment (i.e., dually uncommitted) displayed significantly higher levels of intention to leave than cosmopolitans. Negative outcomes such as employee turnover are stronger when the link to both the organization and career is weak than when there is unilateral commitment (e.g., organizational or professional commitment). Deriving from the substantive theoretical (e.g., Gouldner, 1957, Grimes & Berger, 1970) and empirical (e.g., Carson et al., 1999; Somers & Birnbaum, 2000) arguments, we propose three hypotheses:

Hypothesis 1:   *Locals will display lower turnover than cosmopolitans.*

Hypothesis 2:   *Individuals who are classified as cosmopolitan/local (i.e., dually committed) will display lower turnover than cosmopolitans.*

Hypothesis 3:   *Individuals who are classified neither cosmopolitan/local (i.e., dually uncommitted) will display higher turnover than cosmopolitans.*

Control Variables

In examining these hypotheses, we control for other demographic, job-related, environmental, and contextual variables (collected from organization records) across 405 schools that have been linked with voluntary turnover. In terms of the demographic variables, as education reflects the human capital of employees, we hypothesize a positive relationship with turnover (Cotton & Tuttle, 1986; Hom & Griffeth, 1995). Although research is rather scant, there is evidence to affirm that female teachers demonstrate higher turnover rates than their male counterparts (Murnane, Singer, Willett, Kemple, & Olsen, 1991). In terms of race, Adams and Dial (1994) employing event history analysis observed that white teachers were significantly more likely to leave than their minority colleagues. The job-related variable of promotional advancement is defined as the degree of movement between status levels in an organization (Martin, 1979). As promotional advancement focuses on the retention of employees via the organization's internal labor market, we expect a negative relationship with turnover (Stumpf & Dawley, 1981). The environmental variable, job opportunity, refers to the availability of jobs outside the organization (Price & Mueller, 1986). The supply and demand created by the job market influences the ability of employees to leave. Where employees perceive there to be job opportunities, greater voluntary turnover is anticipated (Griffeth, Hom, & Gaertner, 2000; Mueller, Price, Boyer, & Iverson, 1994). In relation to the contextual variables, the Metropolitan Life Survey (MLS) (1985) reported that high schools are characterized by problems such as poor student quality, student discipline, alcoholism, drugs, violence, and overcrowded classrooms. Hence, deriving from these problems, we hypothesize high school teachers to resign at greater rates than their elementary school counterparts (Corcoran, Walker, & White, 1988). Finally, as evidence indicates that aspects such as student attendance rates and student performance (graduation and promotion rate of students) are associated with teacher satisfaction and commitment (Ostroff, 1992), we anticipate a negative effect on teacher turnover (Gritz & Theobald, 1996).

METHODS

Method

Research Setting and Sample.   The site for this research was an urban public school district located in a major city in the Midwestern United States. The sample consisted of 838 classroom teachers. Seventy-nine percent of the sample was female, with 83 percent being elementary teachers. The average age, tenure, and education were 38.3 years (SD = 9.3), 4.4 years (SD = 3.7), and 17.3 years (SD = 1.1), respectively. Chi-square analysis was undertaken to evaluate the representativeness of the sample. Data for the population were obtained from the school district records. There were no gender differences between the population and sample ($\chi^2(1) = 1.86, p > .05$).

Data Collection. Fifteen hundred teachers were randomly selected to be surveyed from the personnel records of the school district. Respondents were informed in a covering letter that participation was voluntary and all information collected was confidential. Accompanying the questionnaire was an answer sheet with an identification number for follow-ups which was electronically scanned. Questionnaires were mailed to teachers at their schools in early January 1991. A total of 838 (from 405 different schools) were returned by the closeout date, representing a corrected response rate of 57%. Contextual variables were also obtained from the records of the State Board of Education 1989–1990 school year report card and the racial/ethnic survey of the school district. The contextual variables were then matched with the 405 schools in our survey.

Measurement. The variables used were constructed using established scale. Cronbach's alpha (1951) was used to estimate the reliability of multiple-item measures. Table 3.1 presents the descriptive statistics and reliability of the survey measures.

The dependent variable of voluntary turnover was measured as the duration of the teacher's stay in the school system during period of January 15, 1991 to November 13, 1996. The employment status of each teacher (as of November 13, 1996) was determined from personnel records. Employees who voluntarily left for reasons other than job related (e.g., spouse moving) were deleted from the analysis as these were considered to be beyond the control of the employee and the organization (i.e., unavoidable turnover) (Abelson, 1987; Iverson & Pullman, 2000; Shaw, Delery, Jenkins, & Gupta, 1998). During the study period, 151 teachers left the school district, of which 108 were voluntary. This corresponds to a voluntary turnover rate of 15.85%.[3]

The independent variables comprised organizational and professional commitment. Four items (i.e., the school in which I work is the best of all possible places to work; I do not care about the fate of the school in which I work (R); I speak highly of the school in which I work to my friends; and I am proud to tell others that I am part of the school in which I work) from the organizational commitment scale of Porter, Steers, Mowday, and Boulian (1974) (1 = *strongly disagree* to 5 = *strongly agree*) was used to tap commitment to the school ($\alpha = .79$). To measure professional commitment we employed the same strategy as Wallace (1997) in which reference to the "school" was substituted with reference to the "teaching profession." Based on the coefficient alpha (Cronbach, 1951) analysis, the second item (i.e., I do not care

Table 3.1. Descriptive Statistics and Correlations Among Variables[a,b]

Determinants	No. of Items	Mean	s.d.	1	2	3	4	5	6	7	8	9	10	11	12	13
1. Turnover	1	.15	.35	—												
2. Local	1	.21	.41	-.09	—											
3. Cosmopolitan	1	.16	.37	.09	-.22	—										
4. Cosmopolitan/local	1	.26	.44	-.09	-.31	-.26	—									
5. Neither Cosmopolitan/local	1	.36	.48	.09	-.39	-.33	-.45	—								
6. Education	1	17.31	1.07	.00	-.04	-.02	.01	.03	—							
7. Female	1	.81	.39	-.05	-.03	.01	.06	-.04	-.11	—						
8. White	1	.54	.50	.05	-.01	.05	-.04	.01	-.02	-.06	—					
9. Promotional advancement	3	3.48	.80	-.08	.09	-.06	.35	-.34	-.08	.04	-.21	.69				
10. Job opportunity	3	3.13	.94	.09	-.11	.15	-.17	.13	.08	-.09	-.01	-.23	.81			
11. High school	1	1.17	.38	.04	.02	-.05	-.08	.10	.07	-.30	.00	-.11	.07	—		
12. Attendance rate	1	9.47	5.73	-.01	.03	.02	.10	-.14	-.06	.24	.07	.05	-.12	-.76	—	
13. Student performance	1	.49	.50	-.03	.04	-.03	.06	-.06	.01	.03	.04	-.03	-.01	.00	.21	—

[a] Reliabilities are reported along the diagonal.
[b] Correlations above [.06] are significant at $p < .05$ one-tailed test

about the fate of the teaching profession (R)) was deleted (α = .76). The scales have displayed acceptable reliability and validity (Wallace, 1997).

In terms of the control variables, the demographic characteristics consisted of teachers' education (in years), female (1 = female, 0 = male), and white (1 = white, 0 = minority). Both promotional advancement and job opportunity (1 = *strongly disagree* to 5 = *strongly agree*) were assessed using Price and Mueller's (1981, 1986) scales. The psychometric properties of these scales have been demonstrated (Iverson & Maguire, 2000; Iverson & Pullman, 2000). The contextual variables allowed us to control for objective conditions of the 405 schools in the sample. These were obtained from records of the school district and included elementary (coded 1 for elementary and 0 for high school), attendance rate (coded as the aggregate days of student attendance divided by the sum of the aggregate days of student attendance and aggregate days of student absence multiplied by 100), and student performance (coded as 1 for high student performers and 0 for low student performers).

Confirmatory factor analyses were undertaken using Linear Structural Relations (LISREL VIII) (Jöreskog & Sörbom, 1996a) to assess the convergent (i.e., the degree of association between measures of a construct) and discriminant validity (i.e., the degree to which measures of constructs are distinct) of the multiple-item measures of organizational commitment, professional commitment, promotional advancement, and job opportunity. We initially employed the program of PRELIS (Jöreskog & Sörbom, 1996b) to transform the raw data. In terms of the convergent validity, the hypothesized four-factor model was found to significantly better fit the data than both the null ($\Delta\chi^2$ (18) = 3756.26, p < .001), one factor ($\Delta\chi^2$ (6) = 1328.37, p < .001), and three factor (organizational and professional commitment combined) ($\Delta\chi^2$ (3) = 375.04, p < .001) models.[4] Examination of the parameter estimates (factor loadings) of the best fitting four-factor model were all significant (p < .05) and ranged from .53 to .91. These results provided support for the convergent validity of the model. The discriminant validity was also affirmed.[5] The constructs of organizational and professional commitment, for example, had an χ_d^2 (1) = 325.34, p < .001. The measurement model demonstrated acceptable fit: goodness-of-fit index (GFI) of .92, a normed fit index (NFI) (Bentler & Bonnett, 1980) of .91, and a root-mean-square error of approximation (RMSEA) (Browne & Cudeck, 1993) of .08 (Browne & Cudeck, 1993; Gerbing & Anderson, 1993). The average reliability of the multiple-item measures displayed a good internal consistency of .76.

Analytical Procedures

We employed the survival analysis technique of event history analysis (Allison, 1984; Tuma & Hannan, 1984; Yamaguchi, 1991). Event history analysis estimates two related functions: the survival function, which at time t estimates the probability that an employee will stay beyond time t, and the hazard function, which estimates the probability that an employee will quit at time t (given that the employee survives to time t). The advantage of event history analysis is that it simultaneously predicts whether employee turnover occurred, as well as building in the exact time at which this turnover did occur (i.e., converts turnover into a continuous variable). As the model includes continuous, categorical, and time-dependent variables, the regression-analog method is utilized in the analysis (Morita, Lee, & Mowday, 1993). We adopt a single-event model as we focused on predicting the resignation of employees.[6]

RESULTS

Using median splits for the two commitment measures, we created four categories of the local-cosmopolitan construct with the following cell sizes: local ($n = 141$), cosmopolitan ($n = 108$), cosmopolitan and local ($n = 180$), and neither cosmopolitan nor local ($n = 248$). Before proceeding to the event history analysis, we first provide a discussion of some descriptive results.

Chi-square Results

We initially analyzed the difference among the four groups for the frequency of turnover behavior. The chi-square results indicated that there were significant group differences (χ^2 (3) = 16.65, $p < .001$). Compared to the average group turnover rate of 15%, both cosmopolitans (22%) and those individuals classified neither cosmopolitan/local (i.e., dually uncommitted) (19%) were over-represented in their turnover rate, while locals (9%) and those individuals classified as cosmopolitan/local (i.e., dually committed) (9%) were under-represented in their turnover rate. These results provide some support at the outset for our hypotheses.

Bivariate Results

Examination of the correlations also offers preliminary confirmation of our hypotheses (see Table 3.1). We observed that both the profiles of local and cosmopolitan/local had significant negative associations ($r = -.09$, $p <$ .05), while cosmopolitan and neither cosmopolitan/local had significant positive associations with employee turnover ($r = .09$, $p < .05$). The direction of the relationships are consistent with our taxonomy.

Event History Results

The product limit (Kaplan-Meier) estimates of the hazard function for all four dimensions of the cosmopolitan-local construct are displayed in Figure 3.2. As can be seen from the plots, both the profiles of locals and dually committed (i.e., cosmopolitan/local) appear to differ from cosmopolitans and those dually uncommitted (neither cosmopolitan/local) in survival. This observation was supported by the log rank which tests the equality of survival distributions (16.85, df = 3, $p < .05$) (Norušis, 1994). To detect the direction of these differences we therefore undertook additional pair wise log rank tests among the four profiles. Significant differences were found between locals and cosmopolitans (9.81, $p < .05$) and between locals and dually uncommitted teachers (7.6, $p < .05$). A similar pattern of results was demon-

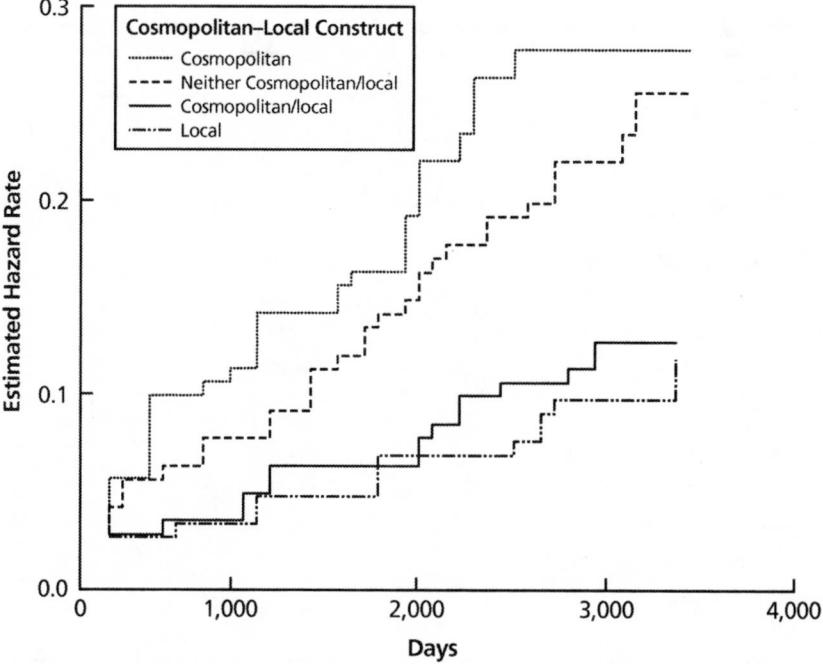

Figure 3.2.   Hazard function for the four categories of the Cosmopolitan–Local construct.

strated between dually committed teachers and cosmopolitans (9.18, $p < .05$) and dually uncommitted teachers (7.71, $p < .05$), respectively.

The event history results are presented in Table 3.2. With respect to our categories of the cosmopolitan-local construct, Hypotheses 1 and 2 were affirmed. First, locals were less likely to leave than their cosmopolitan counterparts (omitted category) ($\beta = -1.026$, $p < .01$). More specifically, exponentiating the coefficient (i.e., antilog), we find that turnover for cosmopolitans was 179% larger than that for locals. In addition, teachers who were dually committed (i.e., cosmopolitan/local) were also 46% less probable to resign than cosmopolitans ($\beta = -.771$, $p < .05$). Further, we observed no significant differences in turnover behavior ($\beta = -.215$, $p > .05$) between locals and those who were dually committed. This pattern of non-significance was also found between teachers who were dually uncommitted (i.e., neither cosmopolitan/local) and those who were cosmopolitans ($\beta = -.092$, $p > .05$). In terms of the control variables, we found only support for job opportunity ($\beta = .245$, $p < .05$). Each additional unit change in perceived job opportunity increases the likelihood of turnover by 28%. Consistent with expectations, when jobs are perceived to be plentiful in the labor market, turnover is increased (Griffeth et al., 2000; Mueller et al., 1994). The explained variance was small but significant (.033).[7]

Table 3.2.   Cox Proportional Hazards Model of Voluntary Turnover

Variables	β	SE
Control Variables		
Education	−.043	.100
Female	.117	.134
White	−.116	.111
Promotional advancement	−.013	.140
Job opportunity	.245*	.121
High school	.204	.224
Attendance rate	.032	.033
Student performance	.130	.114
Predictor Variables		
Local	−1.026**	.386
Cosmopolitan and local	−.771*	.339
Neither Cosmopolitan nor local	−.092	.261
Model chi-square	27.837**	
D	.033	

[a] Cosmopolitan was the referenced category.
[b] Global chi-square (null hypothesis that all of the coefficients are 0 can be rejected at $p < .05$).
* $p < .05$ level. ** $p < .01$ level. *** $p < .001$ level.

DISCUSSION

This study provides further support for Gouldner's (1957) original cosmopolitan-local construct. We extended the cosmopolitan-local construct by the two additional categories of cosmopolitan/local, and nether cosmopolitan/local (Blau & Scott, 1962; Grimes & Berger, 1970). Using organizational and professional commitment to operationalize these categories, it was proposed that the various types of commitment would be differentially associated with employee turnover. Employing event history analysis, the results indicated that locals displayed lower turnover than cosmopolitans, as did teachers who were characterized as cosmopolitan/local. The theoretical and practical implications for disentangling the cosmopolitan-local construct are discussed.

In accordance with Gouldner's (1957) original formulation, locals demonstrated lower turnover than their cosmopolitan counterparts. This finding is consistent with our expectations that locals are more committed to the school than to the profession and are regarded as membership "pillars." The result has a number of implications. First, engendering a local identity (i.e., organizational commitment) can assist firms in their human resource planning, as well as in reducing turnover costs (Cascio, 1991). Importantly, there is now evidence to suggest that organizational commitment can be managed via appropriate HR practices (Meyer & Allen, 1997). Given that locals can behave like cosmopolitans in later stages of their careers (Cornwall & Grimes, 1987), organizations need to foster HR practices (e.g., family-friendly) that meet the changing requirements of employees throughout their organizational tenure.

In contrast to Gouldner's (1957) single cosmopolitan-local continuum, we observed that dual commitment (i.e., organizational and professional commitment) was associated with a decline in employee turnover. Researchers should not overlook the powerful role of dual commitment in reducing turnover compared to other forms of unilateral commitment such as organizational commitment (i.e., local). Turnover was observed to decrease in situations where employees do not experience conflicting allegiance between their organization and career. This is an important finding given that we controlled for the labor market variable of job opportunity. Moreover, the current emphasis of organizations to improve efficiency and to cut costs by restructuring and delayering can lead to the unintended consequence of increased voluntary turnover. That is, we are seeing the emergence of a "new" psychological contract in which employee expectations about the employment relationship is changing. Employees now enter this new contract with the understanding that their loyalty to the organization and effort are less likely to be rewarded (Noer, 1993). As noted by Capelli (2000), as organizations further dismantle internal labor markets and career paths, they turn their attention to poaching rather the retaining employees. Employees become less committed to the organization and more committed to their profession.

Yet we must be careful not to go beyond the scope of the study. First, the data comes from a single school district comprising mainly female elementary teachers. This was mitigated somewhat by data being collected across 405 sites. Another limitation pertains to the relatively low base rate of turnover. Although it was comparable to current studies (e.g., Cohen, 1999; Iverson & Pullman, 2000; Somers & Birnbaum, 1999; Vandenberghe, 1999), it does make it more difficult to establish relationships. Our measure of professional commitment requires improvement. We had to delete one of our three-items because of poor reliability. A further problem relates to using cutoff points for dividing scores on our measures of professional and organizational commitment into four groups. Gordon and Ladd (1990) note that cutoff points are arbitrarily determined (i.e., median and midpoint splits are commonly used), making categorization problematic. Moreover, information is lost as a result of dichotomous categorization of continuous variables (commitment was measured on a five-point Likert type scale). A final limitation concerns the specification of our model. As we were unable to decompose the direct and indirect effects of the various commitment profiles on turnover, alternative models with multiple decision paths (e.g., Lee & Mitchell, 1994; Price & Mueller, 1986) could not be tested.

Nevertheless, this paper contributes to our understanding of the local-cosmopolitan construct in a number of ways. First, in keeping with Gouldner's (1957) original thesis, unlike much of previous research, we focused our attention on predicting turnover. We also found support for the original category of local as well as the expanded category cosmopolitan/local. Together these findings indicate that the application of latent role theory is still very much relevant in today's environment. A relevant example is the current move toward contingent employment (e.g., temporary and part-time work). While being associated with decreased costs on the one hand, contingent employment is also associated with increased turnover. This primarily occurs due to the failure of organizations to engender local and dually committed identities. Finally, researchers need to study other negative outcomes (e.g., loafing) if we are to truly understand the ramifications of such failures.

ACKNOWLEDGMENTS

An earlier version of this paper was presented at the 2002 Annual Academy of Management Meetings in Denver. Financial support was provided by the

Lloyd A. Fry Foundation of Chicago, Illinois and the Presidents Research Grant at Simon Fraser University. Direct all correspondence to Roderick D. Iverson, Faculty of Business Administration, Simon Fraser University, 8888 University Drive, Burnaby, B.C. V5A 1S6, CANADA, E-Mail: riverson@sfu.ca; Fax: (604) 291-4920.

NOTES

1. Researchers employ the terms of professional, career, and occupational commitment interchangeably (Lee, et al., 2000).

2. Although Somers and Birnbaum (2000) found no group differences for frequency of turnover behavior, the small turnover cell sizes of 9 for cosmopolitan and local (i.e., dually committed), 4 for locals, 5 for cosmopolitans, and 11 for neither cosmopolitan nor local (i.e., dually uncommitted) casts doubt on these findings.

3. Due to the matching of data (turnover and school level) and listwise deletion of missing data, the final sample size used in the analysis was 681.

4. When testing for convergent validity, Bagozzi and Yi (1988) recommend a nested test of the hypothesized, three factor, one factor, and null model.

5. The discriminant validity was calculated by estimating the difference between one model which allowed the correlations between the constructs to be constrained to unity (i.e., perfectly correlated) and another model, which allowed the correlations between the constructs to be free (see Bagozzi & Yi, 1988).

6. We estimated models for each variable (see Blossfeld, Hamerle, & Mayer, 1989 for procedure) and found the plotted hazard functions to be approximately proportional to each other. This indicates that the proportionality assumption was not violated as the "hazard function is only dependent upon the duration $v = t - t_{k-1}$ and that the baseline hazard rate as well as the coefficients β are the same for all episodes" (Blossfeld et al., 1989, p. 143).

7. Current research considers that "D is similar to the R^2 value used regression models: $D = \chi^2 / (n - K + \chi^2)$, where n = sample size and K = number of variables" (Sheridan, 1992, p. 1047).

REFERENCES

Abrahamson, M. (1965). Cosmopolitanism, dependence- identification and geographic mobility. *Administrative Science Quarterly, 10*, 98–106.

Adams, G.J., & Dial, M. (1994). The effects of education on teacher retention. *Education, 114*(3), 358–364.

Allison, P.D. (1984). *Event history analysis.* Beverly Hills, CA: Sage.

Bagozzi, R.P., & Yi, Y. (1988). On the evaluation of structural equation models. *Academy of Marketing Science, 16*, 74–94

Bentler P.M., & Bonett, D.G. 1980, Significance tests and goodness of fit in the analysis of covariance structures. *Psychological Bulletin, 88*, 588.

Blau, P.M., & Scott, W.R. (1962). *Formal organizations.* San Francisco: Chandler.

Blossfeld, H.P., Hamerle, A., & Mayer, K.U. (1989). *Event history analysis.* Hillsdale, NJ: Lawrence Erlbaum.

Browne, M.W., & Cudeck, R. (1993). Alternative ways of assessing model fit. In K.A Bollen & J.S. Long (Eds.), *Testing structural equation models* (pp. 136–162). Newbury Park, CA: Sage.

Cappelli, P. (2000). Managing without commitment. *Organizational Dynamics, 28*(4), 11–24.

Carson, K.D., Carson, P.P, Roe, C.W., Birkenmeier, B.J., & Phillips, J.S. (1999). Four commitment profiles and their relationship to empowerment, service recovery, and work attitudes. *Public Personnel Management, 28,* 1–13.

Cascio, W. (1991). *Costing human resources,* Boston, MA: PWS-Kent.

Cohen, A. (1999). Turnover among professionals: A longitudinal study of American lawyers. *Human Resource Management, 38*(1), 61–75.

Corcoran, T.B., Walker, L.J., & White, J.L. (1988). *Working in urban schools.* Washington, DC: Institute for Educational Leadership.

Cotton, J.L., & Tuttle, J.M. (1986). Employee turnover: A meta-analysis and review with implications for research. *Academy of Management Review, 11,* 55–70.

Cronbach, L.J. (1951). Coefficient alpha and the internal structure of tests. *Psychometrika, 16,* 297–334.

Gerbing, D.W., & Anderson, J.C. (1993). Monte Carlo evaluations of goodness- offit indices for structural equation models. In K.A Bollen & J.S. Long (Eds.), *Testing structural equation models* (pp. 40–65). Newbury Park, CA: Sage.

Glaser, B.G. (1963). The local-cosmopolitan scientist. *American Journal of Sociology, 69,* 249–259.

Gouldner, A.W. (1957). Cosmopolitans and locals: Towards an analysis of latent social roles-I. *Administrative Science Quarterly, 2,* 281–306.

Gouldner, A.W. (1958). Cosmopolitans and locals: Towards an analysis of latent social roles-II. *Administrative Science Quarterly, 2,* 444–480.

Gordon, M.E., & Ladd, R.T. 1990. Dual allegiance: renewal, reconsideration, and recantation. *Personnel Psychology, 43,* 37–69.

Griffeth, R.W., Hom, P.W., & Gaertner, S. (2000). A meta-analysis of antecedents and correlates of employee turnover: Update, moderator tests, and research implications for the next millennium. *Journal of Management, 26,* 463–488.

Grimes, A.J., & Berger, P.K. (1970). Cosmopolitan-local: Evaluation of the construct. *Administrative Science Quarterly, 15,* 407–416.

Grtiz, R.M., & Theobald, N.B. (1996). The effects of school district spending priorities on length of stay in teaching. *Journal of Human Resources, 31*(3), 477–512.

Hom, P.W., & Griffeth, R.W. (1995). *Employee turnover.* Cincinnati, OH: South-Western College.

Iverson, R.D., & Maguire, C. (2000). The relationship between job and life satisfaction: Evidence from a remote mining community. *Human Relations, 53*(6), 807–839.

Iverson, R.D., & Pullman, J.A. (2000). Determinants of voluntary turnover and layoffs in an environment of repeated downsizing following a merger: An event history analysis. *Journal of Management, 26*(5), 977–1003.

Jöreskog, K.G., & Sörbom, D. (1996a). *LISREL 8: user's reference guide.* Chicago: Scientific Software International.

Jöreskog, K.G., & Sörbom, D. (1996b). *PRELIS 2: User's reference guide.* Chicago: Scientific Software International.

Larwood, L., Wright, T.A., Desrochers, S., & Dahir, V. (1998). Extending latent role and psychological contract theories to predict intent to turnover and politics in business organizations. *Group & Organization Management, 23,* 100–123.

Lee, K., Carswell, J.J., & Allen, N.J. (2000). A meta-analytic review of occupational commitment: Relations with person- and work-related variables. *Journal of Applied Psychology, 85,* 799–811.

Lee, T.W., & Mitchell, T.R. (1994). An alternative approach: the unfolding model of voluntary employee turnover. *Academy of Management Review, 19,* 51–89.

Martin, T.N. (1979). A contextual model of employee turnover intentions. *Academy of Management Journal, 22,* 313–324.

Mathieu, J.E., & Zajac, D.M. (1990). A review and meta-analysis of the antecedents, correlates and consequences of organizational commitment. *Psychological Bulletin, 108,* 171–194.

Merton, R.K. (1957). Patterns of influence: Local and cosmopolitan influentials. In R.K. Merton (Ed.), *Social theory and social structure,* 368–380. Glencoe, IL: Free Press.

Metropolitan Life Survey. (1985). *Strengthening the profession.* New York: Louis Harris and Associates.

Meyer, J.P., & Allen, N.J. (1997). *Commitment in the workplace: Theory, research, and application.* Thousand Oaks, CA: Sage.

Morita, J.G., Lee, T.W., & Mowday, R.T. (1993). The regression-analog to survival analysis: A selected application to turnover research. *Academy of Management Journal, 36,* 1430–1464.

Mueller, C.W., Boyer, E.M., Price, J.L., & Iverson, R.D. (1994). Employee attachment and noncoercive conditions of work: The case of dental hygenists. *Work and Occupations, 21,* 179–212.

Murnane, R.J., Singer, J.D., Willett, J.B., Kemple, J.J., & Olsen, R.J. (1991). *Who will teach? Policies that matter.* Cambridge, MA: Harvard University.

Noer, D. (1993). *Healing the wounds: Overcoming the trauma of layoffs and revitalizing downsizing organizations.* San Franscisco: Jossey-Bass.

Norušis, M. J. 1994. *SPSS Advanced Statistics Guide.* Chicago: SPSS.

Ostroff, C. (1992). The relationship between satisfaction, attitudes, and performance: An organizational level analysis. *Journal of Applied Psychology, 77,* 963–974.

Porter, L. W., Steers, R. M., Mowday, R. T., & Boulian, P.V. (1974). Organizational commitment, job satisfaction and turnover among psychiatric technicians. *Journal of Applied Psychology, 59,* 603–609.

Price, J.L., & Mueller, C.W. (1981). A causal model of turnover for nurses. *Academy of Management Journal, 24,* 543–565.

Price, J.L., & Mueller, CW. (1986). *Absenteeism and turnover of hospital employees.* Greenwich, CT: JAI Press.

Ritti, R.R. (1968). Work goals of scientists and engineers. *Industrial Relations, 7,* 116–131.

Sheridan, J.E. (1992). Organizational culture and employee retention. *Academy of Management Journal, 35*, 1036–1056.

Somers, M., & Birnbaum, D. (2000). Exploring the relationship between commitment profiles and work attitudes, employee withdrawal, and job performance. *Public Personnel Management, 29*, 353–365.

Somers, M., & Birnbaum, D. (1999). Survival versus traditional methodologies for studying employee turnover: Differences, divergences and directions for future research. *Journal of Organizational Behavior, 20*, 273–284.

Stumpf, S.A., & Hartman, K. (1984). Individual exploration to organizational commitment or withdrawal. *Academy of Management Journal, 27*, 308–329.

Tuma, N.B., & Grimes, A.J. (1981). A comparison of models of role orientations of professionals in a research-oriented university. *Administrative Science Quarterly, 26*, 187–206.

Tuma, N.B., & Hannan, M.T. (1984). *Social dynamics.* New York: Academic Press.

Vandenberghe, C. (1999). Organizational culture, person-culture fit, and turnover: A replication in the health care industry. *Journal of Organizational Behavior, 20*, 175–184.

Wallace, J.E. (1997). Becker's side-bet theory of commitment revisited: Is it time for a moratorium or a resurrection? *Human Relations, 50*, 727–749.

Wallace, J.E. (1988). Professional and organizational commitment: Compatible or incompatible? *Journal of Vocational Behavior, 42*, 333–349.

Yamaguchi, K. (1991). *Event history analysis.* Newbury Park, CA: Sage.

CHAPTER 4

JOB MARKETS AND TURNOVER DECISIONS

Robert P. Steel

ABSTRACT

A "read-and-react" view of the turnover decision process is proposed. This view holds that the steps in an individual's turnover decision process vary as a function of interactions between (1) personal circumstances (i.e., skill sets) and (2) salient features of the *relevant* labor market.

INTRODUCTION

Lee and Mitchell (1984) proposed a model of the turnover process that is, in some respects, a conceptual departure from its many predecessors. Before Lee and Mitchell, turnover models were generally intended to describe a more-or-less universal turnover process. By way of contrast, Lee and Mitchell's (1984) framework describes four different decision paths that apply to the turnover decisions of different populations. In essence, their framework is suggesting that the process of turnover is different for people in different kinds of situations.

Innovative Theory and Empirical Research on Employee Turnover, pages 73–82
Copyright © 2004 by Information Age Publishing
All rights of reproduction in any form reserved.

The current article takes a cue from Lee and Mitchell (1984). In this article I will suggest that the behavioral process people follow as they move toward a decision to quit varies as a function of interactions between (1) personal circumstances and (2) labor market factors. Instead of following the kind of carefully scripted, linear decision process that traditional turnover theory has usually envisioned, individuals may actually be performing an adaptive process—an adaptation that is molded by both life circumstances and personally-relevant job-market conditions.

EMPIRICAL LITERATURE

How much do we really know about the impact of labor markets on individual decisions? The answer is, not much. The empirical literature relating to this issue is surprisingly skimpy. Dreher and Dougherty (1980) published one of the first studies focusing on the effects of labor market factors on individual turnover decisions. They used data compiled by the U.S. Department of Labor to investigate the effects of *occupational market demand* on the turnover decisions of oil company workers. As expected, workers in occupations with more favorable labor markets were significantly more likely to quit ($r = -.26$, $p < .05$).

Gerhart (1990) focused on a different facet of the labor market. He evaluated the effects of *regional labor markets* on the turnover decisions of young adults. Gerhart found that objective data describing labor-market opportunity (i.e., regional unemployment) added significantly to the turnover predictions of perceptual labor-market variables (e.g., perceived alternatives). In this study the correlation between regional unemployment and turnover was $-.12$ ($p < .05$).

While studying the same group as Gerhart (1990), Trevor (2001) used a two-variable operationalization of the labor market to predict turnover decisions. Trevor's labor-market variable combined data on regional unemployment with scores reflecting levels of occupational unemployment. Trevor reported a small, but significant relationship ($r = .04$, $p < .05$) between turnover and his measure of labor-market opportunity.

Dreher and Dougherty (1980) and Gerhart (1990) used one-variable operationalizations of the labor market. Trevor (2001) attempted to develop a two-variable measure. My own work (Steel, 1996) involved the use of four different measures of employment-market activity. This set of indices included a measure of the volume of newspaper advertising for jobs targeted by my study, data on regional unemployment, measures of occupational demand (as reported by the Department of Labor), and institutional data on historical retention rates. Data segmenting the market on a regional basis (i.e., regional unemployment rates) were not significantly correlated with the turnover decisions of individuals in my study, but several market variables rooted primarily in occupational mechanisms (e.g., job advertising, Department of Labor statistics, historical retention rates) were significant predictors of the study's retention criterion ($rs = .10$–.14, $p < .05$). Effectively replicating Gerhart (1990), the study also found that perceptual and objective measures of employment opportunity explained unique variance in turnover data.

Studies by Gerhart (1990) and Trevor (2001) found regional unemployment to be significantly correlated with turnover. My study (Steel, 1996) did not. Why the difference? One viable explanation for inconsistent findings might be problems with predictor variance. If the measure of regional unemployment in my study suffered from restriction in range (i.e., low variance), this could explain why my findings did not agree with the other studies. The measures used by Gerhart (1990) and Trevor (2001) had more than ample variance. They were based on a national cohort of young adults. But, my study of military personnel ($N = 402$) also performed a national sampling. My dataset included individuals from virtually every region in the continental United States. Hence, this explanation does not appear to account for differences in study findings.

Another possible explanation is that the retention decisions of my military personnel were not much influenced by regional considerations. Compared to run-of-the-mill civilian populations, military populations are more mobile. Military personnel experience frequent assignment rotations, and, because of these practices, they become less inclined to sink roots in any specific geographical location. Because, as a group, military personnel tend to have weaker geographical preferences, they may be less inclined than their civilian workforce counterparts to focus on *regional dimensions* of labor markets. Stated as a general principle, there may be interactive effects between labor market structures and how people in different kinds of life circumstances react to those structures.

Carsten and Spector (1987) used a creative approach in their study of the effects of labor market factors on turnover decisions. Their meta-analysis evaluated the moderating effects of unemployment rates (regional, occupational, and industrial) on two kinds of turnover relationships, job satisfaction-turnover relationships and quit intentions-turnover relationships. Consistent with the work of other researchers (e.g., Dreher & Dougherty, 1980, Gerhart, 1990; Steel, 1996), they found that occupational unemployment had a greater effect on satisfaction-turnover relationships ($r = -.52$) than did regional unemployment ($r = -.18$). However, these differences were not present in the quit intention-turnover data. Instead, moderating effects of the two kinds of market variables (i.e., occupational unemployment; regional unemployment) in this analysis were similar.

The discussion so far has suggested that market structures may have differential effects on the turnover decision process. Existing data, while admittedly scanty, appear to suggest that occupational labor markets tend to have a greater effect on turnover decisions than regional markets. However, I have also noted that the inclination to attend to a particular market segment (e.g., occupational market, regional market) may be accentuated or diminished by personal circumstances (e.g., membership in the military).

Before concluding our review of the empirical literature, we turn to examination of data relating to a central question underlying market-turnover interfaces. Do individuals base perceptions of the labor market on objective labor market realities? Michaels and Spector (1982) are doubtful. Their article raised the possibility that labor-market perceptions have little relationship with actual market realities. This issue is central to the current paper's thesis because I am suggesting that individuals take different paths to turnover decisions as a result of perceptions of their unique labor market. Hence, labor-market perceptions drive the process.

Findings reported recently bear on this question. In a recent article (Steel, 2002), I reanalyzed some of the military retention data that had been previously published in Steel (1996). This reanalysis showed that, for some groups (i.e., leavers), perceptions of the employment market were significantly correlated with objective characteristics of the market. In other words, the study showed that people actively engaged in the process of quitting are better informed about labor-market realities. These data, some of the first of their kind, indicate that perceptions of employment opportunity are systematically related to market realities.

LABOR MARKETS AND THE TENDENCY TOWARD PERCEPTUAL SEGMENTATION

In an article some years ago (Steel & Griffeth, 1989), Rodger Griffeth and I argued that it was a mistake to think of "the labor market" as a homogenous construct. Instead, we argued that the perceptual referent we are accustomed to calling "the labor market" would be more correctly seen as a complex mosaic of occupational, industrial, and regional job markets.

We didn't expect anyone to disagree with this point, and, to our knowledge, no one actually has. But, we didn't make the statement to provoke an argument. We made it to raise levels of awareness. Researchers need to be aware that conceptual and empirical practices have never done full justice to the intricate complexity of the "labor market" or to its pervasive effects on turnover decisions.

Data illustrating how really shallow our understanding is of this pivotal mechanism are plentiful. Consider, for example, standard practice in the domain of turnover theory. Turnover models give nodding acknowledgment to the effects of employment markets by including stand-alone mechanisms with labels like "opportunity" (Price & Mueller, 1986), "economic and market conditions" (Steers & Mowday, 1981), and "probability of alternatives" (Mobley, Horner, & Hollingsworth, 1978).

Each of these authors would probably admit that the market mechanisms shown in their models are oversimplifications. They might even concede that, in reality, labor markets have a structural complexity akin to Steel and Griffeth's (1989) "mosaic" notion. But, even if our models were able to reproduce every minute detail of the market, we might still find that progress in this area of study is stunted. Why? Because, above all else, turnover decision models need to understand *how* individuals make use of information about their labor markets.

The U.S. job market is an incredibly complex perceptual referent. It is too vast and too complex for any, but the most superficial, of perceptual assessments. The market's scope and intricacy conspire against the kind of rich detail that holistic impressions would need to be actionable. Because the full market is a fundamentally unknowable perceptual target, individuals devote relatively little scanning activity to holistic appraisals.

Instead, job searchers mainly derive their conclusions about employment opportunity from labor market segmentations. To manage the process of job market perception, decision makers divide the labor market into homogenous segments. Then, through a process of selective attention, they focus on some aspects of the market while ignoring others.

As Simon (1976) noted some years ago, when individuals are confronted by perceptual arrays that exceed their limited processing capacities, they utilize selective attention as a means of scaling decisional arrays down to a manageable level. Simon dubbed this propensity for perceptual simplification "bounded rationality."

Bounded rationality leads job searchers to divide their perceptual array into segments. However, individuals do not review each segment, one at a time. Instead, they concentrate on segments of the market that have a direct bearing on their ability to find replacement employment. Because job search is an inherently self-referential process, they focus primarily on *personally-relevant market segments*. For the most part, segments of the labor market that are not deemed relevant get ignored. Registered nurses searching for jobs will focus on the occupational market for nurses. They pay little or no attention to segments of the market that have no informational utility for the job search being conducted (e.g., general economic conditions, the occupational market for airline pilots).

However, individuals differ substantially with regard to which market segments (e.g., an occupational labor market, a regional labor market, etc.) they define as relevant. A complex of factors (e.g., personal factors, occupational factors, skill sets, etc.) affect these choices. But, once this determination has been made, the segment (or segments) chosen can have a profound effect on the form of subsequent steps in the turnover process.

Role of Personal Factors

Skill sets define who we are vis-à-vis the market. They can condition one's access to occupational markets. For example, job advertisements for tool and die makers ordinarily specify experience as a tool and die maker (or, at minimum, appropriate technical training). Experience as a nurse doesn't help. Knowledge of accounting principles won't work. The skill set must be of such a nature as to materially overlap the occupational requirements. Other skill sets, no matter how complex or how "in demand," will not substitute for the occupationally-necessary skill set in question.

Sometimes, social institutions formalize these ideas. For example, access to some occupations is controlled by licensure. Successful completion of licensing examinations is required for admission to the occupation. The skill sets of nurses, physicians, licensed psychologists, lawyers, and so forth are scrutinized in this way before entry into the occupation is permitted.

Occupational skill sets are the main driver behind cross-occupation variability in employment opportunity, but *experiential skill sets* are the main driver of variability within occupational markets. Individuals with more experience and more accomplishments are often "more marketable" than individuals with comparatively less experience and/or fewer accomplishments. Experiential skill sets often have a monotonic relationship with individual marketability (i.e., greater experience is associated with more job access and higher pay), but this relationship may sometimes also become an inverted U-shaped function because individuals may become prohibitively expensive at the upper reaches of job experience.

A TALE OF THREE MARKETS

Traditional models of the turnover process (e.g., Mobley, 1977) envisioned a universal decision process. Recent models (e.g., Lee & Mitchell, 1994; Steel, 2002) have increasingly suggested that alternative paths may be possible. But, even the newest models may be incomplete. They still fail to acknowledge that the election of alternative paths may be triggered by attention to different market foci. To show how job markets differ and to illustrate how these differences may affect the decision process itself, I will describe three different occupational labor markets.

The first occupational job market we will consider will be the market for registered nurses (RNs). Entry into this occupation is tightly controlled. A program of demanding baccalaureate study and successful completion of a professional certification exam is necessary for entry into the profession (i.e., a high premium on occupational skill sets). These factors tend to suppress the available supply of nurses. At the same time, demand for skilled nurses is accelerating rapidly in response to a variety of demographic and societal forces (e.g., nurses exiting the profession, increasing numbers of geriatric patients, etc.). Because the number of vacant RN positions far surpasses the number of qualified individuals seeking employment, demand for RNs is very high. It is so high, in fact, that signing bonuses have become a familiar aspect of the occupation's employment-market landscape.

My wife Bev is an RN. When we were moving to Detroit, MI from Dayton, OH a couple of years ago, Bev picked the names of three hospitals out of a Detroit phone book. She called each hospital and requested an interview on a specific day that we were to be in the Detroit area. All requested interviews were granted. When the date of our Detroit visit arrived, she left for her interviews at 8:00 a.m. By 2:00 p.m. that day, she had three offers on the table, all with tempting signing bonuses.

The job market for nurses evidences several distinctive qualities. Demand for individuals in this profession is mostly impervious to fluctuations in the levels of *general economic conditions*. As such, nurses are free to ignore downturns in the general economy when planning a job move. What's more, the demand for skilled nursing personnel remains at constant levels as one moves about the country. East-west, north-south, urban-rural; it makes little difference. Appeals for skilled nursing personnel are everywhere. For the most part, therefore, licensed RNs can also discount *regional variations* when determining their employment prospects.

The unique set of circumstances defining their job market invites nurses to concentrate full attention on the one aspect of the labor market that will be personally-relevant to their search (i.e., their occupational labor market) and to virtually ignore all other factors defining employment opportunity in the U.S. labor economy (e.g., regional factors, industrial markets, etc.) What's more, the constant and unvarying demand within their occupational market emboldens RNs to plan job moves with impunity. New jobs are available in abundance, and they may be obtained at short notice. There is no compelling reason to arrange alternative employment prior to quitting. Nurses have no reason to fear periods of between-job unemployment (Steel, 2002). Because of all of this, nurses often conduct *low intensity* job searches (i.e., less job prospecting, fewer resumes sent out, fewer requests for interviews are made).

Some might take the position that the employment market for nurses represents an extreme example. They might argue that there are few, if any, occupational markets that resemble this particular one. I would disagree. The markets for airline pilots in the 70s and for computer engineers during the .com era resembled, in many respects, the high-demand market for nurses in the current labor economy. Lest we forget, all labor markets, even the hottest ones, are subject to change.

My wife and I were making the move to Detroit because I had just completed my own job search. Whereas her search lasted about six hours, mine had taken about three years to complete.

The employment market for business school professors with an organizational behavior (OB) specialty is, in some respects similar, and other respects dissimilar, to the market for nurses. It is similar in the sense that entry into the occupation is restricted to individuals with advanced education and specialized credentials (i.e., appropriate doctoral degree). Hence, this profession also places a premium on occupational skill sets. However, in this profession experiential skill sets can produce marketability differentials that are not nearly so apparent among nurses.

The occupational market for OB professors is softer than the market for nurses. There is usually a surplus of applicants for each position. To locate employment, individuals must ordinarily invest substantially more effort in searching the employment market (i.e., high intensity job search) than must their nurse counterparts. Within any given geographical region, the number of jobs for people in this profession tends to be few in number. As such, OB professors usually plan national job searches. They mostly ignore regional aspects of the employment market. The OB faculty market is not particularly sensitive to business cycles, but it is more so than the market for nurses.

Once again, properties of the market shape the turnover decision process. Attention among OB job searchers is mainly focused on occupational markets. They will probably not pay close attention to *regional dimensions* of employment opportunity or to *general-economy factors*. However, employment search in this job market generally requires higher levels of *search intensity* and *search perseverance*. Hiring lead times are long in this business (i.e., whole academic years). In fact, they are some of the longest lead times faced by any profession. Coupled with the general softness of demand in this employment market, there is almost no chance of rapid turnarounds in the job search process. Hence, OB job searchers must take great care to guard against periods of between-jobs unemployment. They are, therefore, far less likely than nurses to quit without an alternative job offer in hand.

For the sake of comparison, we consider one final job market, the market for counter help in fast food restaurants. For all intents and purposes, entry into this occupation is unrestricted. Limited occupational skill sets are desirable, but not really essential for successful search. Because there are many duplicate jobs of this type in any local economy, large-scale job searches (e.g., national searches) are not indicated.

Because occupational skill sets have little or no bearing on employment, job searchers pay scant attention to *occupational markets*. Instead, decisions to search for employment will probably be controlled by *business cycle mechanisms* (i.e., the general lack or abundance of similar openings), alternative job visibility, and, perhaps, some consideration of *regional issues* (i.e., when a locational preference exists).

JOB SEARCH AS AN INTERACTIVE PROCESS

The prevailing approach to modeling the labor market's effect on turnover decisions could be called a "passive data-gather" model. It views individuals as passive gatherers of job market data (e.g., "lots of adds for my career field right now"). Individuals gather such data as they advance through the job search component of a pro forma turnover process. However, the approach proposed in the current paper is that of a "read-and-react" model of job search. This view suggests that, instead of following a preordained sequence, individuals actually construct their own decision process in response to (1) salient features of the *relevant* labor market and (2) factors that define their personal marketability (i.e., skill sets).

Individuals use information about their occupational skill sets and experiential skill sets to decide which segments of the market will be treated as personally-relevant. Once this step has been completed, properties of the chosen segment (or segments) may then shape remaining steps of the turnover process.

The Evolutionary Model of Job Search proposed in an earlier article of mine (Steel, 2002) suggested that individuals adjust their beliefs about personal marketability as a result of feedback originating in the employment market. As individuals interact with potential employers, they gain insight into their own market status. While a step in the right direction, this view does not go far enough. I am herein suggesting that information gleaned from the job market (i.e., perceptions derived from relevant market segments) can affect the eventual shape of the turnover decision process itself.

REFERENCES

Carsten, J.M., & Spector, P.E. (1987). Unemployment, job satisfaction, and employee turnover: A meta-analytic test of the Muchinsky model. *Journal of Applied Psychology, 72*, 374–381.

Dreher, G.F., & Dougherty, T.W. (1980). Turnover and expected competition for job openings: An exploratory analysis. *Academy of Management Journal, 23,* 766–772.

Gerhart, B. (1990). Voluntary turnover and alternative job opportunities. *Journal of Applied Psychology, 75,* 467–476.

Lee, T.W., & Mitchell, T.R. (1994). An alternative approach: The unfolding model of employee turnover. *Academy of Management Review, 19,* 51–89.

Michaels, C.E., & Spector, P.E. (1982). Causes of employee turnover: A test of the Mobley, Griffeth, Hand, and Meglino model. *Journal of Applied Psychology, 67,* 53–59.

Mobley, W.H. (1977). Intermediate linkages in the relationship between job satisfaction and employee turnover. *Journal of Applied Psychology, 62,* 237–240.

Mobley, W.H., Horner, S.D., & Hollingsworth, A.T. (1978). An evaluation of precursors of hospital employee turnover. *Journal of Applied Psychology, 63,* 408–414.

Price, J.L., & Mueller, C.W. (1986). *Absenteeism and turnover of hospital employees.* Greenwich, CT: JAI Press.

Simon, H.A. (1976). *Administrative behavior* (3rd ed.). New York: Free Press.

Steel, R.P. (1996). Labor market dimensions as predictors of the reenlistment decisions of military personnel. *Journal of Applied Psychology, 81,* 421–428.

Steel, R.P.(2002). Turnover theory at the empirical interface: Problems of fit and function. *Academy of Management Review, 27,* 346–360.

Steel, R.P., & Griffeth, R.W. (1989). The elusive relationship between perceived employment opportunity and turnover behavior: A methodological or conceptual artifact? *Journal of Applied Psychology, 74,* 846–854.

Steers, R.M., & Mowday, R.T. (1981). Employee turnover and postdecision accommodation processes. In L. Cummings & B. Staw (Eds.), *Research in organizational behavior* (Vol. 3, pp. 235–281). Greenwich, CT: JAI Press.

Trevor, C.O. (2001). Interactions among actual ease-of-movement determinants and job satisfaction in the prediction of voluntary turnover. *Academy of Management Journal, 44,* 621–638.

CHAPTER 5

STRESS MEASURES AS PREDICTORS OF INTENTION TO LEAVE AND TURNOVER

Meni Koslowsky and Meyrav Marom

ABSTRACT

Using a longitudinal design, the present study examined three types of popular stressors—chronic, hassles, and life events—as predictors of intention to leave and turnover. A total of 201 nurses in central Israel completed stress questionnaires, controlled for order, administered eight months apart. Findings indicated that the different types of stressors are independent constructs, the best predictor of turnover was intention to leave at time 2 ($r = .41$), and critical life events at time 1 showed the highest correlation with intention to leave at time 2. Analysis of change showed that all stress variables showed change over time with chronic stress and hassles increasing and life events decreasing. Theoretical and practical considerations of the results were discussed.

INTRODUCTION

As a very popular outcome variable in the OB literature, and frequently, the last step in a stage-wise process, many models of turnover have been

Innovative Theory and Empirical Research on Employee Turnover, pages 83–101

suggested with most of them focused on identifying the individual, organizational, or extra-organizational variables that directly or indirectly lead to or are associated with turnover (e.g., Mobley, 1982). Generally, turnover is considered as the most extreme form of organizational withdrawal behavior (along with lateness and absence, all three behaviors are sometimes lumped under the category of *physical* withdrawal; see, Rosse, & Noel, 1996) with antecedents such as personality, attitudes (especially job satisfaction and commitment), job alternatives, ease of leaving, intention to leave, considered the major components in such formulations (Hom, Caranikas-Walker, Prussia, & Griffeth, 1992; Jenkins, 1993; Tett & Meyer, 1993). Although work related stressors have been mentioned as a possible antecedent (Jamal, 1990), few researchers have examined the impact of various types of stress in the same investigation. The present study uses a longitudinal design to examine several common stressors—chronic, hassles, and life events—as predictors of intention to leave and turnover.

Although in a few studies, turnover was seen as producing a positive gain for the organization or the individual (Dalton & Todor, 1981; McEvoy & Cascio, 1987), it is, generally, viewed as a negative outcome with considerable psychological and financial costs involved. In one recent formulation, Hom and Griffeth (1995) describe two main paths, one, a traditional, analytical route where withdrawal cognitions lead the worker to consider several available options with leaving the organization one of the possible outcomes and a second, more impulsive path where turnover is the only possible outcome of withdrawal cognitions. In both paths, stressors are seen as affecting satisfaction that, in turn, leads to withdrawal behavior.

Rosse and Noel argue that individual difference variables play a more important role than envisaged by Hom and Griffeth. In particular, dispositional and affective reactions to specific stimuli, such as the discomfort or dissatisfaction that follows stress at work, are suggested as possible causes of turnover and other withdrawal behaviors (Rosse & Noel, 1996, pp. 480–483). When stress is included in such a formulation, the main role of leaving the organization (or, for that matter, other behavioral withdrawal indicators, as well), is to remove the stressors. Nevertheless, the big question remains: is relieving stress, an adequate reason for leaving the organization? Perhaps, but the status of the present research does not allow us to answer this question adequately. In discussing the direction that research on individual differences and turnover should pursue, Hom and Griffeth argue that longitudinal studies are needed so as to determine the actual direction of cause and effect in withdrawal research.

As the relationship between measured organizational antecedents and actual behavior has often yielded poor associations, it behooves the researcher to include a measure of intention to perform a specific behavior. Thus, McGuire (1985) argues that other factors, some of which are difficult to gauge, have an impact on whether or not an individual decides to act out a specific behavior. By including intentions to leave, a measured construct, as an additional outcome, we can provide a construct that has cognitive and affective components that, in a broader sense, have components that overlap with stress. For example, although attitude-turnover correlations are often quite small, attitude-intentions to leave correlations often yield moderately high values (George & Jones, 1997; Steel & Rentsch, 1995). Moreover, in a large study of staff nurses, intention to leave the place of employment which, in itself, was predicted by several different types of variables, was also seen as the best and most "immediate determinant" of turnover (Parasuraman,1990).

Although our focus here is examining the role of stress as an antecedent of turnover, to the organizational psychologist, stress is seen both as a consequence of a series of variables, individual and organizational ones, as well as a causal or predictor of various behaviors and performance (Fox, Dwyer, & Ganster, 1993; Kahn & Byosiere, 1992). These separate roles have also been assigned different names that help clarify what the intentions of the researcher are in a particular study. Thus, researchers distinguish between the terms stress and strain with the former referring to its role as an independent variable and the latter as an outcome measure (Jex, Beehr, & Roberts, 1992).

Why would we expect that a worker who has experienced or is experiencing stress be more likely to leave the organization? Stated more scientifically, what underlying theoretical process can explain the stress-turnover link? Lee and Mitchell (1991, 1994), in presenting a model of employee turnover, argue that employees attempt to interpret environmental events by integrating them with past cognitions. After "aversive" events are integrated, a cognitive process is started that involves mental comparisons among the present job situation, values, and expectations. If a certain level of satisfaction exists, then one will likely continue in the present situation; if dissatisfied, then alternatives may be sought.

Although Lee and Mitchell do not mention stress, per se, much of what the authors describe as an employee's attempt to manage aversive environmental events or stimuli is consistent with Lazarus and Folkman's (1984) description of stress. In their well-known formulation, stress is the result of environmental demands that are perceived by the individual as either threatening or potentially damaging. Although Lee and Mitchell's approach contains two main work-related components—negative events/ situations preceding the decision to leave and the cognitive process that is produced (all quite consistent with the Hom and Griffeth dual path approach)—other types of stimuli are posited as potentially important, too. The model is wide-ranging and can easily include stimuli that do not emanate from the job or organization and also the general category of stress.

Bedeian and Armenakis (1981) present a second, more straightforward approach for understanding the impact of stress on turnover. When an individual experiences stress, there is an attempt to either reduce the stressor or distance oneself from it. Within the work environment, a possible consequence of this process is leaving the organization. These authors perceive stress as acting both directly and indirectly on the dependent variable. Nevertheless, the authors do not make a distinction between the various types of stress and similar to other stress investigators in I/O psychology, the focus is on chronic (work-related) stressors.

Over the years, several investigators have suggested that non-work related variables be included in models of organizational behavior (Bolger, Delongis, Kessler, and Wethington, 1989; Crouter, 1984). One of the first researchers to recommend the inclusion of variables such as the home and family as predictors of turnover was Bhagat, Mcquaid, Lindholm, and Sergovis (1985). Although data on behavior were not available, the latter investigators reported that the evidence indicated that stressors from all aspects of life have an impact on job satisfaction and organizational commitment.

Three major categories of stressors have been identified: critical life events, hassles, and chronic stressors (Pratt & Barling, 1988; Wheaton, 1996).Critical life events are relatively rare but powerful events that may have a major effect on the individual (e.g., death of a spouse, losing one's job, etc.). When confronted with these events, the individual is, generally, required to change or modify some specific aspect of his or her life. Hassels are quite common but relatively benign events that tend to occur at specific points in time (e.g., noise made by neighbors, waiting on a line at a bank, short electric blackouts, etc.). Chronic stressors are continuous, range from relatively benign to powerful events found in one's environment. Although some of the items in the latter category have components found in the previous two, the focus here is more personal and include non-work related factors such as raising a disabled child or taking care of an aging parent and, the more common, work related factors such as difficulty in finding a job or a boss who overworks the employee.

One additional perspective of stress was considered here. Recently, Cavanaugh, Boswell, Roehling, and Boudreau (2000) found that certain types of stress factors do indeed predict outcomes, including job satisfaction, job search, and voluntary turnover. Their findings focused on the distinction between stress that has a challenge or work-focused component associated with the work itself and stress factors that are not directly related to the work content and serve as a hindrance to the worker. Although overlapping somewhat with the aforementioned hassles measure, chronic stress is more continuous and is not focused on specific points in time. Whereas Cavanaugh et al. did not find an association between turnover and challenge, there was a positive and significant relationship with the hindrance measure. The analysis reported by the Cavanaugh group is somewhat non-traditional as it breaks stress into several components that are quite specific to certain job categories, such as managers where challenge is a meaningful construct. It is unclear, according to Cavanaugh et al. (2000), whether these findings generalize to non-managerial types. In the present study, we have expanded the concept somewhat to include overload, which, for a nurse, relates specifically to the work content and is part and parcel of their job. In any case, Cavanaugh et al. (2000), who limited their stress measures to two types only, explicitly state the need to examine the distinction they found with other samples as well as to identify other specific components of stress that can be expected to correlate with outcome.

For our purposes, four components of stress (chronic stress, overload, hassles, and life events) measured at two time periods served as the main antecedents. The research on the effects of different types of stress on mental health can offer some theoretical and empirical insights on the relative contribution of each stress type for the prediction of withdrawal. There the data seems to indicate that chronic stress is the best of all stress predictors. The empirical findings in longitudinal studies support the claim that chronic stress, as compared to critical life events, is the better predictor of mental health (e.g., Avison & Turner, 1988; Sherbourne, 1988). Also, as expected from Freeman and Webster's (1994) theorizing, chronic stressors, when compared to hassles, are expected to be the superior predictors of health as the former are more proximate to the individual and surround him constantly.

In addition, focusing on the influence of stress during the employees' first months of work in the organization provided us with several clear advantages. First, high levels of perceived stress usually characterize this period because employees are required to learn new tasks and adapt to new demands while maintaining an acceptable level of performance (Nelson, 1987; Nicholson, 1990). The study of stress during this time and its long-term influences may be particularly important because of the salience of environmental demands and stressors during this period. Secondly, by controlling for tenure, a somewhat similar group is created which helps to moderate not only the influence of tenure but also other variables that are confounded with it including the availability of coping resources, such as support systems, control, and predictability of stressful demands. Finally, there is some evidence that during the very early phases of one's organizational career, intention to leave, is more closely associated with actual turnover (Steel & Ovalle, 1984) and tends to be higher as compared to later phases (Arnold & Davey, 1999).

In summary, the application of a longitudinal design here assumes that stress, initially, and its change over time can be significant predictors of the intent to leave and actual turnover. Although it is difficult to suggest clear differential hypotheses, as few researchers have investigated all these stress measures simultaneously with turnover, it would appear, at least from the literature on mental health, that the measures are relatively independent and that chronic stress may be the best predictor of outcome. It is also expected that change scores in each of the stress measures would provide additional prediction, both for intention to leave and actual turnover.

METHOD

Participants

The study was conducted among academically certified nurses who were working in one of 25 general hospitals in Israel. At the start of study, none had been in their jobs for more than five months. A total of 201 nurses completed questionnaires twice. In the sample, 90% were females, the average age was 27.4, with a range from 21 to 50, and approximately 57% were married. Nearly 70% of the participants were employed full-time at their hospital and about 10% worked less than 50% of the time.

Measures

Although each of the measures discussed below was based on existing scales, when necessary, items were added or modified slightly to reflect the situation of nurses working in Israel. Pretesting and forward-backward translation from English to Hebrew was used to maximize the psychometric properties of the scales. Moreover, the scales were carefully devised so as to best represent independent dimensions. As suggested by Wheaton (1996) and Herbert and Cohen (1996), the items found within any particular scale, especially those developed locally, were carefully examined so as to minimize as much as possible any contamination or artificial overlap with the other stress scales in the study.

1. *Hassles (HS)*.   This questionnaire consisted of 33 items, 24 of which were derived from work conducted in this area by Kanner et al. (1981) with the other items developed locally. Examples of items included "Some appliance in your house needed fixing" and "The telephone in your house rings at inappropriate times." The alternatives ranged from 1 "hardly ever" to 5 "very often." Reliability (Cronbach alpha) was .89.

2. *Chronic Stressors (CS)*.   Items in this questionnaire were originally derived from a wide range of scales in the literature including those

developed by Gray-Toft and Anderson (Nursing Stress Scale, NSS, 1981), Kushnir and Kagan (1993), Frone, Russell, and Cooper (1992), and Koslowsky, Alzer, and Krausz (1996). Examples here include "I receive inconsistent instructions" and "I am not consulted when important decisions are made." The alternatives ranged from 1 "never" to 5 "very frequently."

Based on the recommendation of Cavanaugh et al. (2000), the chronic stress measure was divided into two components: one, gauging *overload* at work, consisted of five items (e.g., "not enough time to do quality work") and, the other, the more traditional indicators of *chronic stress* which contained 41 items. Cronbach alpha reliability for the former was .83 and, for the latter, .90.

3. *Critical Life Events (CLE).*   This questionnaire contained 39 items, 31 based on the work of Levav, Krasnoff, and Dorenwend (1981) and the rest of the items derived locally. Respondents were asked the number of times they experienced one of the events described in the questionnaire. Examples include "Divorce or separation from significant other" and "Moved to a new home." As expected the reliability here, .63, was the lowest of all the scales as many, though, by no means, all the items are independent of each other.

4. *Intention to Leave.*   A short four-item scale based on the turnover literature and adapted for a nurse population was used here. The items included "Are you planning to reduce the number of hours that you will be working in the hospital?" (1 "Definitely no" to 5 "Definitely yes"), "What are the chances that you will leave the hospital in the coming year? (1 "Very unlikely" to 5 "Very likely"), "Are you planning to find work in another hospital?" (1 "Definitely no" to 5 "Definitely yes"), and "What is the probability that you will work the same number or, even more hours by the end of the year?" (1 "very unlikely" to "very likely"). The reliability here was .77.

5. *Turnover.*   The data on turnover was obtained from the head nurses' files at each hospital.

Procedure

After receiving approval from the Israel Department of Health for conducting the study (required in Israel today), contact was made, either personally or by telephone, with the head nurse in all major hospitals in the country. A letter guaranteeing confidentiality (no person in the hospital hierarchy would be allowed to see any of the nurses' responses) and anonymity was sent to each hospital. Nurses were then contacted, by mail, over a two-month period. The purpose of the study was explained in detail and an incentive of 15 dollars (approximate conversion from the local currency to dollars) was promised to each nurse that agreed to complete and return both mailings.

The questionnaires were mailed in two different orders. Chronic stress was the first scale for one form and hassles, for the second one. Later analysis indicated that no order effects were present. One telephone reminder three weeks after the first mailing helped produce a return rate of 72% or 234 total respondents. About eight months after the first mailing, this group was mailed a second questionnaire and again a high rate of response, 86%, or 201 respondents were obtained. This final group represented 62% of the original list of 324 nurses who were contacted in the first stage, a percentage considered quite high in a longitudinal study. A final letter thanking the nurses for their participation was sent and it included the small gift mentioned before. (It should be noted that we received many letters from nurses who were most happy to participate in a study that measured stress in their lives, a topic that is, naturally, very prominent in their everyday conversations). So as to ascertain if any bias was present in the group that was analyzed, we examined the responses of all study variables for the group that answered only the first questionnaire with those that completed both measures. For one measure, years of education, a significant difference was obtained. Such a difference could very well be a chance finding, and from the comparison analysis, we inferred that the groups were essentially equivalent.

In the final stage, one year after the first mailing, a letter was sent to each head nurse asking them to describe the present position of each nurse on their staff, and if no longer there, to state this fact clearly.

Analysis

Data analysis was performed by using hierarchical multiple regression and SEM (structured equation modeling by means of the AMOS procedure; Arbuckle, 1997). In step 1 of all regressions, the stress level at Time 1 was entered and at step 2 the same component of stress measured at Time 2 was entered. Studies show that this is the preferred statistical technique for examining changes from Time 1 to Time 2 (Edwards, 1995; Edwards & Perry, 1993). The additional variance explained at Time 2 can be considered as the contribution of *change* for explaining variance in the dependent variable. If there were a perfect correlation between a measure at Time 1 and Time 2, then the second measure could not explain any additional variance. Besides the inclusion of Time 1 variables as an aid in examining change, studies have shown that these variables are important predictors in their own right. In their longitudinal study of turnover, Holton and Russell (1999) showed that organization entry factors and attitudes measured the first year explained a large percentage of turnover variance at the end of the first year. The model examined with AMOS was the theoretical one suggested by the research hypotheses, namely that the four stressors, and their change over time, are predictors of intention to leave. The theoretical research model, was compared with an alternative one, where the time 2 measures of stress were left out. The significance of the difference of the chi square values of the various models was then examined.

Also, as many researchers have suggested, logistic regression analysis is the preferred method when a skewed measure such as turnover is the dependent variable (Cavanaugh et al., 2000; Holton & Russell, 1999; Morrow et al., 1999). According to Tabachnick and Fidell (1989, p. 271), this is particularly true when the dependent variable is dichotomous and the split is quite skewed (more extreme than 25%–75%) as was true here where only about 15% were left by the end of the time period.

RESULTS

The first stage of the study included a descriptive analysis of all relevant variables in the study. In Table 5.1, the means, standard deviations, and intercorrelations are presented. A secondary purpose of the present study, though important for understanding the predictability of each type of stress, was to determine the uniqueness of each measure of stress in the study. By viewing the intercorrelation portion of Table 5.1 as analogous to a convergent-discriminant analysis, we can expect similar measures of stress (even though separated by time) to correlate higher with each other than do dissimilar ones. Using a modified form of the multi-trait multi-method approach to determining convergent and discriminant validity (Campbell & Fiske, 1959), a data pattern where the same measures across different time periods correlate more highly than do different measures across time periods is indicative of convergent validity. Discriminant validity is indicated when the correlations among different stress measures within the same time period traits is relatively low.

A perusal of the table shows that, as expected, the highest correlations were among the time 1 and time 2 scales assessing the same component of stress. For example, the two measures of chronic stress showed a correlation of .62 and the two measures of hassles correlated .76; the findings, generally, supported the convergent validity among the scales. Moreover, within each time period, the intercorrelations were relatively low. However, hassles was significantly correlated with chronic stress (correlations near .50 within

Table 5.1.   Means, Standard Seviations, and Intercorrelations among Time 1 and Time 2 Stress, Intention to Leave, and Turnover Variables (N = 201)

Variable	M	SD	1	2	3	4	5	6	7	8	9	10
1. Chronic Stress—1	1.97	.45										
2. Overload—1	2.74	.42	39									
3. Hassles—1	2.17	.17	52	29								
4. Life Event—1	1.25	.17	19	06	33							
5. Intention to Leave—1	3.01	.39	13	04	14	–07						
6. Chronic Stress—2	2.12	.45	62	31	39	11	17					
7. Overload—2	2.86	.84	21	58	16	15	–07	29				
8. Hassles—2	2.21	.46	47	31	76	18	12	49	27			
9. Life Event—2	0.31	.19	26	14	45	51	–02	29	20	47		
10. Intention to Leave—2	1.99	.96	10	19	13	27	00	19	25	17	14	
11. Turnover	0.15	.36	–05	11	15	07	–08	–04	07	08	13	41

(0 = No, 1 = Yes)

Note. Decimals were left out in the intercorrelations part of the matrix. Correlations above .14 are significant at $p < .05$, and above .20 are significant at $p < .01$.

each time period) and even across time periods still showed substantial correlations (the correlation of hassles, time 1 with chronic stress, time 2 equals .39, and the correlation of hassles, time 2 with chronic stress, time 1 equals .46). Although considerably lower than its correlation with itself, the hassles scale appears to have a conceptual overlap with chronic stress. As expected, the best predictor of turnover was intention to leave at time 2 ($r = .41$). Among the stress measures, critical life events at time 1 showed the highest correlation with intention to leave at time 2 ($r = .27$, $p < .01$). None of the stress variables showed a significant correlation with intention to leave at time 1. Actual turnover was correlated significantly with hassles at time 1 ($r = .15$, $p < .05$). As mentioned above, turnover with its skewed (0.1) distribution is not readily amenable to analyses that assume a normal distribution. Thus, all reported Spearman correlations with turnover must be viewed with caution.

Before examining the effects of change in time with the preferred statistical method as described above, it may, nevertheless, be informative to test the change in time with a simple *t*-test for paired means. In all cases, the change was significant with chronic stress ($t = -5.20$, $p < .01$), overload ($t = -2.40$, $p < .03$), and hassles ($t = -2.10$, $p < .04$) increasing over time whereas life events ($t = 74.00$, $p < .01$) and intention to leave ($t = 13.82$, $p < .01$) decreasing over time. In particular, the change in the last two variables should be noted. The decrease in life events may very well represent the fewer opportunities for such events occurring between the two measures. Also, the decrease in intention to leave from time 1 to time 2, while most stress measures were increasing, may indicate that the nurses have adjusted, to some extent, to their jobs.

Hierarchical multiple regression was used for analyzing the effect of the stress variables, and their change measures, on intention to leave at time 2. Table 5.2 presents the findings when the stress variables were considered individually and Table 5.3 considers the simultaneous case where time 1 stress variables were entered at one step and time 2 stress variables at another step. In Table 5.2, the dependent variable is intention to leave at time 2 and Table 5.3 the dependent variables are intention to leave at time 1 and intention to leave at time 2.

Table 5.2.   Hierarchical Regression Analysis of Intention to Leave on Individual Stress Variables

	Step 1		Step 2	
Predictors	β	ΔR^2	β	ΔR^2
1. Hassles	.13	.01	.17	.02
2. Chronic Stress	.00	.00	.21*	.03*
3. Overload	.19	.04**	.21*	.03*
4. Life Events	.27**	.07**	.00	.00

Notes: * $p < .05$, ** $p < .01$
In step 1, the time 1 measure of stress was entered and in step 2, the time 2 measure of the same stress variable was entered.

From the individual analyses, one can see that life events at time 1 ($\beta = .27$, $p < .01$) and the change over time of chronic stress ($\beta = .21$, $p < .05$) and overload ($\beta = .21$, $p < .05$) were significant predictors of intention to leave at time 2. From the simultaneous analyses, the data showed that among the time 1 variables, life events ($\beta = .26$, $p < .01$) and chronic stress ($\beta = .18$, $p < .05$) were significant predictors. The entry of time 2 variables into the regression analysis, which gauged the influence of change, showed that chronic stress ($\beta = .16$, $p < .01$) and overload ($\beta = .14$, $p < .01$) were significant predictors. When intention to leave at time 1 was used as the dependent variable, only hassles was found to be significant ($\beta = .15$, $p < .05$).

One further analysis was performed with this last set of data. For the simultaneous case at time 2, structural equations modeling was used to determine the goodness of fit produced by including the time 1 and time 2 data as predictors of intention to leave. The largest standardized coeffi-

Table 5.3. Hierarchical Regression Analysis of Intention to Leave on all Stress Variables Simultaneously

	Intention to Leave-1		Intention to Leave-2	
A. Step 1	β	ΔR^2	β	ΔR^2
Hassles–1	.15*		.01	
Chronic Stress–1	.09		.01	
Overload–1	–.03		.18*	
Life Event–1	–.14	.040	.26**	.10**
B. Step 2				
Intention To Leave–1			.01	.00
C. Step 3				
Hassles–2			.13	
Chronic Stress–2			.16*	
Overload–2			.14*	
Life Event–2			.10	.04*
Total R^2		.040		.15**

Notes: * $p < .05$, ** $p < .01$

cients are observed between the time 1 and time 2 measures of the same variables, all of which were highly significant. Also, the overload measure at time 2 was significantly associated with intention to leave at time 2 (ß = .20, $p < .05$). A final comparison between the model that includes the time 2 variables with one that doesn't showed a highly significant improvement in fit ($\Delta\chi^2 = 95.6$, $\Delta df = 19$, $p < .001$).

The logistic regression analysis for turnover indicated that none of the attitudinal variables, individually, was a significant predictor of turnover. However, as can be seen in Table 5.4, the change over time of the intention to leave indicator increased the classification accuracy from approximately 85% to close to 91%. The overall model (with all stress variables and intention variables included) was significant ($\chi^2 = 50.28$, $p < .01$) as was the individual contribution made, in the last step, by intention to leave ($\chi^2 = 35.15$, $p < .01$).

DISCUSSION

Much of the literature on the effects of different types of stressors has focused on psychological functioning, especially measures of well being. In the present study, we examined differential stress effects on two common

Table 5.4.   Logistic Regression with Turnover as the Dependent Variable and Time 1 and Time 2 Measures of Stress and Intention to Leave as Predictors

Predictors	Step χ^2	Model χ^2	Classification Accuracy (%)
A. Step 1 (Time 1) Hassles, Chronic stress, Overload, Life events	12.04*	12.04*	85.4
B. Step 2 (Time 1) Intention to Leave	1.55	13.58*	85.4
C. Step 3 (Time 2)[a] Hassles, Chronic stress, Overload, Life events	1.56	15.14	84.9
D. Step 4 (Time 2) Intention to Leave	35.15**	50.28**	91.0

Note: * $p < .05$, ** $p < .01$

organizational measures: intention to leave and actual turnover. By comparing the predictions afforded by stress variables individually and as a group, we were able to draw some inferences concerning the relative contribution of each stressor to understanding withdrawal intentions and behavior.

First, it appears that the various types of stress studied here are independent constructs and it would argue for analyzing them separately. As expected from the definitions of the measures, hassles correlates rather significantly with chronic stress but still less than it does with itself over time. The distinction in predictability between chronic stress and overload, as suggested by Cavanaugh et al. (2000), was not observed here, but this may be attributed to the different definitions used here. Somewhat unexpectedly, the critical life events measure served as the best predictor of intentions to leave at a later time period. Also, for predicting intention to leave, a model that included stress change measures was better than a model that did not include the change measures. Finally, we found that, when using logistic regression, the change in intention to leave at time 2 was the only significant predictor of turnover. Overall, the data support the notion that stress is a weak to moderate predictor of withdrawal intentions but does not contribute directly to predicting actual turnover.

The findings concerning the impact of critical life events on turnover relative to the other types of stress could be explained by assuming that the unexpected/uncontrollable events that occurred to the worker may require a quick, not well thought out, "fix." According to Lee and Mitchell's (1994) formulation, a worker may decide to leave the organization in an attempt to manage aversive environmental events or stimuli. Thus, critical life events are seen as a trigger that indirectly leads to actual turnover whereas chronic stress or hassles are perceived as more or less continuous and coping reactions other than trying to leave the organization are probably sought by the workers. Another possible explanation focuses on the characteristics of the respondents rather than the content of the scale. Respondents in our study, mostly in their early twenties, were as yet inexperienced in coping with unexpected and largely uncontrollable life events likely to disrupt their professional career, like separation from a spouse or loss of parent. It could be that for older nurses, the prediction regarding the stronger predictive power of chronic stresses and hassles will hold. Hypotheses concerning the various aspects of life events and different ages for the samples need to be formulated and studied. Future research may want to move away from generic types of stress that we used, to much more specific categories of life events, such as types of marital changes that constitute critical life events for this age group of nurses.

The fact that intention to leave at time two shows a higher correlation with actual turnover than does the first intention measure is also quite consistent with the literature. Time lag between the attitude and behavior measures was originally mentioned by Ajzen and Fishnbein (1977) as a key element influencing the attitude-behavior correspondence. Nearly all models that posit a network of links between various antecedents and actual turnover place the intention to leave measure as one of the last predictors. Besides indicating its importance, its position in these models would also imply that, for many investigators, intention to leave, or the more general construct of withdrawal cognitions, must reach some critical mass right before the actual behavior takes place (see, e.g., Parasuraman, 1990; Rosse & Noel, 1996).

The study's findings have several implications for hospital human-resources management. The significant rise in nurses' stress level after their first months of work indicates the need for stress-management intervention. It also suggests that nurses should be offered training programs that provide them with ways to cope efficiently with the types of stress that affect directly or indirectly the decision to leave the company. The levels of work overload, role ambiguity, and other chronic stresses could be reduced, as could those critical life events and hassles that are under the organization's control. Also, the fact that stress did not necessarily lead to actual turnover but did relate to intention to leave indicates that management may very well have time to act. This intermediate stage allows for a 'breathing space' and, although its duration is hard to gauge, the organization has some extra time to prevent attitudes from turning into negative behaviors.

Several distinct advantages to the present design can be identified. First, four different types of stress were measured simultaneously. Second, we examined these stress measures at two separate times, in a longitudinal design. Third, we attempted to enhance the study's internal validity by applying a variety of techniques. The longitudinal data were measured at meaningfully spaced intervals. Data were analyzed so each subject constituted a control of himself or herself, through the use of changes in the level of stress as predictors. In such an analysis of change scores, various statistical artifacts, such as the unreliability of indices, regression toward the means, and others, is substantially reduced (Edwards, 1995). Finally, the relatively high response rate obtained in the study adds a degree of meaningful external validity to the specific population that was sampled.

One of the limitations of the current research is that we focused on measuring the frequency of major or minor potentially stressful events only as perceived by the respondent. Actual objective indicators of the stressors in the environment were not obtained. As suggested by Frese and Zapf (1989) and Koslowsky (1998), objective measures are often viewed as the starting point in a stress-strain models. Besides being less prone to distortion, they may also explain a portion of outcome variance that is not mediated by perceived stress. Koslowsky (1998) argued that such stressors might emanate from the job, the home, the organization, and even from without the organization. Structural equations along with longitudinal designs are the best way for ferreting out these causal links.

One other potential methodological issue here relates to the use of self-report scales for obtaining all relevant measures. If a respondent provides all study data rather than having the investigator glean information from other sources such as company files, personnel records or, even colleagues at work, then distortion or bias may enter the picture. As discussed by several researchers (e.g., Crampton & Wagner, 1994), percept-percept studies, i.e., the use of self-reports for both variables in a correlation, may yield findings reflecting common method variance rather than true or actual associations. In such a case, the observed correlation between the measures might be inflated artificially. Crampton and Wagner (1994), in their wide-ranging study, were not able to collect enough data to compare the potential correlation inflation in stress studies that use only self-report measures as compared to studies that use self-report and behavioral measures. In a sense, our investigation can shed some light on this topic as we were able to compare the correlation among the three stress measures and intention to leave at time 2 (self-report), the closest in time to the behavior, with the correlation among the three stress measures and actual turnover. The average correlation for the former was .18 and for the latter .06 consistent with Crampton and Wagner's conclusion that, in many case, one can expect an increase in percept-percept calculations as compared to multi-source studies. Nevertheless, this difference is not only a function of artificial inflation but also actualization of the turnover intention. As already mentioned, the two measures, though highly related ($r = .41$, in our study) may also have different antecedents that play a role in moderating the observed association. General economic situation, availability, personality, tenure, and opportunity are some of the variables that have been studied previously in this regard. These variables may deter or, conversely, encourage a worker to actually leave an organization but not really have much influence on intention to leave.

From a theoretical perspective, the data provided some support to several commonly held propositions in the I/O literature, generally, and withdrawal behavior literature, specifically. Similar to others who have previously analyzed worker stress as a predictor in areas outside of mental health functioning, it does indeed explain some of the variance of intention to leave yet intervening variables, acting as moderators and/or mediators, not examined here must be considered in the future so as to better understand the turnover process. A multivariate design where other personal and situational variables are considered simultaneously is necessary before we can verify or reject with certainty the role of stress in the withdrawal process. For example, individual difference measures such as personality may play a role, either directly or indirectly, on the stress-turnover relationship. Rosse and Noel (1996) cite emotional stability as a potential moderator that affects how workers react and even cope with stress. For emotional stability to act as a true moderator, then, we would expect to observe higher stress-turnover correlations among subjects with low emotional stability as compared to those high on this moderator.

Similarly, it may be productive to investigate the role of potentially important attitudinal variables that are often assumed to be affected by the different types of tressors and, in turn, are potential antecedents of withdrawal outcomes (Kemery et al., 1985; Koslowsky, 1998). These include attitudes such as job satisfaction, commitment, job involvement, job security and many similar variables in the I/O literature. A nurse who is experiencing stress may leave the organization but only if dissatisfied. Or, she may become dissatisfied (i.e., serve as a mediator) because of the perceived stress and then, after dissatisfaction reaches a certain level, decide to leave. The role of attitudes in the model can be assumed to vary by the stress measure and investigators need to test the possibility that they act as moderators or mediators (partially or fully) or, perhaps, both. It would appear that the next step in the study of stress and withdrawal is the inclusion of such intervening variables. It may very well be that a link between a particular type of stress and withdrawal is strengthened or weakened in the presence of one of these personal/attitudinal variables.

ACKNOWLEDGMENT

This paper is part of the second author's doctoral dissertation completed at Bar-Ilan University.

REFERENCES

Ajzen, I., & Fishbein, M. (1977). Attitude-behavior relations: A theoretical analysis and review of empirical research. *Psychological Bulletin, 84,* 888–918.

Arnold, J., & Davely, K.M. (1990). Graduate's work experience as predictors of organizational commitment, intention to leave, and turnover: Which experiences really matter? *Applied Psychology: An international Review, 48,* 211–238.

Arbuckle, J. (1997). *Amos User's Guide* (Version 3.6). Chicago: SPSS.

Avison, W.R., & Turner, R.J. (1988). Stressful life events and depressive symptoms: Disaggregating the effects of acute stressors and chronic strains. *Journal of Health and Social Behavior, 29,* 253–264.

Bedeian, A.G., & Armenakis, A.A. (1981). A path-analytic study of the consequences of role conflict and ambiguity. *Academy of Management Journal, 24*(2), 417–424.

Bhagant, R.S., Mcquaid, S.J., Lindholm, H., & Segovis, J. (1985). Total life stress: A multimethod validation of the construct and its effects on organizational value of outcomes and withdrawal behaviors. *Journal of Applied Psychology, 70,* 202–214.

Bolger, N., DeLongis, A., Kessler, R.C., & Schilling, E. A. (1989). Effects of daily stress on negative mood. *Journal of Personality and Social Psychology 57,* 808–818

Campbell, D.T., & Fiske, D.W. (1959). Convergent and discriminant validation by the multitrait-multimethod matrix. *Psychological Bulletin, 56,* 81–105.

Cavanaugh, M.A., Boswell, W.R., Roehling, M.V., & Boudreau, J.W. (2000). An empirical examination of self-reported work stress among U.S. managers. *Journal of Applied Psychology, 85,* 65–74.

Crampton, S.M., & Wagner, J.A. III. (1994). Percept-percept inflation in microorganizational research: An investigation of prevalence and effect. *Journal of Applied Psychology, 79,* 67–76.

Dalton, D.R., & Todor, W.R. (1981). Functional turnover: An empirical assessment. *Journal of Applied Psychology, 66,* 716–721.

Edwards, J.E. (1995). Alternatives to difference scores as dependent variables in the study of congruence in organizational research. *Organizational Behavior and Human Decision Processes, 64,* 307–324.

Edwards, J.E., & Perry, M.E. (1993). On the use of polynomial regression equations as an alternative to difference scores in organizational research. *Academy of Management Journal, 36,* 1577–1613.

Fox, M.L., Dwyer, D.J., & Ganster, D.C. (1993). Effects of stressful job demands and control of physiological and attitudinal outcomes in a hospital setting. *Academy of Management Journal, 36,* 289–318.

Freeman, L.C., & Webster, C.M. (1994). Interpersonal proximity in social and cognitive space. *Social Cognition, 12,* 223–247.

Frese, M., & Zapf, D. (1988). Methodological issues in the study of work stress: Objective vs. subjective measurement of work stress and the question of longitudinal studies. In C.L. Cooper & R. Payne (Eds.), *Causes, coping, and consequences of stress at work* (pp. 375–412). New York: Wiley.

Frone, M.R., Russell, M., & Cooper, M.L. (1992). Relationship of work and family stressors to psychological distress: The independent moderating influence of social support, mastery, active coping, and self-focused attention. In PL Perrewe (Ed.), *Handbook on Job Stress* (special issue). *Journal of Social Behavior and Personality, 6,* 227–250.

George, J.M., & Jones, J.R. (1997). Experiencing work: Values, attitudes, and moods. *Human Relations, 50,* 393–416.

Gray-Toft, P., & Anderson, J.G. (1981). The nursing stress scale: Development of an instrument. *Journal of Behavioral Assessment, 3,* 11–23.

Herbert, T., & Cohen, S. (1996). Measurement issues in research on psychological stress. In H.B. Kaplan (Ed.) *Psychosocial stress: Perspectives on structure, theory, lifecourse, and methods* (pp. 295–232). San Diego, CA: Academic Press.

Holton,E.F., & Russell, C.J. (1999). Organizatinal entry and exit: An exploratory longitudinal examination of early careers. *Human Performance, 12,* 311–341.

Hom, P.W., & Griffeth, R.W. (1995). *Employee turnover.* Cincinnati,OH: South-Western.

Hom, P.W., Caranikas-Walker, F, Prussia, G.E., & Griffeth, R.W. (1992). A meta-analytical structural equations analysis of a model of employee turnover. *Journal of Applied Psychology, 77,* 890–909.

Jamal, M. (1990). Relationship of job stress and Type-A behavior to employees' job satisfaction, organizational commitment, psychosomatic health problems, and turnover motivation. *Human Relations, 43,* 727–738.

Jenkins, J.M. (1993). Self-monitoring and turnover: The impact of personality on intent to leave. *Journal of Organizational Behavior, 14,* 83–91.

Jex, S.M., & Beehr, T.A., & Roberts, C.K. (1992). The meaning of occupational stress items to survey respondents. *Journal of Applied Psychology, 77,* 623–628.

Kahn, R.L., & Byosiere, P. (1992). Stress in organizations. In M.D. Dunnette & L.M. Hough (Eds.), *Handbook of industrial and organizational psychology* (pp. 573–580). Palo Alto, CA: Consulting Psychologists Press.

Kanner, A.D., Coyne, J.C., Schaeter, C., & Lazarus, R.S. (1981). Comparison of two modes of stress measurement. *Journal of Behavioral Medicine, 7,* 375–389.

Kemery, E.R., Bedian, A.G., Mossholder, K.W., & Touliatos, J. (1985). Outcomes of role stress: A multisample constructive replication. *Academy of Management Journal, 28,* 363–375.

Koslowsky, M., Aizer, A., & Krausz, M. (1996). Stressor and personal variables in the commuting experience. *Journal of Manpower, 17,* 4–14.

Kushnir, T., & Kagan, R. (1993). Major sources of stress among women managers,clerical workers, and working single mothers: Demands versus resources. *Public Health Reviews, 20,* 215–229.

Lazarus, R.S., & Folkman, S. (1984). *Stress, appraisal, and coping.* New York: Springer.

Lee, T.W., & Mitchell, T.R. (1991). The unfolding effects of organizational commitment and anticipated job satisfaction on voluntary employee turnover. *Motivation and Emotion, 15,* 99–121.

Lee, T.W., & Mitchell, T.R. (1994). An alternative approach: The unfolding model of voluntary employee turnover. *Academy of Management Review, 19*, 51–89.

Lee, T.W., Mitchell, T.R. , Wise, L., & Fireman, S. (1996). An unfolding model of voluntary employee turnover. *Academy of Management Journal, 39*, 5–36.

Levav, U., Krasnoff, L., & Dohrenwnd, B. S. (1981). Israeli PERI life event scale: Ratings of events by a community sample. *Israeli Journal of Medical Sciences, 17*, 176–182.

McEvoy, G.M., & Cascio, W.F. (1987). Do good or poor performers leave? A meta-analysis of the relationship between performance and turnover. *Academy of Management Journal, 30*, 744–762.

McGuire, W.J. (1985). Attitudes and attitude change. In G. Lindzey & E. Aronson (Eds.), *Handbook of social psychology* (Vol. 2, pp. 223–246). New York: Random House.

Mobley, W.H. (1982). *Employee turnover: Causes, consequences, and control.* Reading, MA: Addison-Wesley.

Morrow, P.C., McElroy, J.C., Laczniak, K.S., & Fenton, J.B. (1999). Using absenteeism and performance to predict employee turnover: Early detection through company records. *Journal-of-Vocational-Behavior. 55*, 358–374.

Nelson, D.L. (1987). Organizational socialization: A stress perspective. *Journal of Organizational Behavior, 8*, 311–324.

Nicholson, N. (1990). The transition cycle: Causes, outcomes, processes and forms. In S. Fisher & C.L. Cooper (Eds.), *On the move: The psychology of change and transition.* New York: Wiley.

Parasuraman, S. (1990). Nursing turnover: An integrated model. *Research on Nursing and Health, 12*, 267–277.

Pratt, L.I., & Barling, J. (1988). *Differentiating between daily events, acute and chronic stressors: A framework and its implications.* In J.J. Hurrell (Ed.), *Occupational stress* (pp. 41–53). New York: Taylor & Francis.

Rosse, J.G., & Noel, T.W. (1996). Leaving the organization. In K.R. Murphy (Ed.), *Individual differences and behavior in organizations* (pp. 451–504). San Francisco: Jossey-Bass.

Sherbourne, C.D. (1988). The role of social support and life stress events in use of mental health services. *Social Science and Medicine, 27*, 1393–1400.

Steel, R.P., & Ovalle, N.K. (1984). A review and meta-analysis of research on the relationship between behavioral intention and employee turnover. *Journal of Applied Psychology, 69*, 673–686.

Steel, R.P., & Rentsch, J.R. (1995). Influences of cumulation strategies on the long range prediction of absenteeism. *Academy of Management Journal, 38*, 1616–1634.

Tabachnick, B.G., & Fidell, L.S. (1989). *Using multivariate statistics.* Cambridge, MA: Harper & Row.

Tett, R.P., & Meyer, J.P. (1993). Job satisfaction, organizational commitment, turnover intention, and turnover: Path analyses based on meta-analytic findings. *Personnel Psychology, 46*, 259–293.

Wheaton, B. (1996). The domains and boundaries of stress concepts. In H.B. Kaplan (Ed.), *Psychosocial stress: Perspectives on structure, theory, life-course, and methods* (pp. 29–70). Sand Diego, CA: Academic Press.

part III

INNOVATIVE NEW WAYS OF THINKING ABOUT TURNOVER

CHAPTER 6

FIVE ANTECEDENTS NEGLECTED IN EMPLOYEE TURNOVER MODELS

Identifying Theoretical Linkages to Turnover for Personality, Culture, Organizational Performance, Occupational Attachment, and Location Attachment

Carl P. Maertz, Jr.

ABSTRACT

There are many potential antecedents for voluntarily leaving an organization that have been suggested or implied in the organizational literature. However, some of these have been underrepresented in turnover models or neglected altogether in the turnover literature. The purpose of this chapter is to elucidate five (5) of these neglected antecedent categories in the interest of creating a more complete view of voluntary turnover behavior. Specifically, I review turnover literature related to personality, culture (i.e., organizational and national), organizational performance, occupational attachments, and loca-

Innovative Theory and Empirical Research on Employee Turnover, pages 105–151
Copyright © 2004 by Information Age Publishing
All rights of reproduction in any form reserved.

tion attachments. I then propose theoretical linkages between these categories of antecedents and turnover using proximal motivational mechanisms from a recent model (i.e., Maertz, 2001) as key mediating constructs. Finally, I discuss the implications of the resulting turnover models for future research.

INTRODUCTION

There have been many proposed models of voluntary turnover in the literature and even more proposed antecedents (Griffeth, Hom, & Gaertner, 2000; Maertz & Campion, 1998). Most of these models and antecedents focus on variations of March and Simon's (1958) antecedents of perceived desirability and ease of movement (e.g., Hom & Kinicki, 2001; Lee & Mitchell, 1994). Researchers translate these as work attitudes (e.g., job satisfaction, organizational commitment) and as perceived job alternatives (Allen & Griffeth, 2001), respectively. Much has been learned about these constructs and they have been firmly established as key antecedents of turnover, both as main (e.g., Allen & Griffeth, 2001) and interactive effects (e.g., Trevor, 2001). These lines of research have proven very fruitful, and yet many important variables beyond job satisfaction and alternatives have been neglected (Mitchell, Holtom, Lee, Sablynski, & Erez, 2001) and left out of multivariate turnover models (Maertz & Campion, 1998). With such omissions, models risk empirical estimation problems (James, 1982), perhaps contributing to the problem of low explained variance in turnover behavior (e.g., Hom, Caranikas-Walker, Prussia, & Griffeth, 1992).

To avoid such problems and to more fully understand voluntary turnover, researchers must focus more on antecedents other than work attitudes and job alternatives. Research must better enumerate neglected but relevant antecedents and link them conceptually to turnover decisions. The purpose of the current chapter is to help do this. The chapter's main contribution is providing a theoretical and empirically testable framework for the relatively neglected antecedents of personality, organizational and national culture, organizational performance, occupational attachment, and location attachment. Specifically, I review turnover-related literature on each and explain through what mechanisms each may influence voluntary turnover intention, and thereby behavior. Through these conceptual linkages, I build several non-traditional models that can be integrated with current turnover theory. First though, I introduce a framework to help link the antecedent constructs to turnover intention.

PROXIMAL MOTIVES OF TURNOVER INTENTIONS

Research has long held that turnover intention is the proximal cause of turnover behavior (e.g., Hom et al., 1992; Mobley, 1977; Steel & Ovalle, 1984). Nevertheless, research must identify the different motives that drive turnover intention to truly expand our understanding (Vandenberg & Nelson, 1999). To identify and clarify these proximal causes of turnover intention, Maertz (2001) along with Maertz and Griffeth (under review) reviewed the content turnover and work attitude research to distill the distinctive motives that drive turnover decisions. They proposed a framework of seven proximal motive categories that apply to both the organization and its constituents. According to this framework, these motive categories act as key mediators of more distal antecedent constructs on turnover intentions. Accordingly, I will utilize this framework to link the five neglected antecedent categories to turnover intentions, and thus help expand content turnover theory. First though, I briefly review the motive categories in Maertz' (2001) framework. See Figure 6.1 and Table 6.1.

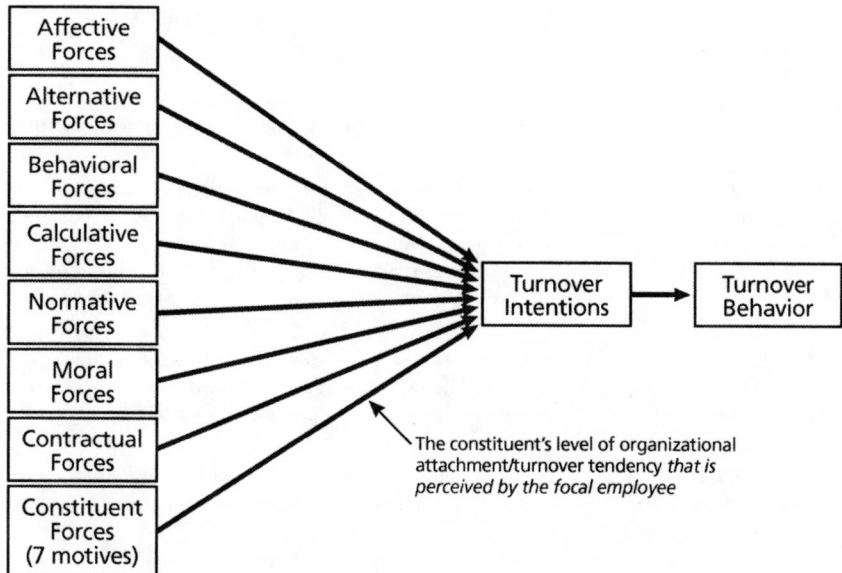

Figure 6.1.   The 8 motivational forces of attachment and withdrawal.

Table 6.1. Type of Force, Related Research Studies, and Motivational Mechanisms

Type of Force—Research Studies	Psychological Motivational Mechanism for Attachment or Withdrawal
Affective Forces (Meyer & Allen, 1991; Mowday et al., 1979; Tett & Meyer, 1993)	Hedonistic approach-avoidance mechanism: Positive/negative emotional responses cause psychological comfort/discomfort with membership. Comfort causes one to approach or stay with the organization. Discomfort causes one to avoid or quit the organization. (affect ➤ comfort/discomfort ➤ approach/avoidance)
Alternative Forces (March & Simon, 1958; McGee & Ford, 1987; Steel & Griffeth, 1989)	Magnitude and strength of self-efficacy beliefs about obtaining alternative jobs/roles: whether one/or more alternatives will provide some *level* of benefit combined with *certainty* of obtaining such alternatives. In the case of certainty that *zero* alternatives are available, (amount of) fear of unemployment acts as the motive.
Behavioral Forces (Becker, 1960; Meyer & Allen, 1991; Salancik, 1977)	Conscious or subconscious desire to avoid the explicit and psychological costs of behavioral change, in this case, quitting. Investments in membership or behaviors favoring membership cause these perceived costs, which range from zero to very high.
Calculative Forces (Forrest et al., 1977; Mobley et al. 1979; Vroom, 1964)	Expectancy-type calculation of attaining valued benefits and goals in the future through continued membership. High expectancy of achieving goals in the future at the current organization increases motivation to stay. Low expectancy of future value attainment at the organization increases motivation to withdraw.
Normative Forces (Fishbein, 1967; Prestholdt et al., 1987)	Desire to meet the perceived expectations of others (outside the organization) and avoid disappointing them with respect to staying or quitting. This force involves perceiving normative expectations from one or more people that imply or suggest staying or quitting, and feeling some motivation to comply with these expectations.
Moral Forces (Jaros et al., 1993; Morrow, 1983; Triandis, 1975)	Maintaining consistency between behavior and values regarding employment. These values range from "quitting is bad/persistence is a virtue" to "changing jobs regularly is good/staying long causes stagnation".
Contractual Forces (Meyer & Allen, 1991; Rousseau, 1989; Scholl, 1981; Wiener, 1982)	Desire to fulfill perceived obligations to the organization under the psychological contract through staying. Or conversely, the desire to dissolve a psychological contract or to respond to violations through quitting. These desires depend on some perceived obligation or violation and some adherence to a norm of reciprocity.
Constituent Forces (Becker, 1992; Clugston et al., 2000; Reichers, 1985)	Desire to maintain or end relationships with a constituent(s) by staying or quitting. This category is a hybrid of one or more motivational forces: affective, alternative, behavioral, calculative, normative, moral, and contractual forces. The net force to stay or leave may depend on relationships with many constituents and the attachment/withdrawal tendency of these constituents themselves.

Affective Forces: Hedonistic Approach-Avoidance

At any given point in time, an individual has a feeling or affective state with respect to his/her organization. Along with evaluative cognitions, such affective responses are often captured by measures of job satisfaction, organizational commitment, or other global work attitude measures (e.g., Weiss & Cropanzano, 1996). Depending on the direction, this affective response triggers either a level of psychological comfort or discomfort with one's current employment. This comfort/discomfort drives a hedonistic approach-avoidance mechanism. An employee who feels good about an organization and enjoys membership is drawn toward the organization (Meyer & Allen, 1991). Conversely, a person who is unhappy with or dislikes some aspect of the organization wants to avoid this displeasure by withdrawing (e.g., Mobley, 1977). The driving force is that people want to continue doing things that make them feel good and avoid doing things that make them feel bad or uncomfortable (positive/negative affect ➤ comfort/discomfort ➤ approach/avoidance).

Alternative Forces: Self-Efficacy Beliefs about One's Alternative Jobs or Roles

Many antecedents in the literature reflect that good or plentiful alternative opportunities may attract or psychologically pull employees away from their current organizations, even ones that are well liked (e.g., Bretz, Boudreau, & Judge, 1994). Conversely, an employee who believes that there are few or low quality jobs available to them will be less apt to quit the current organization (March & Simon, 1958). Presumably, this relationship is partially driven by the fact that many employees fear unemployment and would be less willing to quit without having another job. Beyond fear (or lack thereof) as a motivational factor, there is clearly an element of desire and attraction concerning alternatives. People tend to be attracted to opportunities that they perceive will allow them to achieve valued outcomes. Thus, the positive side of this motive is attraction, based on a belief that an alternative can provide valued outcomes. The belief may be based on extensive or vague information and may relate to alternative jobs or non-work roles (e.g., going back to school).

The motivational construct of self-efficacy reflects both the fear and attraction aspects of job/role alternatives. Self-efficacy "refers to beliefs in one's capabilities to mobilize the motivation, cognitive resources, and courses of action necessary to meet situational demands" (Wood & Bandura, 1989, p. 408), in this case, beliefs about capabilities for obtaining alternative jobs/roles. Self-efficacy has at least two dimensions, magnitude and strength. Magnitude is the belief in the *level* of accomplishment that can be attained, and strength is the belief in the *certainty* of achieving a level of accomplishment (Stajkovic & Luthans, 1998). Thus, alternative forces are the self-efficacy beliefs about whether one or more alternatives will provide a *level* of benefit combined with beliefs about *certainty* of obtaining such alternatives. To the extent that magnitude and strength are higher, there is a greater motivation to quit. To the extent that magnitude and strength are lower, there is a greater motivation to remain.

Behavioral Forces: Behavioral-Continuance Commitment

The behavioral approach to commitment maintains that individuals are bound to "consistent lines of activity" by past behaviors (Becker, 1960). Specifically, one may be attached to the organization by past behaviors that create costs incurred by leaving (Becker, 1960). Recent research indicates these binding costs, or "side bets," may be economic, like vested pension benefits, or adjustment-related, like company-specific training time (Shore, Tetrick, Shore, & Barksdale, 2000). For Salancik (1977) the costs of leaving were psychological, involving cognitive dissonance brought on by volitional, explicit, irreversible, and public behaviors favoring membership. The general motivational mechanism to stay in behavioral forces is that one wants to avoid costs, explicit or psychological, incurred by leaving (Meyer & Allen, 1991). Conversely, perceiving no significant costs of leaving may create motivation to quit (Shore et al., 2000).

Calculative Forces: Expectations Regarding Future Benefits of Membership

Calculative forces are based on rational self-interest. They take the form of an expectancy-like calculation of one's chances for achieving goals and values in the future at the current organization (e.g., Van Eerde, & Thierry, 1996; Vroom, 1964). If an employee feels that he or she can advance, develop, or achieve goals and values in the future through continued membership, the person becomes more psychologically attached to the organization. A calculation that one or more valued goals will not be met in the future, at the current organization, increases motivation to quit.

Unlike affective forces that reflect past and current emotional responses, calculative forces are future-oriented and based on rational self-interest. An employee may be currently satisfied with the job and organization, but also may be very worried about his or her future prospects there. Thus, calculative forces can be meaningfully distinguished from affective forces and each should have a distinct influence on turnover decisions (Aquino, Griffeth, Allen, & Hom, 1997). Calculative forces may also be distinguished from behavioral forces (McGee & Ford, 1987). One may want to avoid considerable costs of leaving the organization (e.g., lost pension benefits) but also perceive that the chances are low for fulfilling objectives there (e.g., promotion to vice-president).

Normative Forces: Expectations of Family and Friends Regarding Turnover Behavior

Turnover decisions often affect the lives of other people outside the organization as well as the employee (e.g., family, friends, and associates). To the extent that this is true, an employee is likely to perceive desires and expectations from these people with respect to his/her turnover behavior. In Fishbein's (1967) model, normative beliefs are perceived expectations of others regarding the employee's behavior. Empirical research has found that such perceptions of normative expectations had even stronger linkages to turnover intentions than attitude measures did (Hom, Katerberg, & Hulin, 1979; Newman, 1974; Prestholdt et al., 1987). Compliance with someone's expectations may require or imply either staying with or quitting the organization. Such expectations can be perceived from several sources within and outside the organization. However, normative forces are perceived expectations of non-coworkers, *not* of people at work, which are captured under constituent forces.

Thus, normative forces in the current model refer to the perceived expectations from family or friends about remaining or quitting, *combined with* some motivation to comply with these expectations (Fishbein & Azjen, 1975). If the expectations are for the employee to stay in the current job, there is motivation to remain. If the expectations are for the employee to leave, there is motivation to quit.

Moral Forces: Consistency with General Values Regarding Quitting or Staying

While normative forces depend on perceived expectations of *others* with regard to staying or quitting, moral forces are based on an internalized general value about turnover behavior. One possibility for a turnover-related value is generalized persistence. One important value in the "protestant work ethic" and other religious/moral traditions is that it is good in itself to persevere and work hard regardless of circumstances (Morrow, 1993; Niles, 1999). This value implies that being fickle or "job-hopping" is morally deficient or indicative of weak character. There is some precedent for this type of value as an antecedent of turnover intention (Hom et al., 1979; Triandis, 1975). At the opposite end of the spectrum is an internalized value that change in general, and *changing jobs* in particular, is a virtue (e.g., "a rolling stone gathers no moss"). These values may be strongly or weakly held. Assuming that one of these values is held by the employee to some extent, the psychological mechanism impacting turnover decisions is the desire to do the "right thing" and avoid dissonance caused by acting inconsistently with one's values (Festinger, 1957). Maintaining behavioral consistency with a generalized value of persistence is a motive to stay. Maintaining consistency with the "change is good" value is a motive to quit.

Contractual Forces: Perceived Obligations under or Breach of the Psychological Contract

Perceived agreements with the organization to fulfill certain obligations, combined with a norm of reciprocity (Gouldner, 1960; Scholl, 1981) can create a motivational force. In the research literature, perceived obligations to the organization and obligations expected from the organization are often conceptualized within a psychological contract (Rousseau, 1989; Rousseau & Parks, 1992). Felt obligations to the organization may arise from its making prepayments, from its past need fulfillment, or simply from its having hired the employee (Meyer & Allen, 1991). The employee then becomes indebted to the organization as part of his psychological contract. A sense of obligation to an organization, "...acts to hold a person into a particular system until the debt is repaid" (Settoon, Bennett, & Liden, 1996, p. 220). Paying back the organization would usually imply at least some continuing membership, and thus, increased psychological attachment. In fact, an employee may perceive that he is actually paying back an obligation directly through continuing membership (Robinson, Kraatz, & Rousseau, 1994). In contractual forces, the essential motivation to stay depends on felt obligations that include or imply staying with the organization for some period.

Conversely, a perceived breach of the psychological contract is an employee's cognition that the organization has failed one or more of its obligations (Morrison & Robinson, 1997). These breaches are relatively common and can result in decreased feelings of obligation to the employer and intentions to quit (Robinson et al., 1994; Turnley & Feldman, 2000). This contractual relationship is characterized by a mirroring and balanced exchange, whereby each party maintains its side of the bargain *only* to the extent the other party does (Robinson & Morrison, 2000). Thus, any breach reduces or negates any obligations that employees feel they owe, including obligations to stay with the organization (Turnley & Feldman, 2000). In fact, the employee may feel so betrayed that, out of revenge, he or she quits to "even the score" or strike back at the organization. In these ways, perceived psychological contract breaches by the organization can cause employee motivation to quit.

Constituent Forces: Attachment to or Desire to Withdraw from Organization Constituents

Constituent forces are a hybrid motive category composed of the seven forces just discussed, but directed toward sub-components of the organization salient to the employee, rather than toward the organization itself. Reichers (1985) suggested that employees become committed to constituents within the organization, apart from commitment to the organization as a whole. There is considerable evidence that employees meaningfully distinguish between their relationships with people or groups in the organization and their relationship with the organization itself (e.g., Ellemers, de Gilder, & van den Heuvel, 1998; Settoon et al., 1996; Wayne et al., 1997). As such, these relationships with constituents may be conceptualized as independent from the organization itself and may have independent effects on turnover intentions (Becker, 1992; Maertz, Mosley, & Alford, 2002).

In constituent forces, attachment or withdrawal tendency may result from any or all of the motives proposed previously. The employee may: (1) like or dislike constituents (affective), (2) be attracted to or repelled by constituents associated with an alternative role (alternative), (3) wish to avoid losing investments made in constituent relationships (behavioral), (4) determine that constituents are beneficial or a liability to their future achievement (calculative), (5) perceive expectations from the constituent with regard to staying or leaving (normative), (6) be motivated to continue working with constituents because it is "the right thing to do" (moral), and/or (7) feel obligated to remain/quit because previous agreements were made with constituents or broken by them (contractual). The net effect on turnover intentions would depend on a subjective combination or weighting of different motives across different constituents.

A key point is that constituent force effects on turnover intention depend on whether the constituent has stable attachment to the current organization. For example, if employees are attached to a coworker who they believe will soon quit, any motivational forces to stay would begin to dissolve, or change to forces of withdrawal (Krackhardt & Porter, 1985, 1986). Likewise, if employees are motivated to withdraw from a union and learn that it will soon decertify, union forces of withdrawal would dissolve or change into forces of attachment. Thus, employees' perceptions about whether the constituent will remain or leave the organization conditions the strength and direction of constituent forces on turnover intentions.

FIVE NEGLECTED ANTECEDENTS AND THEIR RELATION WITH TURNOVER INTENTION

These eight motive categories, or forces of attachment and withdrawal, represent proximal causes of turnover intention and mediate the effects of antecedents on turnover intentions. In the next sections, I briefly review definitions and findings relevant to turnover (if any) for (1) personality, (2) organization and national culture, (3) perceived organization performance, (4) occupational attachments, and (5) location attachments. Then, based on empirical findings, some existing theory, and conceptual reasoning, I propose causal linkages for each antecedent construct to turnover intention, using the eight forces as mediating mechanisms.

Personality

An important question for research and practice is whether personality significantly affects turnover behavior and, if so, what is the mechanism at work behind this relationship. Some practitioners claim that they have developed measures that can predict turnover behavior at time of hire, based on a "turnover personality"(e.g., *Personnel Journal,* 1992). Although using personality measures to screen out dysfunctional quitters is attractive, such measures must be based on theoretical dimensions and empirical validation research in order to draw conclusions about the usefulness of such measures. Research reviews have traditionally concluded that personality variables are poor predictors of turnover (Mobley et al., 1979; Muchinsky & Morrow, 1980) and most turnover models do not explicitly include personality (Hom & Griffeth, 1995). However, dimensions of the "Big Five" factor model of personality (e.g., Barrick & Mount, 1991) have demonstrated significant empirical findings with turnover and offer a basis to theorize about relationships with turnover. Personality dimensions probably do not directly cause turnover intentions, but rather are mediated through other more proximal antecedents (Day, Bedeian, & Conte, 1998). These proximal antecedents are the motive categories, or forces. Specifically, I propose that the "Big Five" personality dimensions influence various forces of attachment, and in turn, these motivate turnover intentions and behavior (see Figure 6.2).

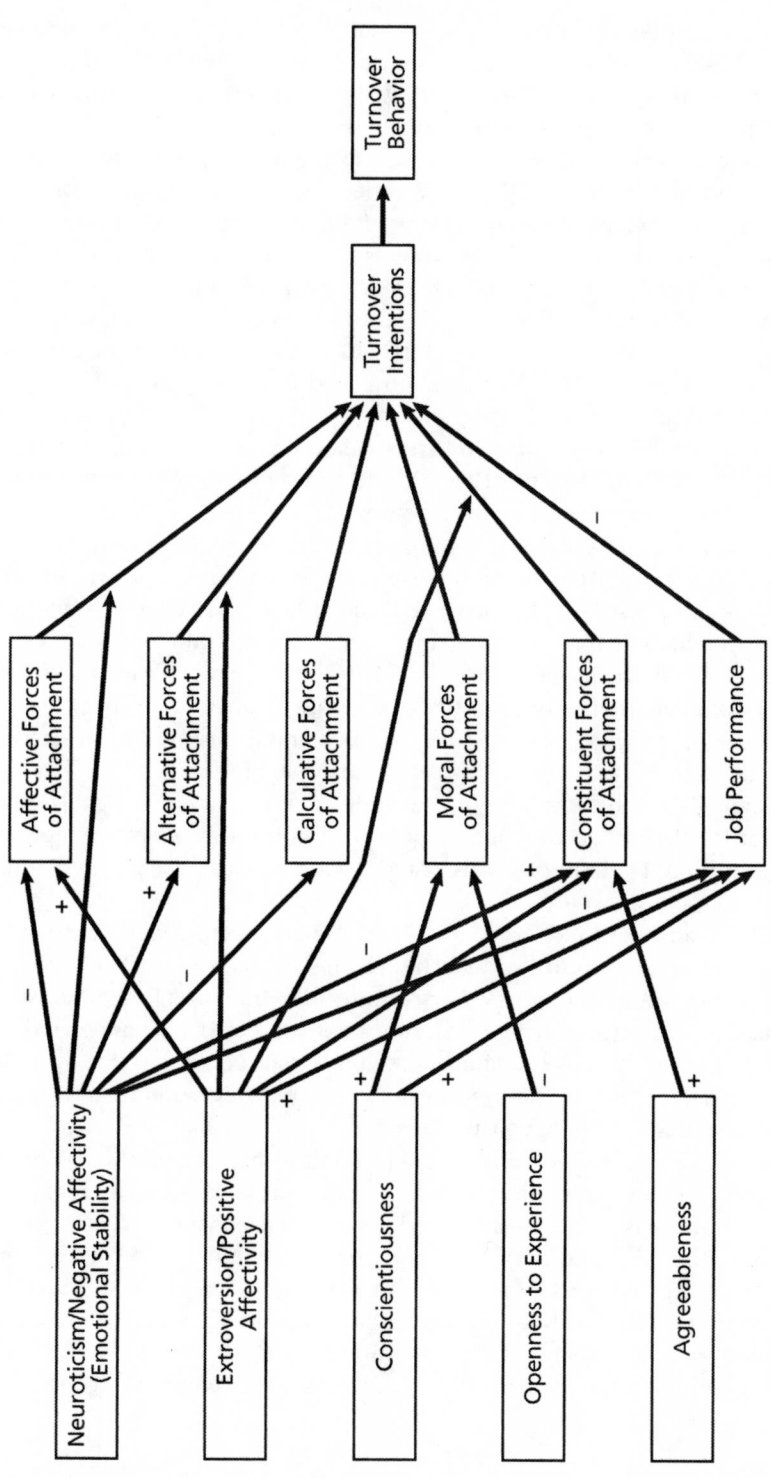

Figure 6.2. Linkages among the "big five" personality dimensions and turnover.

Neuroticism/negative affectivity (emotional stability).   Personality traits such as aggression and anxiety have demonstrated positive relationships with turnover (Muchinsky & Tuttle, 1979; Porter & Steers, 1973). Such traits are captured within the dimension of neuroticism. Neuroticism is the tendency to experience negative affectivity as related to anxiety, subjective distress, and dissatisfaction (Kanfer, Wanberg, & Kantrowitz, 2001; McCrae & Costa, 1997). Neurotics tend to be rigid, unadaptable, timid, insecure, and dependent (Wiggins, 1996). Neuroticism is also usually equated with trait negative affectivity (e.g., Iverson & Deery, 2001; Watson, Clark, & Tellegen, 1988). Emotional stability is at the opposite end of the continuum from neuroticism (Barrick & Mount, 1991). Representative traits for emotional stability are calm, unemotional, secure, and not angry (Barrick & Mount, 1996). Hough, Eaton, Dunnette, Kamp and McCloy (1990) found that emotional adjustment was positively related to job involvement (retention). Barrick and Mount (1996) found that emotional stability (neuroticism) was negatively related to turnover.

To explain these empirical findings, there are at least four (4) direct theoretical linkages between neuroticism and voluntary turnover. First, McCrae and Costa (1991) noted that individuals high on neuroticism are predisposed to experience negative affect. This could include negative affect toward the organization, reducing the average level of affective forces of attachment for neurotics (e.g., Hom & Griffeth, 1995).

Second, individuals high in neuroticism tend to respond to stress by giving up attempts to reach their goals (Watson & Hubbard, 1996). This may indicate that neurotics believe that they cannot reach their goals. These doubts could extend to reaching goals through future membership at the organization. By definition, this would decrease calculative forces of attachment to the organization.

Third, another mediator of the neuroticism effect may be negative relations with coworkers. Individuals high in neuroticism may tend to respond to stress by complaining to others (Watson & Hubbard, 1996). Consistent complaining and negativity may cause coworkers to dislike and avoid neurotics. This would likely damage relations between neurotics and their coworkers, thereby generally weakening the neurotic's potential for attachments to organizational constituents.

Fourth, despite generally negative relationships between neuroticism and attachment types, there is a potentially positive effect on attachment as well. Neuroticism has been linked to problem-solving deficits, timidity, career indecision, and fearfulness of novel situations (Tokar, Fischer & Subich, 1998; Wiggins, 1996), possibly leading to less job search behavior (Kanfer et al., 2001). But neuroticism also indicates more anxiety, possibly leading to more search behavior (Boudreau, Boswell, Judge, & Bretz, 2001). Despite these contradictory findings on job search, neuroticism has been negatively related to receiving job offers in two studies (Kanfer et al., 2001). With fewer job offers from job search, neurotics are likely to feel low confidence for obtaining attractive employment alternatives. Thus, I propose that neuroticism should be positively related to alternative forces of attachment.

Extroversion/positive affectivity. Extroversion is equated with positive affectivity (e.g., Watson et al., 1988). "Extroversion represents the tendency to be sociable, assertive, forceful, active, and experience positive affects such as energy, zeal, and excitement" (Boudreau et al., 2001, p. 30). Extroverts tend to experience positive affective states more than introverts (e.g., Watson et al., 1988). Thus, we might expect that extroverts would generally have greater positive affect toward the job and organization than introverts. Thus, extroversion should be positively related to affective forces of attachment.

Because of their inherent sociability, extroverts are more likely to form friendships at work than introverts (Tokar & Fischer, 1998). They tend to prefer team-oriented cultures (Judge & Cable, 1997). Thus, extroverts may more easily form attachments to coworkers, groups, and leaders (constituents) than introverts do. However, it should be noted that extroverts may also be aggressive, lacking sensitivity and tact (Judge & Cable, 1997), which could inhibit building strong relationships. Because of this, extroverts will not always have stronger constituent attachments than introverts, but they should still have more of them. Thus, I still hypothesize a positive relationship between extroversion constituent forces of attachment.

Conscientiousness. Conscientiousness includes facets of achievement, dependability (Boudreau et al., 2001), and tendency to persevere (McCrae & Costa, 1997). This latter tendency could lead to endorsing the value that perseverance in work is good for its own sake, similar to the Protestant Work Ethic (e.g., Morrow, 1983; Niles, 1999). This tendency could cause adoption of the value that being fickle or "job-hopping" is bad. Assuming employees want to maintain behavioral consistency with this value and avoid cognitive dissonance (Festinger, 1957), they will be motivated to remain with the organization through moral forces. Conversely, low conscientiousness may indicate low dependability and lack of focus and planning (Barrick & Mount, 1991). This behavioral tendency may prohibit strong adherence to a value of persistence, implying lower moral attachment. Thus, conscientiousness should be positively related to moral forces of attachment.

Effects on job performance. Job performance has been consistently found to be negatively related to voluntary turnover (Griffeth et al., 2000), although the causal effects behind this meta-analytic finding are complex and involve moderators (see Allen & Griffeth, 2001). Nevertheless, this negative relationship is well established and can be explained by the fact that good performers are likely to be more satisfied than bad performers and thereby less likely to leave (e.g., Judge, Thoresen, Bono, & Patton, 2001). Research has shown that neuroticism is negatively related to job performance (e.g., Barrick & Mount, 1996; Judge & Bono, 2001), that conscientiousness is positively related to job performance (e.g., Barrick & Mount, 1991, 1996), and that extroversion is positively related to job performance, especially in high autonomy jobs where interaction with others is important (e.g., Barrick, Mount, & Strauss, 1993; Mount, Barrick, & Stewart, 1998). Thus, these three dimensions should also have indirect effects on turnover intention through job performance.

Openness to experience.   Individuals high on openness have intellectual curiosity and a preference for variety, while individuals low on openness tend to be conventional, conservative, and prefer the familiar to the novel (Costa & McCrae, 1992). Curiosity and preference for variety or newness may lead to the endorsement of a "change is good" value. This could extend to the realm of changing jobs (e.g., Ghiselli, 1974). In other words, openness could lead to adoption of an instrumental value that changing jobs frequently is good, based on an end value of variety and accumulation of experience. Maintaining consistency with such a value would cause moral forces to withdraw from the organization after a period of time. Thus, openness to experience should be negatively related to moral forces of attachment.

Agreeableness.   This dimension is largely composed of tendencies regarding interpersonal relationships. Agreeable people are altruistic, sympathetic, eager to help, cooperative, kind, considerate, and trusting of others, while disagreeable people are egocentric, competitive, skeptical of others' intentions (Costa & McCrae, 1992; McCrae & Costa, 1997). It is clear that agreeable people would be more able and likely than disagreeable people to make good friendships with others, including coworkers within the organization. Judge and Cable (1997) found that individuals high on agreeableness were more attracted to team-oriented organizational cultures. This may suggest a propensity to form attachments to work groups/teams, as well as individuals. Thus, agreeableness should be positively related to constituent forces of attachment.

Moderator effects.   In addition to the direct effects just discussed, personality dimensions may also moderate the effects of various forces of attachment on turnover intention (e.g., Jenkins, 1993). This may be particularly true of relationships between affective attachment and turnover intention. That is, affect may be a more or less important determinant of turnover intention depending on neuroticism/negative affectivity and extroversion/positive affectivity.

Weitz (1952) hypothesized that those with high negative affectivity are less likely to withdraw when they experience job dissatisfaction than those with low general dissatisfaction (emotional stability). This is because negative affect would be less salient to neurotics' intentions because it could be more a function of their disposition than the job or the organization (e.g., Judge, 1993). Thus, the relationship between affective forces and turnover intention should be weaker for neurotics than for "emotionally stables."

Similarly, it has been hypothesized that job satisfaction may be more predictive if an individual's predisposition to be generally satisfied (i.e., positive affectivity) is considered in the analysis (e.g., Staw, Bell, & Clausen, 1986). Judge (1993) found that positive affective people (i.e., extroverts) exhibit a stronger negative job satisfaction-turnover relationship, than those without a positive-affective disposition. This may be because a relatively larger contrast between negative organizational affect and generally positive life affect is more likely to violate expectations, create more tension, and trigger more quitting (e.g., Porter & Steers, 1973). Thus, the relationship between affective forces and turnover intent should be stronger for extroverts than for introverts.

In addition, extroverts gear their lives toward being actively social in relationships with others. This sociability may lead to placing more importance on such relationships than on the job itself (Judge, Martocchio, & Thoresen, 1997). Further, work relationships may be more salient for extroverts than introverts, who are more reserved and independent (Costa & McCrae, 1992). Thus, the relationship between constituent forces of attachment and turnover intention should be stronger for extroverts than for introverts.

Other effects mediated by job search.   One additional way that personality can relate to the forces of attachment is through its effects on job search (Boudreau et al., 2001). In their meta-analysis, Kanfer et al. (2001) found medium-sized positive effects on job search for extroversion (corrected r = .46) and for conscientiousness (corrected r = .38). Kanfer et al. (2001) and Boudreau et al. (2001) also found statistically significant, but smaller and practically less significant, positive correlations for agreeableness and openness to experience on job search. In turn, job search behaviors are positively related to number of job offers received (corrected r = .28, Kanfer et al., 2001). Job offers directly increase the strength of self-efficacy for obtaining alternative jobs. Therefore, through this process, extroversion, conscientiousness, agreeableness, and openness to experience should be negatively related to alternative forces of attachment. For the sake of clarity in the diagram, these four (4) negative paths between these personality dimensions and alternative forces of attachment are omitted from Figure 6.2.

Conclusions.   Clearly, personality dimensions affect turnover intentions through multiple, complex mechanisms. More interesting though is the fact that each dimension may have both positive and negative affects on attachment. There are also several interactive effects for neuroticism and extroversion. Together, if these opposing and interactive linkages are further supported, they seem to undermine the notion that managers can effectively screen out individuals likely to quit by simple top-down selection on certain "Big Five" dimensions. However, emotional stability and conscientiousness seem to have the best potential for selection because they have better established negative linkages to turnover intent and also positive linkages to performance (e.g., Barrick & Mount, 1996). Although not empirically related to turnover intent in the past, openness to experience and agreeableness may have meaningful effects particularly in combination with other dimensions. For example, high openness and low conscientiousness may well lead to a chronic lack of persistence across endeavors and poor, unfocused performance. This combination may explain Ghiselli's (1974) "hobo syndrome" where individuals regularly and almost instinctively drift away from jobs. These dimensions and low moral forces of attachment could be a starting point for determining whether a turnover motive exists that is stable across employment situations. Also, high agreeableness, high emotional stability, and extroversion could comprise a syndrome of attachment to people and groups at work. People high on these dimensions may persist because of attachment to constituents even when they dislike the organization itself or their jobs. For either of these "types" of employees, traditional turnover models, where job dissatisfaction is the driving force (e.g., Mobley, 1977), may not apply.

To assess the full impact of personality we must also examine patterns of turnover intentions and behavior over time and employers. Traits are more likely to predict such patterns of behavior than a specific instance of turnover intention and behavior. Until such research is done, the complete picture of the relationship between personality and turnover will remain hidden.

Organizational Turnover Culture

Organization culture consists of the collective belief, assumption, and value systems/structures regarding organizational reality and effective ways of coping for organizational members (e.g., Pettigrew, 1979; Schein, 1985). Researchers have long suggested that these shared systems/structures can affect the likelihood that applicants will enter the organization and that employees will quit (e.g., Schneider, 1987). However, most of this research that links culture to turnover has taken an interactive approach. That is, the *interaction* of organization culture and individual characteristics affect turnover decisions. Specifically, this interaction is based on similarity between personal and organizational characteristics leading to lower chances of turnover (Schneider, 1987). Researchers have primarily focused on the similarity between employee and organization goals and values, represented in the supplementary P-O fit perspective (Kristof, 1996). Personality dimensions have been reliably associated with values and preferences for certain organizational cultures (Judge & Cable, 1997). Some research has also examined interactive effects of personality, culture, and turnover intentions (Schaubroeck, Ganster, & Jones, 1998). In fact, O'Reilly, Chatman, and Caldwell (1991) found that "misfits" on organization values terminated faster than "fits" after 20 months of tenure.

Although this interactive, P-O fit perspective has been popular and relatively successful in predicting variance in turnover, it is incomplete with respect to explaining the impact of culture. Researchers have argued that an organization's culture may have direct effects on the rate of voluntary turnover within an organization (Abelson, 1993; Kerr & Slocum, 1987; Sheridan, 1992). Kerr and Slocum (1987) proposed that the cultural values of teamwork, security, and respect for individuals would foster loyalty and greater retention than values of initiative and individual rewards. Using newcomer accountants, Sheridan (1992) confirmed that organizational cultures emphasizing interpersonal relationship values improved retention by an average of 14 months over cultures emphasizing work task values. He also questioned the efficacy of the interactive (P-O fit) perspective in light of the strong findings for his situational perspective. Despite these supportive findings, this study does not specify how an organization culture comes to include these turnover-related values. They also do not propose an actual "turnover culture," explicitly formed around turnover-related behavior.

Based on Schein's (1985) model of organizational culture, Abelson (1993) proposed how a turnover culture may develop. First, employees individually perceive an organization's structural characteristics, human resource policies, leadership, and external environment. They respond to stories, symbols, and customs about turnover-related behavior. These individual interpretations along with social information processing lead to individual cognitions, prototypes, scripts, and schemas regarding turnover behavior. For instance, "A lot of managers quit around here; nobody gives two weeks notice before quitting; people quit after conflicts with manager X." These cognitions are then shared with other employees and tested for compatibility. Cognitions affirmed by others are transmitted further, becoming generally shared by the group. This process results in group-level assumptions, schemas, axiomatic knowledge and values relating to turnover from the organization. An example might be, "The organization has broken promises and thus does not deserve employee loyalty, or Quitting is socially acceptable under most circumstances." Finally, these phenomena become organized into a logical and systematic patterns, which in turn, determine subsequent organizational artifacts and creations related to turnover and help determine organizational turnover rates. These processes can occur both at the organization level and at organization sub-group level.

In summary, a turnover culture as a group phenomenon evolves through employees' sense-making and social information processes regarding common environmental cues relating to turnover behavior. Presumably, the resulting group phenomenon then reciprocally influences individual employee perceptions and interpretations that relate to turnover decisions. Despite Abelson's (1993) rich description of turnover cultures, he leaves a key question unanswered, "How does a turnover culture actually influence individual decisions to quit or stay?" I address this question in the following paragraphs (see Figure 6.3).

Patterns of shared norms and values regarding turnover comprise a turnover culture. These may be contingent or absolute. They are contingent if turnover behavior is more or less encouraged under certain conditions. For instance, "One should only quit if they have a higher paying job offer, or people in this organization quit when they get passed over for a promotion." They are absolute if norms and values favor or discourage turnover directly (e.g., "Everybody wants to quit this organization; Quitting this organization at any time is perfectly acceptable or expected; People who quit this organization end up regretting it.").

First, such norms and values may influence affective forces. Employees who are subject to norms and values favoring turnover would likely perceive that the organization is not well liked. For those who have not strongly identified with the organization, this social information would likely lead directly to more negative regard for the organization at the individual level (Salancik & Pfeffer, 1978), reducing affective forces of attachment. In the case of high organizational identification where the employee's self-concept is linked with that of the organization (e.g., Ashforth & Mael, 1989; Turner, 1987), the employee may perceive insufficient justification for their continuing membership within a turnover culture (e.g., Salancik & Pfeffer, 1978). An employee would likely reason, "if turnover is highly acceptable and if I am still employed and identify with this organization, then I must really like the organization." In this case, attitudes and affect toward the organization would likely become more positive (Salancik & Pfeffer, 1978). Thus, for employees with high organizational identification, a turnover culture might lead to increased affective attachment.

Norms and values comprising a turnover culture primarily affect turnover decisions through their impact on the individual's norms and values regarding turnover. Over time, through social information processes (Salancik & Pfeffer, 1978), employees may internalize the prevailing norms and values from the turnover culture. Adherence to the norms and values of the turnover culture may also be facilitated by the threat of sanctions

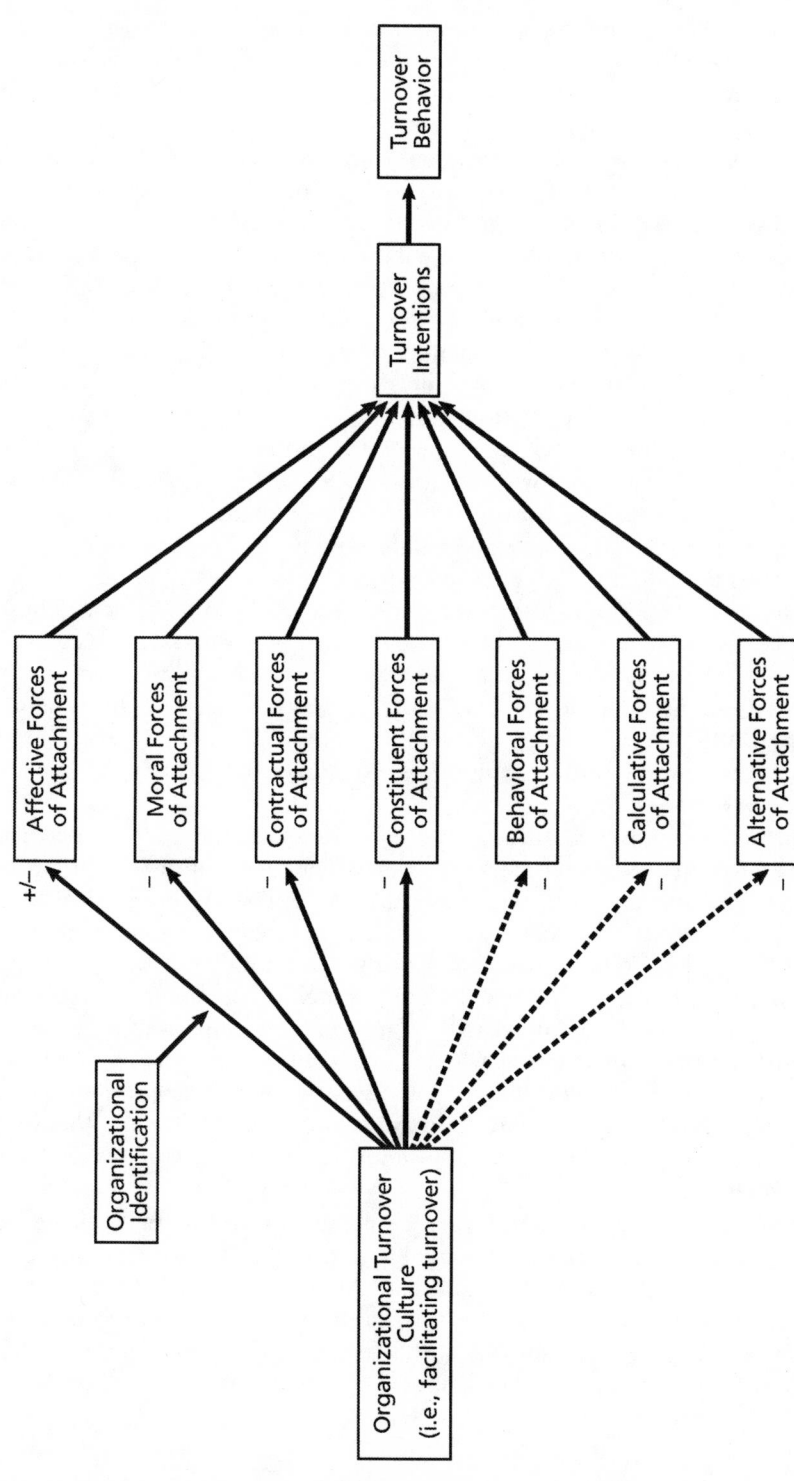

Figure 6.3. Linkages between organization turnover culture and turnover.

123

from coworkers within the organization for resisting cultural norms. In this way, employees within a turnover-favoring culture are more likely to adopt a value that quitting is generally normal, right, or acceptable. This would cause a reduction in moral forces of attachment.

Turnover culture norms and values may also take the form of what is personally owed to the organization, for example: "The employee doesn't owe this organization anything; If the organization breaks a promise to an employee, he or she should quit; or Employees owe this organization at least one year of tenure." In the same ways mentioned above, these shared norms and values may be transmitted to the individual level, affecting the employee's level of personal obligation to stay with the organization. In this way, turnover cultures may reduce one's level of obligation to stay and thus, reduce contractual forces of attachment.

In addition, turnover culture norms and values may take the form of what is owed by the employee to coworkers and other organizational con-stituents (e.g., local union), for example: "Close relations among cowork-ers are not possible because people quit too quickly; Employees don't owe any obligation to stay with people at this organization; or Employees should not leave their coworkers during an important project." These norms and values are transmitted to individual employees. If the cultural norms and values favor loyalty to coworkers and groups, this would increase (moral, contractual, and normative) attachments to constituents. If the cultural norms and values imply little loyalty to coworkers and groups, this would reduce (moral, contractual, and normative) attach-ments to constituents.

Finally, a turnover culture may have some additional and less predict-able effects on how people frame their employment situation. For instance, these elements may influence how employees evaluate their costs of leav-ing or their future at the organization. Specifically, a turnover culture might signal to the employee that there are generally low costs of leaving the organization and there is limited probability of meeting long-term goals there. A turnover culture may even encourage employees to see alter-natives as more attractive than when no such culture or an attachment cul-ture exists. Thus, I suggest that turnover cultures may be negatively related to behavioral, calculative and alternative forces of attachment (because these linkages are more speculative, they are represented with dashed lines in Figure 6.3).

Conclusion. Turnover cultures include norms and values related to turnover behavior that are transmitted to individuals. These make turnover behavior more or less salient and acceptable in employees' minds, prima-rily through effects on affective, moral, contractual, constituent forces, and perhaps, behavioral, calculative, and alternative forces. It is unlikely that turnover cultural norms and values are transmitted to all employees equally. For instance, employees who have little tenure or low job performance may be more marginalized within the organization, reducing cultural transmission. However, such individuals may also be more susceptible to cultural socialization. Such potential moderators should be investigated. Future research should also examine whether the theoretical linkages proposed here apply to turnover cultures that cross organization boundaries. Specifically, it is possible that turnover cultures may also operate at the level of the occupation or labor market. For example, business professors, IT professionals, or nurses may be socialized into prevailing norms that career progression implies inter-organizational movement. Watching colleagues change jobs regularly and sharing beliefs like, "If you want a pay raise in this business, you have to move," may contribute to a professional culture where quitting is well accepted or even expected. Maertz, Stevens, and Campion (2003) found evidence that a prevailing turnover culture may occur among Maquiladora laborers in Mexico, which serves to facilitate turnover decisions. Occupational labor markets with low unemployment and many job opportunities would likely facilitate such turnover cultures (Sheridan, 1992). Researchers should investigate the existence and potential impact of such occupational turnover cultures. If confirmed, these may help explain the effects of labor market on individual turnover decisions (e.g., Gerhart, 1990; Steel & Griffeth, 1989).

National Culture

Like at the organizational and occupational levels, very little theoretical or empirical research has attempted to explain how national culture impacts turnover (cf. Redding, Norman, & Schlander, 1994). In this section, I address this gap by explicating the effects of Hofstede's (1980a,b) cultural value dimensions on the 8 motivational forces, and in turn, on turnover intentions (see Figure 6.4).

Hofstede (1980a) describes national culture as common mental programming that takes place within a society and becomes crystallized within societal institutions. Culture consists of shared norms, values, attitudes, and behavioral patterns. Culture transmits to societal members, ways of thinking and behaving that have worked in the past to cope or adapt (e.g., Triandis, 1995). In Hofstede's (1980a) landmark study, four bipolar dimensions of national culture emerged: individualism-collectivism, high-low power distance, high-low uncertainty avoidance, and masculinity-femininity. The United States scores highest on individualism, medium-low on power distance, low on uncertainty avoidance, and medium-high on masculinity.

Through social learning, societal pressures for conformity, and the social information processes discussed in the previous section, national

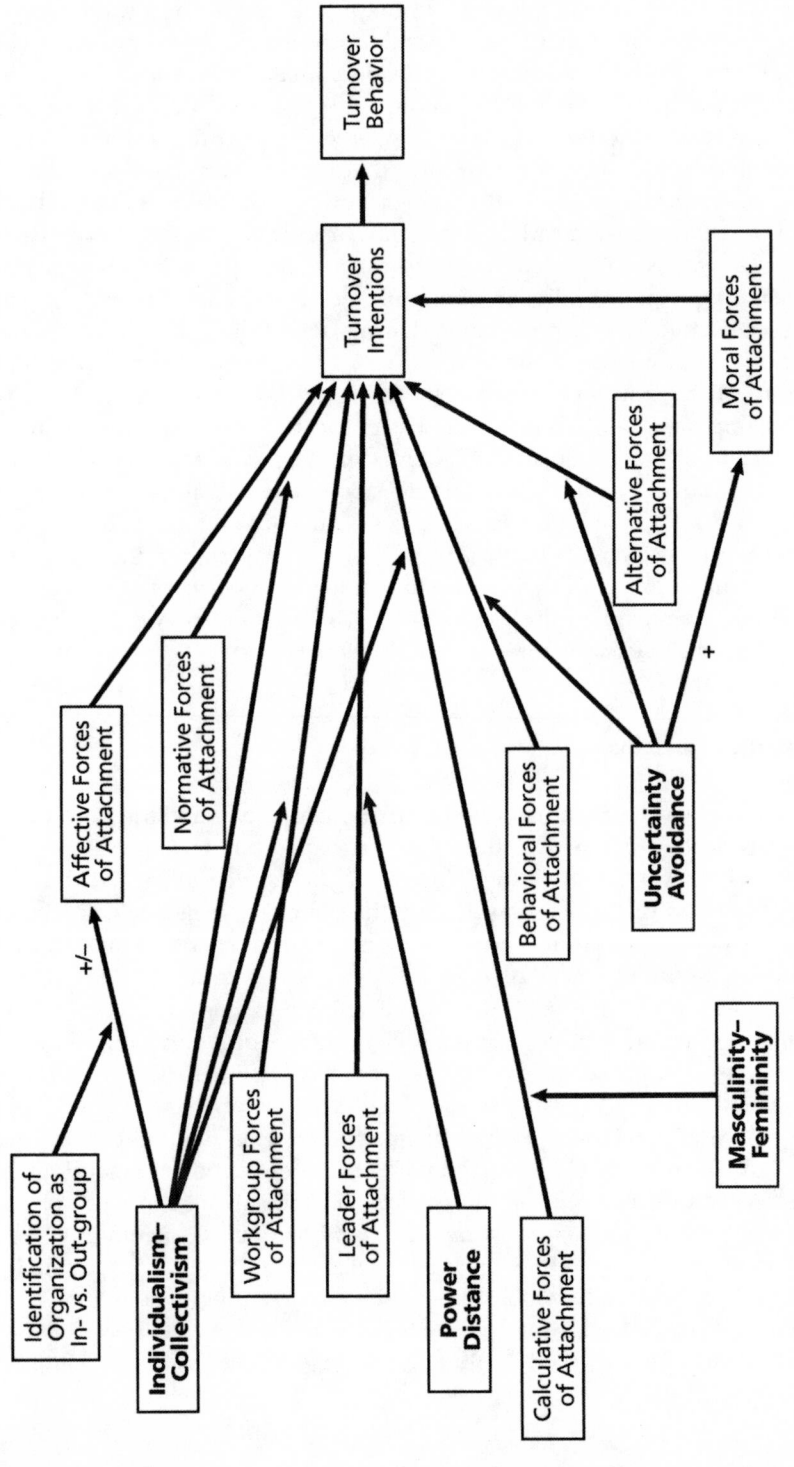

Figure 6.4. Linkages among national culture dimensions and turnover.

culture transmits to the individual, in varying degrees, congruent norms and values (e.g., Earley, 1989). This includes norms and values relevant to turnover behavior. Culture may also transmit norms and values that affect decision-making in general (e.g., Triandis, 1989), and thereby, decisions about turnover.

I propose that the effects of cultural dimensions on the forces of attachment are primarily moderating effects rather than direct effects on mean levels of antecedents (cf. Clugston, Howell, & Dorfman, 2000). Because antecedents may differ in their manifestations across cultures, examining moderating effects of culture is a superior approach to the emic-etic dilemma (Davidson, Jaccard, Triandis, Morales, & Diaz-Guerrero, 1976). Through transmission of norms and values, culture may cause certain motivational forces to be more salient to decisions and more highly weighted in their contribution to behavioral intentions (e.g., Davidson et al., 1976), including turnover intentions. In the next paragraphs, I discuss these moderating effects plus a few direct effects of cultural value dimensions.

Individualism-Collectivism. This dimension deals with the nature of the relationship between the individual and the group in society (Hofstede, 1980a; Triandis, 1995) and norms of how the self is defined (Triandis, 1989). In individualistic cultures, there is an emphasis on values such as autonomy, independence, freedom, achievement, assertiveness, and competition (Markus & Kitayama, 1991; Triandis, 1995; Triandis, McCusker, & Hui, 1990) and the private self predominates (Triandis, 1989). In collectivist cultures, the self is defined in terms of relationships and the collective self predominates (Triandis, 1989). There is an emphasis on values such as belonging, conformity, preserving public image, modesty, along with harmony and cooperation with similar others in interdependent situations (Markus & Kitayama, 1991; Triandis, 1995; Triandis et al., 1990).

With respect to individualism, the value on independence and individual achievement is likely to be more salient to individualists than collectivists (Hofstede, 1980a). Individualists will likely consider personal goals and related cost-benefit analysis of membership to be more important than collectivists, who consider loyalty and group expectations to be relatively more important to membership decisions (Randall, 1993). Thus, calculative forces should be more strongly related to turnover intentions for individualists than for collectivists.

With respect to collectivism, Randall (1993) and Clugston et al. (2000) proposed a direct positive effect on organizational commitment because of a tendency for collectivists to form greater affective attachment to institutions. However, the greater depth of loyalty within collectivist society only applies to in-groups (Triandis, 1989). Thus, if the organization is not identified with as an in-group, there is no reason to expect any more positive affect toward the organization than in individualist countries. There is evidence from several collectivist cultures like South Korea, China, and Mexico, that the organization is *not* seen as an in-group and is far beneath the family and personal friendship groups in terms of influence (Maertz et al., 2003; Redding et al., 1994). In fact, in some collectivist cultures the in-group may not extend far beyond the family (e.g., Gowan et al., 1996; Paik & Teagarden, 1995). In collectivist societies where the organization itself *is* a salient in-group, as may be the case for workers in Japan (Redding et al., 1994), greater positive affect toward the organization would be expected (Randall, 1993). Thus, I propose that collectivist employees who see the organization as an in-group should have greater affective forces of attachment on average than individualist employees or collectivist employees who do not see their organization as an in-group.

It is important to note that affective forces are not equivalent to organizational commitment, on which findings have been mixed with respect to individualist-collectivist comparisons (Redding et al., 1994). Methodological issues with organizational commitment measures and questions about applicability of the construct across cultures cast some doubt on the meaning of these studies (Bozeman & Perrewe, 2001; Near, 1989). A purer (and culturally-equivalent) measure of affect toward the organization than the OCQ is needed to test the previous proposed relationship.

Perhaps the most obvious effect of collectivism is on the salience of the expectations of others, or normative beliefs (e.g., Fishbein & Azjen, 1975). The essential attribute of a collectivist society is that individuals will subordinate their personal interests to the goals of their collective with whom they cooperate and identify (Triandis et al., 1988). These in-groups include family (Triandis et al., 1990) and others outside the organization who have expectations with respect to the employee's retention/turnover behavior. For collectivists, these expectations of in-group members are more influential than for individualists and more likely to be translated into turnover intentions (e.g., Davidson et al., 1976; Triandis, 1989; Triandis et al., 1990). On the other hand, as societies become more complex, affluent, and individualistic, the number of potential in-groups increases and the potency of any particular in-group decreases (Triandis et al., 1988). Thus, I conclude that the relationship between normative forces and turnover intentions should be stronger for collectivists than for individualists.

Moreover, in-group members can also be coworkers within the organization (Triandis, 1989). Thus, collectivism may affect relationships with coworkers (Clugston et al., 2000), assuming they are seen as in-group members. In fact, organizational attachment may be caused by ties to constituents more than for individualists, who tend to be more attached because of the pay system or the work itself (Boyacigiller & Adler, 1991). Attachments to coworkers may even be more important for the turnover decisions of collectivists than attachment to the organization itself (Maertz et al., 2003). Therefore, I propose that the relationship between coworker constituent forces and turnover intentions should be stronger for collectivists than for individualists.

Power distance. Power distance indicates the culture's level of acceptance and expectation of unequal power distributions in society (Hofstede, 1980a). Cultures with high power distance may transmit very specific, definite expectations, values, prototypes, scripts, and schemas for supervisor/leader behavior (e.g., Offermann, Kennedy, & Wirtz, 1994). These may be more definite than in individualist cultures and may include a patriarchal and inaccessible leadership style (Hofstede, 1980b). Well-developed, definite expectations might make leader relations more salient, whether they favor staying with or withdrawing from the leader. If the well-developed expectations are met by the leader, there may be greater attachment and personal loyalty to that leader than in individualist countries (e.g., Morris & Pavett, 1992). On the other hand, a leader who does not meet expectations can be actively repellent and inspire withdrawal more than in an individualist country. Conflict with a supervisor or group leader was the most frequent reason given for quitting in a recent study within Mexico, a high-power distance culture (Maertz et al., 2003). In this country employees may also quit their organization in order to follow a leader to another company (Gowan et al., 1996). In contrast, employees in low power distance cultures have weaker needs for dependence on leaders (Hofstede, 1980a). This implies that relationships with leaders are likely to be less central to behavior than in high power distance cultures. Based on these arguments, I propose that the relationship between leader constituent forces and turnover intentions should be stronger for employees in high power distance cultures than those in low power distance cultures.

Uncertainty avoidance. Uncertainty avoidance indicates the extent to which a society feels threatened by uncertain and ambiguous situations and tries to avoid them (Hofstede, 1980a). High uncertainty avoidance cultures value security in employment whereas low uncertainty avoidance cultures value more risk-taking (Hofstede, 1980b). This dimension will likely influence whether employees frame turnover decisions as avoiding risk vs. accepting risk to maximize benefit (Clugston et al., 2000). For this reason, I propose that uncertainty avoidance helps determine the relative importance of the two components of alternative forces for determining turnover intentions. If uncertainty avoidance is high and the employee is considering quitting he or she is more likely to focus on the certainty of alternative employment, or the strength component of alternative forces. If uncertainty avoidance is low, the employee is more likely to focus on the potential benefits of alternative employment, or the magnitude component of alternative forces. Moreover, under high uncertainty avoidance, the specifics of alternative employment may be generally more important than under low uncertainty avoidance (Clugston et al., 2000). Overall, the relationship between alternative forces of attachment and turnover intentions should be stronger for employees in high vs. employees in low uncertainty avoidance cultures.

High uncertainty avoidance cultures may encourage employees to frame decisions as minimizing losses (Clugston et al., 2000), while low uncertainty avoidance cultures may encourage risk-taking to maximize benefit (Hostede, 1980a). High uncertainty avoidance, then, may influence people to focus on avoiding the costs of quitting when making employment decisions, more than in individualist cultures. Thus, the relationship between behavioral attachment and turnover intentions should be stronger for employees in high uncertainty avoidance cultures than in low uncertainty avoidance cultures.

Uncertainty avoidance may also directly affect levels of moral attachment. Employees in high uncertainty avoidance cultures may view loyalty to an employer as a virtue (Hofstede, 1980a; Randall, 1993). This reflects a value that changing jobs is in many cases unwise or wrong. Employees in low uncertainty avoidance cultures may accept change more easily (Hofstede, 1980b). This may translate into a value that employment change is often good and natural. Thus, I propose that employees in high uncertainty avoidance cultures should have higher moral forces of attachment, on average, than employees in low uncertainty avoidance cultures.

Masculinity-femininity. Masculine cultures favor sex-role differentiation in society with the dominant values being assertiveness and material acquisition; feminine cultures favor more fluid sex-roles in society with the dominant values being nurturing and quality of life (Hofstede, 1980a,b). There is a strong relationship between masculinity and achievement motivation (Hofstede, 1980b). In contrast to feminine cultures, "employees in masculine cultures may express more calculative involvement with the organization" (Randall, 1993, p. 93). This implies that, in masculine cultures, attachment to the organization may depend on the employee's anticipated goal achievement at that organization (i.e., calculative forces). Thus, I propose that the relationship between calculative forces and turnover intentions should be stronger for employees in masculine cultures than in feminine cultures.

Conclusion. Culture dimensions affect multiple motivational forces directly, interactively, or both. It is clear from the proposed model that the effects of national cultural dimensions on the forces of attachment/withdrawal are very complex. Testing such a model implies many samples in multiple countries with both high and low standing on each dimension. I do not even begin to examine the challenges of measuring all the forces across so many cultures. Nevertheless, such ambitious empirical efforts are needed to really examine the complex effects of culture on turnover. Further, the full complexity of cultural effects cannot be adequately captured by any one model, including the model proposed here. First, it is likely that there are more linkages than those proposed. Second, cultural dimensions may affect the nature as well as the salience of the motivational forces. For instance, individualism-collectivism may help determine whether contractual forces are more transactional or relational in nature (e.g., Robinson et al., 1994). Third, national culture will almost certainly interact with other environmental and organizational factors in influencing turnover (Maertz et al., 2003). Finally, the current model examines the effects of the cultural dimensions as independent, but these dimensions are significantly correlated. Hofstede (1980a) found that collectivist countries all had high power distance. Future research must make even more complex predictions and examine the joint effects of cultural dimensions that naturally cluster together.

Finally, Clugston et al. (2000) found significant correlations between cultural dimensions and different types of commitment. However, they did not propose specific causal mechanisms behind these relationships and they only used data from a homogeneous sample within the United States. In contrast, I propose that the primary effects of culture are interactive with respect to motivational forces (e.g., Davidson et al., 1976). The proposed relationships of Clugston et al. and the current model should be tested across cultures to examine whether cultural effects are better conceptualized as moderators, direct causal antecedents, or both.

Perceived Performance of the Organization

The performance of the organization has been completely overlooked as an antecedent in models of individual employee turnover decisions. This lack of inclusion is only important if there is reason to believe that perceived organizational performance relates to turnover intentions. Although there is little research evidence, much anecdotal evidence suggests that this is the case. For example, after employees of Arthur Andersen became aware of the impending obstruction of justice indictment by the Justice Department for shredding documents in the Enron case, they were reportedly e-mailing each other frantically to "abandon ship," or quit the company.

Here, perceived organizational performance is defined as, the employee's conception of the organization's growth, profitability, and continued viability. Generally, employees may be more apt to leave a poor-performing organization for a number of reasons. I describe at least five mediating forces that provide theoretical linkages between employee perceptions of organizational performance and turnover intent (see Figure 6.5).

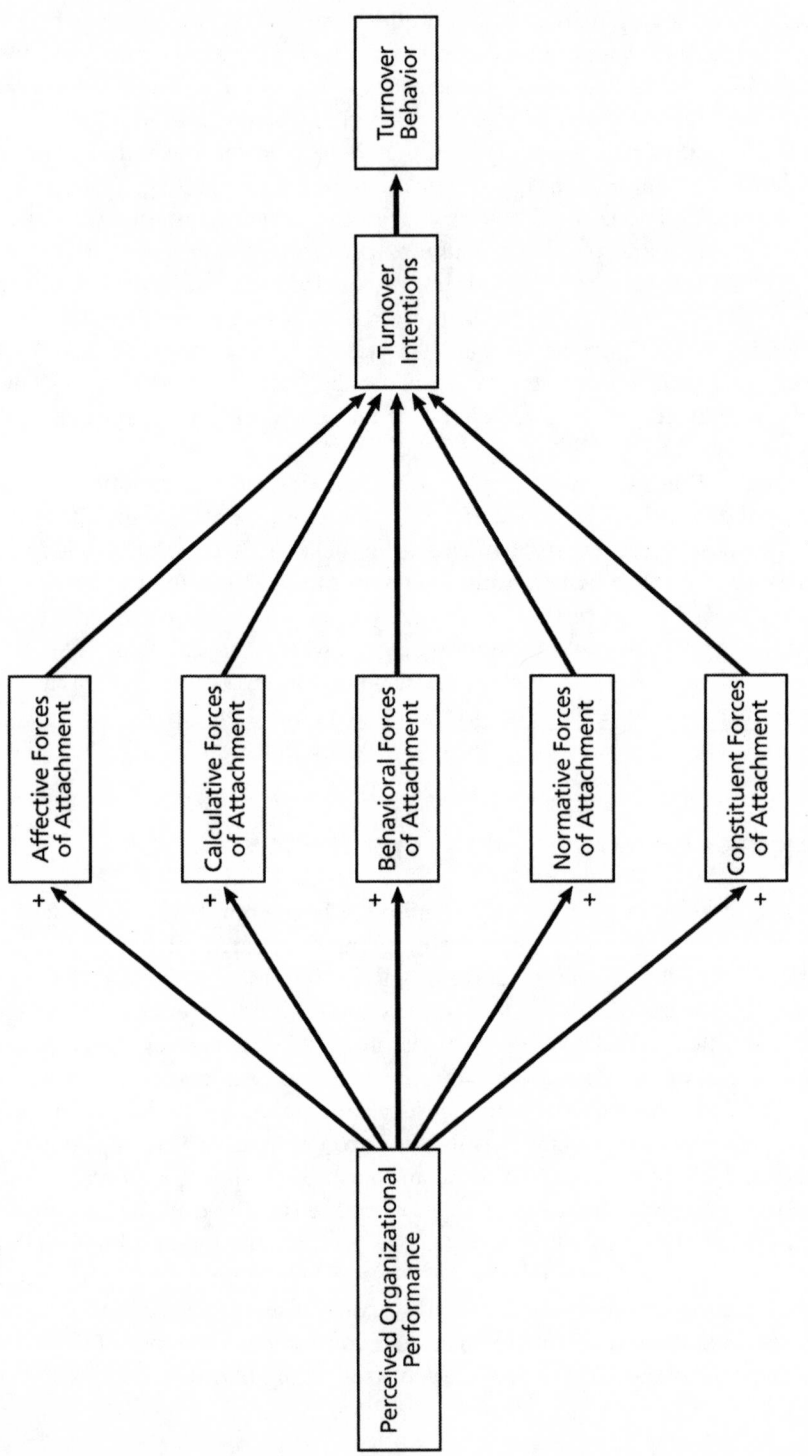

Figure 6.5.   Linkages between perceived organizational performance and turnover.

First, if the employee perceives that the current organization is performing well, the employee may have more respect and positive affect for the organization, particularly for employees with a group-based self-identity (James & Cropanzano, 1994). In addition, an employee may be more likely to identify with the organization after it performs well because it would be positive for their self-concept to be associated with the organization's success (Tajfel & Turner, 1979). In turn, such identification would normally imply positive affect toward the organization (e.g., Ashforth & Mael, 1989; O'Reilly & Chatman, 1986). Conversely, if the organization begins performing badly, employee identification with the organization would likely decrease, leading to less positive affect. For those that have identified closely with the organization already, performance failure could cause feelings of betrayal and resentment. Thus, perceived organizational performance should be positively related to affective forces of attachment.

Second, there is anecdotal evidence from turnover interviews that employees quit organizations that they believe may go out of business. Employees might fear the unemployment that sudden layoffs or bankruptcy might bring. Less extreme, employees may fear not being able to meet future compensation or career goals at an organization with insufficient growth or profitability. In either case, employee perceptions of poor organizational performance may lead to evaluations that meeting their work goals there in the future will be impossible. This may be particularly true for employees in jobs rewarded based on organizational performance and jobs that are easily downsized. Conversely, if an organization is performing well, the employee is likely to see more opportunities for fulfilling goals and values there in the future. Therefore, perceived organizational performance should be positively related to calculative forces of attachment.

Third, positive perceptions of organizational performance may motivate employees to make greater investments in the organization's future success and their membership in it. Given that employees can see a future for themselves in a successful organization they may invest more time and resources in pursuing company opportunities (e.g., company-specific training). Once made, investments that do not transfer to other organizations create costs of leaving and thereby increase behavioral forces of attachment. Conversely, when organizational performance is poor, employees may withhold or devalue current investments made in the organization, reducing their costs of leaving. Thus, perceived organizational performance should be positively related to behavioral forces of attachment.

Fourth, the perceived performance of the organization may have indirect effects through other peoples' expectations. If the employee's family is informed about the organization's performance, they may form expectations about the employee's turnover behavior, out of concern for the employee's career aspirations and concern for the family's financial security. Presumably, the family would expect the employee to stay if the organization performs well and expect the employee to leave if the organization performs poorly. Thus, perceived organizational performance should be positively related to normative forces of attachment.

Fifth, the organization's performance could impact an employee's attachment to leaders within the organization. Good performance may be attributed to good leadership, increasing confidence in and respect for leaders (e.g., Calder, 1977; Offermann et al., 1994). This could, in turn, increase affective and calculative attachments to leaders. Poor organizational performance could cause the opposite effect. Thus, perceived organizational performance should be positively related to constituent leader forces of attachment.

Conclusion.   Given the many potential linkages proposed, it seems that models of employee turnover should include perceived organizational performance. It may increase or decrease: affect toward the organization, the chances of meeting goals there, the costs of leaving the organization, the expectations of family members regarding turnover behavior, and attachment to organizational leaders. If supported empirically, the linkages proposed here imply that organizational success, along with its obvious benefits to owners, represent a potent, multifaceted method to retain employees. Although this suggestion may seem intuitive, it is absent from the current literature and must be tested.

In the future we should explore further moderators of performance-attachment relationships. For example, organizational-performance-contingent compensation or a past history of downsizing during performance downturns could strengthen the negative impact of poor performance on attachment. Researchers should also investigate fluctuations in co-variation between organizational performance and calculative forces to help determine how and when employees feel (or do not feel) that their personal prospects are intertwined with the prospects of the organization.

Occupational Attachment

Occupational attachment has not been conceptualized as comprehensively as organizational attachment has (e.g., Maertz, 2001), primarily relying on affect-loaded measures like occupational commitment. For this and other reasons, studies of occupational attachment and its relationships have been somewhat deficient. Moreover, the causal linkages between occupational attachment and turnover and when these occur remain unclear in the literature. Here, I expand the conceptualization of occupational attachment and clarify its linkages with turnover intention.

Occupation is defined as "an identifiable and specific line of work that an individual engages in to earn a living at a given point in time (e.g., nurse, banker, clerk)" (Lee et al., 2000, p. 800). Most research has examined occupational attachment in the form of occupational commitment. Meyer, Allen and Smith (1993) and Lee et al. (2000) note that occupation, profession, and career have been used interchangeably as the foci of this type of commitment. They recommend that career commitment should not be equated with occupational and professional commitment because the former may involve commitment to multiple lines of work and the latter are related to one line of work. For occupational and professional commitment, like Meyer et al. (1993), I use the term occupational because it applies to both professionals' and nonprofessionals' attachment to their line of work. Most of the measures of occupational commitment have been based on the organizational commitment definition and the OCQ (Mowday, Steers & Porter, 1979), with the "profession" substituted for "organization" in questionnaire items (Wallace, 1993). Lee et al. (2000) defined occupational commitment as, "a psychological link between a person and his or her occupation that is based on an affective reaction to that occupation" (p. 800).

It is clear that occupational commitment captures the affective aspect of attachment to an occupation. However, Meyer et al. (1993) suggested that a more complete understanding of occupational attachment requires expanding research beyond affective forces. They introduced continuance occupational commitment, based on investments lost if one leaves the occupation (behavioral forces) and normative occupational commitment, based on a feeling of obligation to remain in the occupation (contractual forces). Even with this expansion though, the conceptualization of ties to an occupation remains deficient. Using the same logic as Meyer et al. (1993), I propose that a person can be attached to an occupation in all the same ways as they can be attached to an organization or constituent. Besides affective, behavioral, and contractual forces (i.e., Meyer et al., 1993), there are four other potential forces of occupational attachment and withdrawal. A person can perceive that they have no alternative occupations or that they have many good alternative occupations available to them (alternative forces). A person can estimate the probability that the occupation will allow them to meet important future life goals (calculative forces). A person can perceive that valued others expect him or her to stay in or leave the occupation and want to comply with these expectations (normative forces). Finally, a person can believe that the occupation or its activities/goals are an inherent good (moral forces). For instance, doctors or policemen may feel that their occupation provides an invaluable service to society and that their participation in it is also an inherent good. Conversely, people could be apt to withdraw from an occupation if they feel it is corrupt, exploitative, or otherwise immoral. These seven forces of occupational attachment are represented in Figure 6.6.

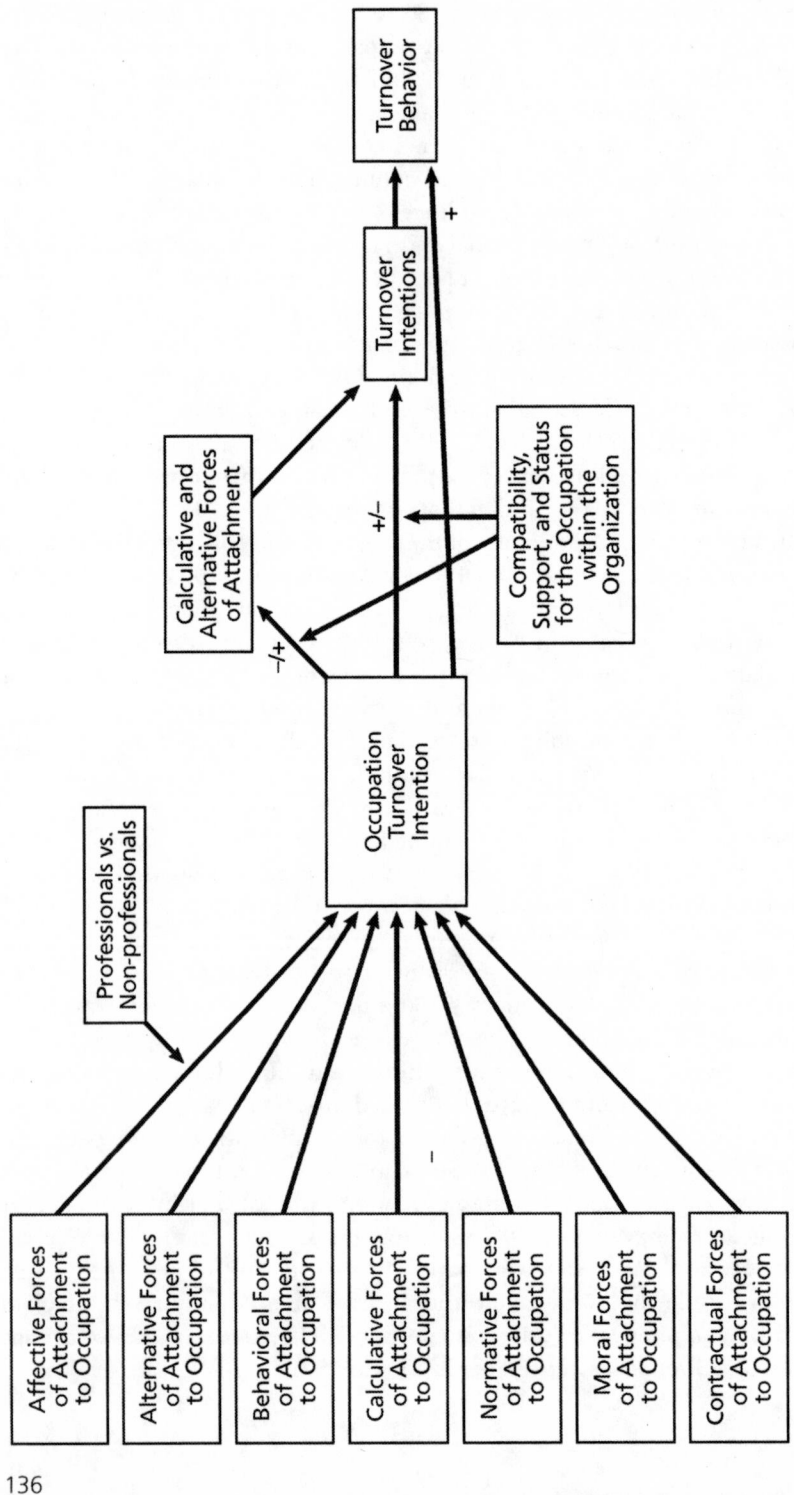

Figure 6.6. Linkages among 7 occupational forces of attachment and turnover.

But the question still remains, why and how would the forces of occupational attachment influence organizational turnover intention and behavior? Early on, commitment research held that occupational commitment might be incompatible with and negatively related to organizational commitment (Wallace, 1993), and in turn, positively related to turnover intention. However, Wallace (1993) and Lee et al. (2000) found in two meta-analyses that the two commitment types were positively correlated (corrected $r = .38$ and .45, respectively), implying an indirect (negative) effect of occupational commitment on turnover intent through organizational commitment. However, Blau (2000) used longitudinal data, along with job and organizational variables as controls, to examine this relationship directly. He found that occupational commitment was *not* significantly related to organizational turnover intent. Lee et al. (2000) did find a significant negative correlation between occupational commitment and turnover intent, but when occupational turnover intent was controlled, this relationship became zero. Occupational turnover intent was substantially and positively correlated with organization turnover intention even when job satisfaction and organizational commitment were controlled (partial $r = .32$). Taken together, these findings indicate that occupational commitment effects on organizational turnover intent are fully mediated through occupational turnover intent.

Using this logic, I propose that the different types of occupational attachments should be negatively related to occupational turnover intention and fully mediated through it. Findings also indicate that the relationship of occupational affective forces to intention should be stronger for professionals than for nonprofessionals (Lee et al., 2000). Additionally, Blau (1989) found that occupational turnover intention may have incremental effects on turnover behavior beyond the effects of organizational turnover intention, so we add this path to the current model as well.

But why is occupational turnover intent positively related to organizational turnover intent? Presumably, this is because changing occupations implies changing organizations because most employees do not have the opportunity to change occupations within a given organization. Consistent with current findings, I propose a direct positive effect from occupational turnover intent to organizational turnover intent, assuming that there is no opportunity to change occupation within the organization.

However, "the more proximal motivating factors of organizational withdrawal intent likely reside in the immediate job context and general organizational context" (Blau, 2000, p. 333), that is, organization level forces. Assuming again no ability to change occupations within the organization, occupational turnover intentions may cause the employee to believe that he or she cannot meet career goals in the future at the organization (i.e., calculative forces of withdrawal) and cause the employee to be attracted to alternative organizations where he or she can pursue a different occupation (i.e., alternative forces of withdrawal). In this way, occupational turnover intent would be negatively related to calculative and alternative forces of attachment.

On the other hand, when an employee is highly attached to an occupation (no or low turnover intention), his/her attachment to the organization will not necessarily be high and organizational turnover intention may even be increased. Occupational attachment will only increase calculative and alternative forces of attachment and reduce turnover intentions when the occupation in question is compatible, supported, and given adequate status within the organization (e.g., Lee et al., 2000). If the employee is highly attached to his or her occupation and the organization is not compatible with, is not supportive of, or awards low status to the occupation, occupational attachment can cause the employee to doubt their future goal achievement at the organization and to be attracted to more occupationally-compatible organizations. Thus, where compatibility, support, or status for the occupation are low, occupational attachment (no turnover intent) may translate into *lower* calculative and alternative forces of attachment and *higher* organizational turnover intention.

Conclusion.   The main conclusion of this section is that the view of occupational attachment should be broadened to reflect all the potential motivational categories in the literature. In addition, occupational attachments and occupational turnover intention must be integrated into multivariate turnover models so that their considerable predictive potency can be brought to bear (Blau, 1989; Lee et al., 2000). It is also important for research to investigate how organizational and occupational forces change and influence each other reciprocally over time (Blau, 2000). The forces of attachment/withdrawal to the occupation are likely to be more stable over time than attachments to the organization (Morrow, 1993). Thus, environmental changes may impact organizational forces before occupational forces. In turn, decreases in calculative and alternative forces of attachment may influence an employee to be less attached to his or her occupation and more willing to try other occupations. Researchers in this area should study these and other potential paths from organizational forces to occupational forces in more detail.

It should be noted that occupational attachment may involve commitment to professional or trade organizations as well as to the occupation itself (e.g., Blau, 1999). However, because all employees are not members of such organizations, the current model does not include this as a universal dimension of occupational attachment. Nevertheless, these occupational organizations and informal groups of professional colleagues may act as constituents of the occupation and inspire occupational-constituent forces of attachment/withdrawal. Thus, attachment to occupational constituents also deserves considerable future attention from researchers in this area.

Location Attachments

The location of the home and workplace have long been suggested as job attributes important to job choice and turnover decisions (e.g., Campion, 1991; Konrad, Ritchie, Lieb, & Corrigall, 2000). However, location attachment has not been specifically included in current turnover models and its effects on turnover remain unspecified. Before examining the linkage between location issues and turnover though, we discuss how people become attached to or develop a withdrawal tendency with respect to a location.

First, many things may cause a person to want to withdraw from a location where they currently live and work. Eby and Russell (2000) recently proposed a model of willingness to relocate with three main categories of antecedents: background factors, employee attitudes, and spouse attitudes. They found that spousal attitudes toward relocation explained the most variance in the employee's willingness to relocate. Other predictors were also significant such as age (-), relocation beliefs (that moving for the company will bring positive outcomes), and employee and spouse satisfaction with the company relocation policy. Their model constructs and measures assume that the employee is relocating for the purpose of a company transfer, where inherent pressure exists to relocate. However, employees do relocate in spite of having to quit their current organization, or in part, to escape their organization. Clearly, a more generally applicable model is needed to explain why people want to leave a given location. Nevertheless, Eby and Russell's (2000) study makes a valuable contribution by underscoring how important spouse/family attitudes are to relocation decisions.

Besides a relative unwillingness to relocate, employees may be actively attached to a location or community. Recently, Mitchell et al. (2001) introduced the idea that employee's become "embedded" within the organization and within the community. This embeddedness in the community comes about through employee "linkages" to it, perceptions of fit with the community, and desires to avoid sacrifices of leaving the community. Mitchell et al. (2001) found that organizational and community embeddedness together predicted turnover beyond job satisfaction, organizational commitment, perceived alternatives, and job search. Given these findings, community embeddedness is certainly a valuable perspective. However, Mitchell et al. (2001) admitted that they focused more on the overall level of embeddedness, rather than specific elements or causes of embeddedness. As a result, this perspective needs to be expanded in several respects. Employee "linkages" to community are not defined clearly. Some types of motives like alternative, normative, and moral forces are neglected. The opposite of embeddedness, or desire to leave a location, is not specifically included. All the motivational mechanisms contributing to embeddedness and location withdrawal tendency need to be specified and integrated to deepen understanding of the construct.

To do this, I suggest that the community may act similarly to an organizational constituent, linked somewhat to the job and organization, but with distinct attachment potential (Reichers, 1985). Employees may become attached to or want to withdraw from a location, potentially independent of attachments to the organization. The findings on willingness to relocate and embeddedness indicate that this attachment/withdrawal tendency depends on multiple motives. Following the pattern with constituents and with occupation, I propose that employees (and their family members) may become embedded within a location or want to withdraw from a location as the result of the seven basic motive categories (see Figure 6.7).

Employees may simply like or dislike the current geographical location or the commute from home to work (e.g., Konrad et al., 2000). They may like or dislike their town, the location of the plant, or the climate in their part of the country, and as a result, be more or less likely to stay (affective forces). Employees may have no locations they like better, or may be very attracted to alternative geographical locations, "I want to live in another part of the country" (alternative forces). They may perceive high or low costs of leaving the current location (Mitchell et al., 2001) and wish to avoid relocation costs (behavioral forces). Employees may evaluate whether the current location is compatible or incompatible with future life goals (calculative forces). Employees may perceive that their family expects to stay in or leave the current location, (e.g., "My family wants to stay here, or move to a different climate") and want to comply with these expectations (normative forces). Employees may hold a value that loyalty to the community and "staying put" is a good in itself, or that moving frequently ("wanderlust") and variety are an inherent good (moral forces). Finally, employees may feel an obligation to stay in the community (or leave) based on what it has provided (or failed to provide) to them (contractual forces). These seven forces determine the employee's overall level of attachment to, or embeddedness within a specific location or community.

But how does location attachment or withdrawal tendency relate to turnover? In the model, level of location embeddedness influences organizational attachment and withdrawal tendency through two primary mechanisms. First, if the employee is embedded in the location, wanting to remain there, the easiest way to accomplish this is usually by staying in the current job and organization. In this way, location embeddedness would make the person want to stay with the organization. Thus, I propose a direct negative relationship between location embeddedness and turnover intention.

Second, the employee being embedded in the community/location would likely imply that the employee's immediate family (if any) would be

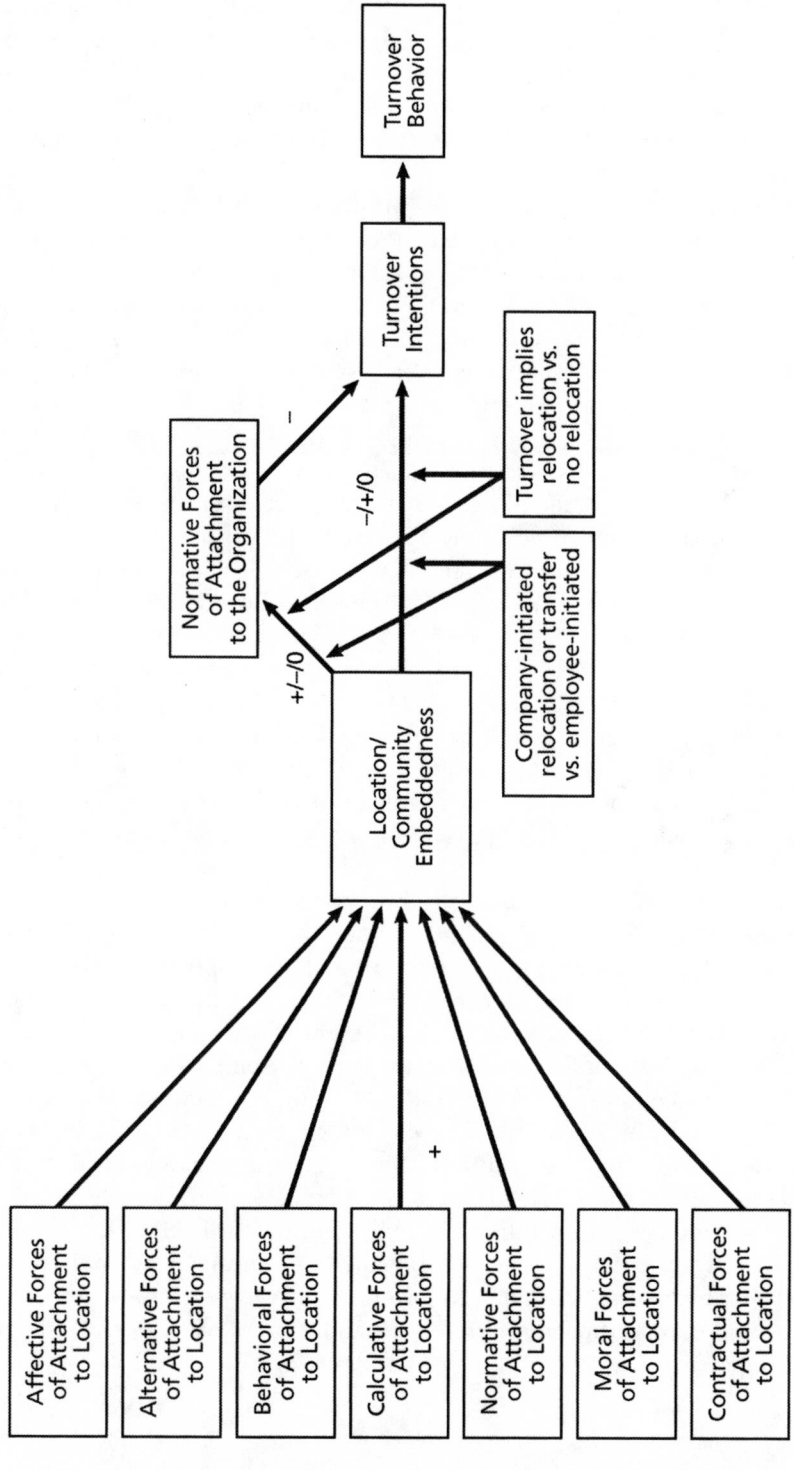

Figure 6.7. Linkages among 7 location forces of attachment and turnover.

embedded in the community as well (Mitchell et al., 2001). If the family is embedded within the community, members are likely to have expectations that the employee should stay in the current organization. This would maximize the family's chances of staying in the current location. Thus, I propose that location embeddedness should be positively related to normative forces of organizational attachment.

However, the direction and strength of these relationships depend on two factors. First, organization-initiated relocation/transfers must be differentiated from employee-initiated relocation. In cases of a proposed company transfer, high attachment to the current location may result in some desire to *refuse the transfer* and perhaps *withdraw* from the organization, particularly if the employee perceives pressure from the organization to accept the transfer. But if a transfer is offered and attachment to the current location is low, this may result in greater attachment to the organization and acceptance of the transfer. In cases of imminent relocation/transfer, location embeddedness will be negatively related to normative forces of attachment and positively related to turnover intention.

Second, cases where quitting the organization implies relocation must be differentiated from cases where quitting does not imply relocation. In most cases the relationship between location embeddedness and organizational attachment would be positive. However, if the employee lives within a local labor market (e.g., a big city) that provides adequate employment alternatives, quitting the organization would not imply relocation. Location embeddedness would have little impact on turnover (Mitchell et al., 2001). Thus, I propose that when quitting does not imply relocation, location embeddedness will not be related to normative attachment and turnover intent.

Conclusion.   Clearly, location attachment and withdrawal tendency can no longer be neglected in models of turnover models. Once again, the proposed model only begins to cover the potential complexity surrounding location attachment and turnover. For instance, the current model assumes that employee and family attachment to location are congruent. Future research should explore the case where the employee wants to leave the current location and his/her family does not, or vice versa. Also, different family members may have varying or conflicting levels of location embeddedness. How these different levels of embeddedness within the family are resolved or consolidated to affect employee turnover decisions is a promising question for future research in this area. Researchers should also investigate which type of location forces are most strongly related to overall embeddedness for different groups of employees. Finally, researchers should explore how the different location forces develop and change over time.

IMPLICATIONS FOR RESEARCH AND PRACTICE

The main contribution of this chapter is in providing theoretical guidance for future empirical research where there was little or none previously. Specifically, the chapter contributes to understanding how personality, culture, organizational performance, occupational attachment, and location attachment relate to employee turnover behavior. These five categories of antecedents had been largely forgotten in turnover models. I proposed causal linkages using Maertz' (2001) model of proximal motives of attachment/turnover, as key mediating mechanisms leading to turnover intention.

The main implication of this chapter for research is to empirically test the linkages proposed. Obviously, for occupation and location attachments the primary challenge is to develop measures of the different motive categories as they relate to occupation and location. Until this is done, the proposed linkages cannot be tested, but measurement issues are beyond the scope of this chapter. However, Maertz' (2001) recommendations to more precisely measure the motive behind each organizational force may be applied to the occupational and location domains as well.

If the proposed linkages are supported empirically, the main challenge for theoretical research is to integrate the proposed linkages with content turnover models. In addition, theoretical and empirical research should investigate interactions among the antecedents discussed. For instance, negative affectivity may interact with collectivism or perceived organizational performance to determine levels and salience of affective forces. There are also many research questions regarding the impact of time within the proposed models. For example, do personality or culture dimensions only influence the forces of attachment over a long period? Because they are relatively stable dimensions, do their effects dissipate after a certain point? Do occupational and location forces only impact turnover intention after a certain period of tenure in occupation or location. To investigate such questions, studies must track turnover across organizations. Even though this chapter represents the most complete consideration to date of how these five antecedent categories influence turnover, it is only a starting point. Fully asking and answering questions related to these areas is beyond the scope of a single chapter and could keep researchers busy for quite some time.

Conclusion.   Often correlates of turnover are assumed to be antecedents based on an empirical relationship alone or based on a post hoc explanation involving some unmeasured constructs. This chapter underscores the need to specify conceptual, causal linkages between antecedents and turnover. This chapter also illustrates that Maertz' (2001) model of proximal turnover motives can be useful for clarifying such theoretical linkages. These forces can be used as central mediating constructs to explain how many different antecedents lead to turnover intention and behavior. Finally, I hope this chapter will help stimulate future empirical research on personality, turnover cultures, national culture, organizational performance, occupational attachments, location attachments, and how they relate to turnover.

REFERENCES

Abelson, M.A. (1993). Turnover cultures. In G. Ferris & K. Rowland (Eds.) *Research in personnel and human resource management* (Vol.11, pp. 339–376). Greenwich, CT: JAI Press.

Allen, D.G., & Griffeth, R.W. (2001). Test of a mediated performance-turnover relationship highlighting the moderating roles of visibility and reward contingency. *Journal of Applied Psychology, 86,* 1014–1021.

Ashforth, B.E., & Mael, F. (1989). Social identity theory and the organization. *Academy of Management Review, 14,* 20–39.

Aquino, K, Griffeth, R.W., Allen, D.G., & Hom, P.W. (1997). Integrating justice constructs into the turnover process: A test of a referent cognitions model. *Academy of Management Journal, 40,* 1208–1227.

Barrick, M.R., & Mount, M.K. (1991). The big five personality dimensions and job performance. *Personnel Psychology, 44,* 1–26.

Barrick, M.R., & Mount, M.K. (1996). Effects of impression management and self-deception on the predictive validity of personality constructs. *Journal of Applied Psychology, 81,* 261–272.

Barrick, M.R., Mount, M.K., & Strauss, J.P. (1993). Conscientiousness and performance of sales representatives: Test of the mediating effects of goal setting. *Journal of Applied Psychology, 78,* 715–722.

Becker, H. (1960). Notes on the concept of commitment. *American Journal of Sociology, 66,* 32–42.

Becker, T.E. (1992). Foci and bases of commitment: Are they distinctions worth making? *Academy of Management Journal, 35,* 232–244.

Blau, G. (1989). Testing the generalization of a career commitment measure and its impact on employee turnover. *Journal of Vocational Behavior, 35,* 88–103.

Blau, G. (1999). Early-career job factors influencing the professional commitment of medical technologists. *Academy of Management Journal, 42,* 687–695.

Blau, G. (2000). Job, organizational, and professional context antecedents as predictors of intent for interrole work transitions. *Journal of Vocational Behavior, 56,* 330–345.

Blau, G., & Lunz, M. (1998). Testing the incremental effect of professional commitment on intent to leave one's profession beyond the effects of external, personal, and work-related variables. *Journal of Vocational Behavior, 52,* 260–269.

Boudreau, J.W., Boswell, W.R., Judge, T.A., & Bretz, R.D. (2001). Personality and cognitive ability as predictors of job search among employed managers. *Personnel Psychology, 54,* 25–50.

Boyacigiller, N.A., & Adler, N.J. (1991). The parochial dinosaur: Organizational science in a global context. *Academy of Management Review, 16*, 262–290.

Bozeman, D.P., & Perrewe, P.L. (2001). The effect of item content overlap on organizational commitment questionnaire-turnover cognitions relationship. *Journal of Applied Psychology, 86*, 161–173.

Bretz, R.D., Boudreau, J.W., & Judge, T.A. (1994). Job search behavior of employed managers. *Personnel Psychology, 47*, 275–301.

Calder, B.J. (1977). An attribution theory of leadership. In B.M. Staw & G.R. Salancik (Eds.), *New directions in organizational behavior* (pp. 179–204) Chicago: St. Clair Press.

Campion, M.A. (1991). The meaning and measurement of turnover: A comparison of alternative measures and recommendations. *Journal of Applied Psychology, 76*, 199–212.

Costa, P.T., & McCrae, R.R. (1992). *Revised NEO Personality Inventory (NEO-PI-R) and NEO Five-Factor (NEO-FFI) Inventory professional manual.* Odessa, FL: Psychological Assessment Resources, Inc.

Clugston, M., Howell, J.P., & Dorfman, P.W. (2000). Does cultural socialization predict multiple bases and foci of commitment? *Journal of Management, 26*, 5–31.

Cotton J.L., & Tuttle, J.M. (1986). Employee turnover: A meta-analysis with implications for research. *Academy of Management Review, 11*, 55–70.

Dalton, D.R., Johnson, J.L., & Daily, C.M. (1999). On the use of "intent to . . ." variables in organizational research: An empirical and cautionary assessment. *Human Relations, 52*, 1337–1350.

Davidson, A.R., Jaccard, J.J., Triandis, H.C., Morales, M.L., & Diaz-Guerrero, R. (1976). Cross-cultural model testing: Toward a solution of the etic-emic dilemma. *International Journal of Psychology, 11*, 1–13.

Day, D.V., Bedeian, A.G., & Conte, J.M. (1998). Personality as predictor of work-related outcomes: Test of a mediated latent structural model. *Journal of Applied Social Psychology, 28*, 2068–2088.

Eby, L.T., & Russell, J.E. (2000). Predictors of employee willingness to relocate for the firm. *Journal of Vocational Behavior, 57*, 42–61.

Ellemers, N., de Gilder, D., & van den Heuvel, H. (1998). Career-oriented versus team-oriented commitment and behavior at work. *Journal of Applied Psychology, 83*, 717–730.

Festinger, L. (1957). *A theory of cognitive dissonance.* Stanford, CA: Stanford University Press.

Fishbein, M., & Azjen, I. (1975). *Belief, attitude, intention, and behavior.* Reading, MA: Addison-Wesley.

Forrest, C.R., Cummings, L.L., & Johnson, A.C. (1977). Organizational participation: A critique and model. *Academy of Management Review, 2*, 586–601.

Gerhart, B. (1990). Voluntary turnover and alternative job opportunities. *Journal of Applied Psychology, 75*, 467–476.

Ghiselli, E.E. (1974). Some perspectives for industrial psychology. *American Psychologist, 29*, 80–87.

Gouldner, H.P. (1960). Dimensions of organizational commitment. *Administrative Science Quarterly, 4*, 468–490.

146 C.P. MAERTZ, Jr.

Gowan, M., Ibarreche, S., & Lackey, C. (1996). Doing the right things in Mexico. *Academy of Management Executive, 10*(1), 74–81.

Griffeth R.W., & Hom, P.W. (1995). The employee turnover process. In G. Ferris & K. Rowland (Eds.), *Research in personnel and human resources management* (Vol. 13, pp. 245–293). Greenwich, CT: JAI Press.

Griffeth, R.W., Hom, P.W., Gaertner, S. (2000). A meta-analysis of antecedents and correlates of employee turnover: Update moderator tests, and research implications for the next millennium. *Journal of Management, 26,* 463–488.

Hofstede, G. (1980a). *Culture's consequences.* Beverly Hills, CA: Sage.

Hofstede, G. (1980b, Summer). Motivation, leadership, and organization: do American theories apply abroad? *Organizational Dynamics,* 42–63.

Hom, P.W., Caranikas-Walker, F., Prussia, G.E., & Griffeth, R.W. (1992). A meta-analytical structural equations analysis of a model of employee turnover. *Journal of Applied Psychology, 78,* 890–909.

Hom, P.W., Griffeth, R.W., & Sellaro, C.L. (1984). The validity of Mobley's (1977) model of employee turnover. *Organizational Behavior and Human Performance, 34,* 141–174.

Hom, P.W., Katerberg, R., & Hulin, C.L. (1979). Comparative examination of three approaches to the prediction of turnover. *Journal of Applied Psychology, 68,* 280–290.

Hom, P.W., & Kinicki, A.J. (2001). Toward a greater understanding of how dissatisfaction drives employee turnover. *Academy of Management Journal, 44,* 975–987.

Hough, L.M., Eaton, N.K., Dunnette, M.D., Kamp, J.D., & McCloy, R.A. (1990). Criterion-related validities of personality constructs and the effects of response distortion on those validities. *Journal of Applied Psychology [Monograph], 75,* 581–595.

Hunt, S., & Morgan, R. (1994). Organizational commitment: One of many commitments or key mediating construct? *Academy of Management Journal, 37,* 57–79.

Iverson, R.D., & Deery, S.J. (2001). Understanding the "personological" basis of employee withdrawal: The influence of affective disposition on employee tardiness, early departure, and absenteeism. *Journal of Applied Psychology, 86,* 856–866.

James, K., & Cropanzano, R. (1994). Dispositional group loyalty and individual action for the benefit of an in-group: Experimental and correlational evidence. *Organizational Behavior and Human Decision Processes, 60,* 179–205.

James, L.R. (1982). Aggregation bias in estimates of perceptual agreement. *Journal of Applied Psychology, 67,* 219–229.

Jaros, S.J., Jermier, J.M., Koehler, J.W., & Sincich, T. (1993). Effects of continuance, affective, and moral commitment on the withdrawal process. *Academy of Management Journal, 5,* 951–995.

Jenkins, J.M. (1993). Self-monitoring and turnover: The impact of personality on intent to leave. *Journal of Organizational Behavior, 14,* 83–91.

Judge, T.A. (1993). Does affective disposition moderate the relationship between job satisfaction and voluntary turnover? *Journal of Applied Psychology, 78,* 395–401.

Judge, T.A., & Bono, J.E. (2001). Relationship of core self-evaluations traits—self-esteem, generalized self-efficacy, locus of control, and emotional stability—

with job satisfaction and job performance: A meta-analysis. *Journal of Applied Psychology, 86,* 80–92.

Judge, T.A., & Cable, D.M. (1997). Applicant personality, organizational culture, and organization attraction. *Personnel Psychology, 50,* 359–394.

Judge, T.A., & Martocchio, J.J., & Thoresen, C.J. (1997). Five-factor model of personality and employee absence. *Journal of Applied Psychology, 82,* 745–755.

Judge, T.A., Thoresen, C.J., Bono, J.E., & Patton, G.K. (2001). The job satisfaction-job performance relationship: A qualitative and quantitative review. *Psychological Bulletin, 127,* 376–407.

Kanfer, R., Wanberg, C.R., & Kantrowitz, T.M. (2001). Job search and employment: A personality-motivational analysis and meta-analytic review. *Journal of Applied Psychology, 86,* 837–855.

Konrad, A.M., Ritchie, J.E., Lieb, P., & Corrigall, E. (2000). Sex differences and similarities in job attribute preferences: A meta-analysis. *Psychological Bulletin, 126,* 593–641.

Krackhardt, D., & Porter, L.W. (1985). When friends leave: A structural analysis of the relationship between turnover and stayers' attitudes. *Administrative Science Quarterly, 30,* 242–261.

Krackhardt, D., & Porter, L.W. (1986). The snowball effect: Turnover embedded in communication networks. *Journal of Applied Psychology, 71,* 50–55.

Kristof, A.L. (1996). Person-organization fit: An integrative review of its conceptualizations, measurement, and implications. *Personnel Psychology, 48,* 1–49.

Lee, K., Carswell, J.J., Allen, N.J. (2000). A meta-analytic review of occupational commitment: Relations with person- and work-related variables. *Journal of Applied Psychology, 85,* 799–811.

Lee, T.W., & Mitchell, T.R. (1994). An alternative approach: The unfolding model of voluntary employee turnover. *Academy of Management Review, 19,* 51–89.

Maertz, C.P. (2001, August). *Why employees quit and stay with an organization.* Paper presented at the 61st annual meeting of the Academy of Management, Washington, DC.

Maertz, C.P., & Campion, M.A. (1998). 25 years of voluntary turnover research: A review and critique. In C.L. Cooper & I.T. Robertson (Eds.), *International review of industrial and organizational psychology* (Vol. 13, pp. 49–83). Chichester: Wiley.

Maertz, C.P., & Griffeth, R.W. (under review). The motivational forces for organizational attachment and turnover: an integrative framework with directions for future research and practice. *Journal of Management.*

Maertz, C.P., Jr., Mosley, D.C., Jr., Alford, B. (2002). Does organizational commitment fully mediate constituent commitment effects: A re-assessment and clarification. *Journal of Applied Social Psychology, 32,* 1300–1313.

Maertz, C.P., & Stevens, M.J., & Campion, M.A. (2003). A turnover model for the Mexican maquiladoras. *Journal of Vocational Behavior, 63,* 111–135.

March, J.G., & Simon, H.A. (1958). *Organizations.* New York: Wiley.

Markus, H.R., & Kitayama, S. (1991). Culture and the self: implications for cognition, emotion, and motivation. *Psychological Review, 98*(2), 224–253.

McCrae, R.R., & Costa, P.T. (1991). Adding *Liebe und Arbeit*: The full five-factor model and well-being. *Personality and Social Psychology Bulletin, 17,* 227–232.

McCrae, R.R., & Costa, P.T. (1997). Conceptions and correlates of openness to experience. In R. Hogan & J.A. Johnson (Eds.), *Handbook of personality psychology* (pp. 825–847). San Diego, CA: Academic Press.

McGee, G., & Ford, R. (1987). Two (or more?) dimensions of organizational commitment: Reexamination of the affective and continuance commitment scales. *Journal of Applied Psychology, 72,* 638–642.

Meyer, J., & Allen, N. (1991). A three-component conceptualization of organizational commitment. *Human Resource Management Review, 1,* 61–98.

Meyer, J., Allen, N., & Smith, C. (1993). Commitment to organizations and occupations: Extension and test of a three-component conceptualization. *Journal of Applied Psychology, 78,* 538–551.

Michaels, C.E., & Spector, P.E. (1982). Causes of employee turnover: A test of the Mobley, Griffeth, Hand, and Meglino model. *Journal of Applied Psychology, 67,* 53–59.

Mitchell, T.R., Holtom, B.C., Lee, T.W., Sablynski, C.J., & Erez, M. (2001). Why people stay: Using job embeddedness to predict voluntary turnover. *Academy of Management Journal, 44,* 1102–1121.

Mobley, W.H. (1977). Intermediate linkages in the relationship between job satisfaction and employee turnover. *Journal of Applied Psychology, 62,* 237–240.

Mobley, W.H., Griffeth, R., Hand, H., & Meglino, B. (1979). Review and conceptual analysis of the employee turnover process. *Psychological Bulletin, 86,* 493–522.

Morrison, E.W., & Robinson, S.L. (1997). When employees feel betrayed: A model of how psychological contract violation develops. *Academy of Management Review, 22,* 226–256.

Morrow, P. (1983). Concept redundancy in organizational research: The case of work commitment. *Academy of Management Review, 8,* 486–500.

Morrow, P. (1993). *The theory and measurement of work commitment.* Greenwich, CT: JAI Press.

Mount, M.K., Barrick, M.R., & Stewart, G.L. (1998). Five-factor model of personality and performance in jobs involving interpersonal interactions. *Human Performance, 11,* 145–165.

Mowday, R.T., Steers, R.M., Porter, L.W. (1979). The measurement of organizational commitment. *Journal of Vocational Behavior, 14,* 222–247.

Muchinsky, P.M., & Morrow, P. (1980). A multidisciplinary model of voluntary employee turnover. *Journal of Vocational Behavior, 17,* 263–290.

Muchinsky, P.M., & Tuttle, M.L. (1979). Employee turnover: An empirical and methodological assessment. *Journal of Vocational Behavior, 14,* 43–77.

Near, J.P. (1989). Organizational commitment among Japanese and U.S. workers. *Organization Studies, 10*(3), 281–300.

Newman, J. (1974). Predicting absenteeism and turnover: A field comparison of Fishbein's model and traditional job attitude measures. *Journal of Applied Psychology, 59,* 610–615.

Niles, F.S. (1999). Toward a cross-cultural understanding of work-related beliefs. *Human Relations, 52,* 855–867.

Offermann, L.R., Kennedy, J.K., & Wirtz, P.W. (1994). Implicit leadership theories: Content, structure and generalizability. *Leadership Quarterly, 5*(1), 43–58.

O'Reilly, C.A., & Chatman, J. (1986). Organizational commitment and psychological attachment: The effects of compliance, identification, and internalization on prosocial behavior. *Journal of Applied Psychology, 71*, 492–499.

O'Reilly, C.A., Chatman, J., & Caldwell, D.F. (1991). People and organizational culture: A profile comparison approach to person-organization fit. *Academy of Management Journal, 34*, 487–516.

Paik, Y., & Teagarden, M. (1995). Strategic international human resource management approaches in the maquiladora industry: A comparison of Japanese, Korean, and U.S. firms. *International Journal of Human Resource Management, 6*(3), 568–587.

Personnel Journal. (1992, April). New behavioral study defines typical "turnover personality." *71*(4), 4–5.

Pettigrew, A.M. (1979). On studying organizational cultures. *Administrative Science Quarterly, 24*, 570–581.

Porter, L.W., & Steers, R.M. (1973). Organizational, work, and personal factors in employee turnover and absenteeism. *Psychological Bulletin, 80*, 151–176.

Prestholdt, P.H., Lane, I.M., & Mathews, R.C. (1987). Nurse turnover as reasoned action: Development of a process model. *Journal of Applied Psychology, 72*, 221–227.

Randall, D. (1993). Cross-cultural research on organizational commitment: A review and application of Hofstede's value survey module. *Journal of Business Research, 26*, 91–110.

Redding, S.G., Norman, A., & Schlander, A. (1994). The nature of individual attachment to the organization: A review of East Asian variations. In M. Dunnette & L. Hough (Eds.), *Handbook of industrial and organizational psychology* (Vol. 4, pp. 647–688). Palo Alto, CA.

Reichers, A. (1985). A review and reconceptualization of organizational commitment. *Academy of Management Review, 10*, 465–476.

Robinson, S.L., Kraatz, M.S., & Rousseau, D.M. (1994). Changing obligations and the psychological contract: A longitudinal study. *Academy of Management Journal, 37*, 137–152.

Robinson, S.L., & Morrison, E.W. (2000). The development of psychological contract breach and violation: A longitudinal study. *Journal of Organizational Behavior, 21*, 525–546.

Rousseau, D.M. (1989). Psychological and implied contracts in organizations. *Employee Rights and Responsibilities Journal, 2*, 121–139.

Rousseau, D.M., & Parks, J.M. (1992). Contracts of individuals and organizations. In B. Staw & L.L. Cummings (Eds.), *Research in organizational behavior* (pp. 1–43). Greenwich, CT: JAI Press.

Salancik, G. (1977). Commitment and the control of organizational behavior and belief. In B. Staw & G. Salancik (Eds.), *New directions in organizational behavior* (pp. 1–54). Chicago: St. Clair Press.

Salancik, G., & Pfeffer, J. (1978). A social information processing approach to job attitudes and task design. *Administartive Science Quarterly, 23*, 224–253.

Schaubroeck, J., Ganster, D.C., & Jones, J.R. (1998). Organization and occupation influences in the attraction-selection-attrition process. *Journal of Applied Psychology, 83*, 869–891.

Schein, E.H. (1985). *Organizational culture and leadership*. San Francisco: Jossey-Bass.

Schneider, B. (1987). The people make the place. *Personnel Psychology, 40*, 437–453.

Scholl, R. (1981). Differentiating organizational commitment from expectancy as a motivating force. *Academy of Management Review, 6*, 589–599.

Settoon, R.P., Bennett, N., & Liden, R.C. (1996). Social exchange in organizations: Perceived organizational support, leader-member exchange, and employee reciprocity. *Journal of Applied Psychology, 81*, 219–227.

Sheridan, J.E. (1992). Organizational culture and employee retention. *Academy of Management Journal, 35*, 1036–1056.

Shore, L.M., Tetrick, L.E., Shore, T.H., & Barksdale, K. (2000). Construct validity of measures of Becker's side bet theory. *Journal of Vocational Behavior, 57*, 428–444.

Stajkovic, A.D., & Luthans, F. (1998). Self-efficacy and work-related performance: A meta-analysis. *Psychological Bulletin, 124*, 240–261.

Staw, B.M., Bell, N.E., & Clausen, J.A. (1986). The dispositional approach to job attitudes: A lifetime longitudinal test. *Administrative Science Quarterly, 31*, 56–77.

Steel, R.P., & Griffeth, R.W. (1989). The elusive relationship between perceived employment opportunity and turnover behavior: A methodological or conceptual artifact? *Journal of Applied Psychology, 74*, 846–854.

Steel, R.P., & Ovalle, N. (1984). A review and meta-analysis of research on the relationship between behavioral intentions and employee turnover. *Journal of Applied Psychology, 69*, 673–686.

Tajfel, H., & Turner, H.C. (1979). An integrative theory of intergroup conflict. In W.G. Austin & S. Worchel (Eds.), *The social psychology of intergroup relations*. Monterey, CA: Brooks, Cole.

Tett, R., & Meyer, J. (1993). Job satisfaction, organizational commitment, turnover intention and turnover: Path analyses based on meta-analytic findings. *Personnel Psychology, 46*, 259–293.

Tokar, D.M., & Fischer, A.R. (1998). More on RIASEC and the five-factor model of personality: Direct assessment of Prediger's (1982) and Hogan's (1983) dimensions. *Journal of Vocational Behavior, 52*, 246–259.

Tokar, D.M., Fischer, A.R., & Subich, L.M. (1998). Personality and vocational behavior: A selective review of the literature. *Journal of Vocational Behavior, 53*, 115–153.

Triandis, H.C. (1975). Culture training, cognitive complexity, and interpersonal attitudes. In R. Brislin, S. Bochner, & W. Lonner (Eds.), *Cross-cultural perspectives on learning* (pp. 39–77). Beverly Hills, CA & New York: Sage and Wiley/Halsted.

Triandis, H.C. (1989). The self and social behavior in differing cultural contexts. *Psychological Review, 96*, 506–520.

Triandis, H.C., (1995). *Individualism and collectivism*. New York: Simon & Schuster.

Triandis, H.C., Bontempo, R., Villareal, M.J., Asai, M., & Lucca, N. (1988). Individualism and collectivism: cross-cultural perspectives on self-ingroup relationships. *Journal of Personality and Social Psychology, 54*, 323–333.

Triandis, H.C., McCusker, C., & Hui, C.H. (1990). Multimethod probes of individualism and collectivism. *Journal of Personality and Social Psychology, 59*, 1006–1020.

Trevor, C.O. (2001). Interactions among actual ease-of-movement determinants and job satisfaction in the prediction of voluntary turnover. *Academy of Management Journal, 44,* 621–638.

Turner, J.C. (1987). A self-categorization theory. In J.C. Turner (Ed.), *Rediscovering the social group* (pp. 42–67). New York: Basil Blackwell.

Turnley, W.H., & Feldman, D.C. (2000). Re-examining the effects of psychological contract violations: Unmet expectations and job dissatisfaction as mediators. *Journal of Organizational Behavior, 21,* 25–42.

Vandenberg, R.J., & Nelson, J.B. (1999). Disaggregating the motives underlying turnover intentions: When do intentions predict turnover behavior? *Human Relations, 52,* 1313–1336.

Van Eerde, W., & Thierry, H. (1996). Vroom's expectancy models and work-related criteria: A meta-analysis. *Journal of Applied Psychology, 81,* 575–586.

Vroom, V. (1964). *Work and motivation.* New York: Wiley Press.

Wallace, J.E. (1993). Professional and organizational commitment: Compatible or incompatible? *Journal of Vocational Behavior, 42,* 333–349.

Watson, D., Clark, L.A., & Tellegen, A. (1988). Development and validation of brief measures of positive affect: The PANAS scales. *Journal of Personality and Social Psychology, 54,* 1063–1070.

Watson, D., & Hubbard, B. (1996). Adaptational style and dispositional structure: Coping in the context of the five-factor model. *Journal of Personality, 64,* 737–774.

Weiss, H.M., & Cropanzano, R. (1996). Affective events theory: A theoretical discussion of the structure, causes and consequences of affective experiences at work. In L. Cummings & B. Staw (Eds.), *Research in organizational behavior* (pp. 1–74). Greenwich, CT: JAI Press.

Weitz, J. (1952). A neglected concept in the study of job satisfaction. *Personnel Psychology, 5,* 201–205.

Wiener, Y. (1982). Commitment in organizations: A normative view. *Academy of Management Review, 7,* 418–428.

Wiggins, J.S. (1996). *The five-factor model of personality: Theoretical perspectives.* New York: Guilford Press.

Wood, R.E., & Bandura, A. (1989). Social cognitive theory of organizational management. *Academy of Management Review, 14,* 361–384.

CHAPTER 7

JOB EMBEDDEDNESS

Current Research and Future Directions

Xin Yao, Thomas W. Lee, Terence R. Mitchell, James P. Burton,
and Chris J. Sablynski

ABSTRACT

This chapter describes Job Embeddedness (JE), a construct related to
employee retention, and indicates research directions. In particular, we
review the theoretical underpinning of JE, including the development of a
program of research, the definition and dimensions of JE, its comparisons
with similar constructs and supportive evidence. We also direct attention to
methodological concerns, including establishing construct validity and refin-
ing the measure. Finally we try to expand the theory on JE by discussing various issues, including how JE is formed, the relative importance of its
dimensions and its relationships with other constructs in various settings.

INTRODUCTION

For most people, work, family, and social relationships are the major factors people consider when it comes to important decisions that will alter

Innovative Theory and Empirical Research on Employee Turnover, pages 153–187 their way of life, including general life style and specific things to do from one moment to the next. What, then, determines the boundaries of one's work and personal life? What are the ties that bind us to our jobs, communities, and family? How do these ties influence one another? More importantly, how can these ties inform management researchers interested in turnover, retention, and organizational attachment?

Recently, we have embarked on a line of research designed to address this topic. We have developed and tested an idea we call Job Embeddedness (JE). JE is a construct that captures how and why people feel "stuck" in their job. In this chapter, we address theoretical as well as methodological issues pertaining to JE in an attempt to organize what people perceive as the things that keep them attached to the place, people and issues at work. In addition, we explore how JE comes into being and circumstances under which JE plays an important role. Specifically, we will first review the theoretical background and roots of JE, then give a conceptual definition and explain its dimensions. Furthermore, we provide a clear picture of where JE stands among other constructs by differentiating it from similar ones. Next, we review empirical evidence for methodological issues of JE. Finally, we discuss future research directions that will bring us greater understanding of the relationships between JE and other constructs as well as processes of interest.

JOB EMBEDDEDNESS: AN OVERVIEW

Theoretical Background

Earlier research on employee withdrawal behavior has its focus on voluntary turnover. The traditional models of voluntary turnover (Mobley, 1977; Price & Mueller, 1981; Steers & Mowday, 1981) state that job attitudes (e.g., job satisfaction and organizational commitment) and ease of movement (e.g., perceived alternatives and job search behaviors) are the major predictors of voluntary turnover. These two groups of antecedents are based on the notions of perceived desirability and ease of leaving (the job) proposed by March and Simon (1958). These models suggest that job attitudes together with job alternatives predict intent to leave, which directly precedes turnover. In this line of research, turnover is thought to develop from the accumulation of (negative) affective reactions over time, which in turn trigger searching behaviors and subsequent quitting. Despite many studies documenting the validity of these theoretical linkages (e.g., Jaros, 1997), the empirical evidence shows limited predictive power. For example, Hom and Griffeth (1995) and Griffeth, Hom, and Gaertner

(2000) report that attitudinal antecedents explain about 4–5% of the variance in turnover.

There has been research effort aiming at broadening both the predictor and the criterion set of employee attachment and withdrawal phenomena. On the one hand, more recent research suggests the use of a set of broader criteria such as absenteeism and job performance in addition to turnover in studying organizational attachment/withdrawal. These variables are conceptualized as part of a general withdrawal construct (Hulin, 1991). On the other hand, the predictor set for voluntary turnover has been expanded to incorporate non-attitudinal variables such as turnover-prompting shocks (Lee, Mitchell, Holtom, McDaniel, & Hill, 1999). Thus the causes for withdrawal behaviors may include a notion of non-predictability (e.g., shock-prompted leaving) as well as variables other than job attitudes (Mitchell, Holtom, Lee, Sablynski, & Erez, 2001).

Within the framework of organizational attachment research, two bodies of research inspired the development of JE. One body of research focuses on off-the-job factors that may influence various attachment attitudes and behaviors, such as non-work commitments (Cohen, 1995) and spillover models (Marshall, Chadwick, & Marshall, 1992). Other research looks at on-the-job non-attitudinal factors such as attachment due to team membership (Cohen & Bailey, 1997). In addition, Lee and Mitchell's (1994) unfolding model of turnover indicates factors (i.e., shocks) other than job dissatisfaction can trigger the decision of leaving. Taken together, these new inquiries and related findings imply factors underlying turnover that are non-work, non-attitudinal, and non-affective. They are related to ease of movement (other than availability of job alternatives) and bring about a sense of obligation. Factors with these characteristics can be further linked to other withdrawal constructs beyond voluntary turnover. Combining these properties, JE is a construct that aims at the diverse aspects of one's life in relation to the job and subsequently predicts one's action and reactions on the job.

A metaphor from the natural world for JE is a spider web. A fly that falls prey on a spider web has a hard time breaking free because (1) the spider silk is sticky and can stretch very far without breaking, and (2) the web is well woven with threads of spider silk connected at many nodes. Like a spider web, other people, things, groups and institutions are at the connecting points of one's network (social web), and one's relations with these entities exert powerful forces resembling stretchy spider silk that prevent one from breaking away, hence constraining one's freedom of movement. Such forces may derive from social norms or a sense of contentment and convenience, making one feel restrained when attempting to leave the network as spider webs take on different shapes and are woven with just different types of spider silk, one's life as a web may differ according to the distance and strength of attachments to people and things. Therefore, the overall "stuckness" for different people develops from various combinations of such distance and strength.

Definition and Dimensions

JE is an overall construct conceptualized as the combined forces that keep a person from leaving his or her job. It subsumes a broad constellation of factors influencing retention. There are three dimensions to this construct: links, fit and sacrifice. Each dimension is related to both on and off-the-job situations, suggesting six separate factors that contribute to JE. Despite its many specific aspects, JE conveys a global sense of difficulty to move out of the current social, psychological and financial structure.

Links.   Links refer to the discernable connections people have both on and off-the-job. Hence there are links to entities (i.e., institutions, other people, environment) in the organization such as being a member of a working team; there are also links to entities in one's community such as having non-work friends. The number of links and the importance of different links contribute to a general degree of embeddedness. Therefore, the more links one has and the more important those links are, the more likely people are heavily embedded. Studies have shown that relations to entities in one's surroundings both on and off the job may result in staying rather than leaving one's job through normative pressure (Maertz, Stevens, Campion, & Fernandez, 1996; Prestholdt, Lane, & Mathews, 1987).

Fit.   Fit is an employee's perceived compatibility with an organization and with his or her environment. It is the extent to which one's job and community are similar to or fit with the other aspects in his or her life space. Such compatibility may entail both affective reactions and non-affective judgments. Fit with one's organization usually relates personal values, career goals and future plans to both macro and micro-level organizational factors like corporate culture and work requirements. Researchers have investigated the relationship between person-organization/person-job fit and turnover and how socialization may influence that relationship. The findings generally support the idea that employees with a better fit stay longer (e.g., Chan, 1996) and people are consciously seeking fit (Cable & Judge, 1996; Cable & Parsons, 1999; Werbel & Gilliland, 1999). Fit with one's community is conceptualized as an independent dimension within fit. This includes one's compatibility with the local weather, culture of the community, entertainment, political and religious activities, and so on. The better the fit, the more likely people will feel professionally and personally tied to their job and not want to seek a job that request them to move.

Sacrifice. Sacrifice is the perceived cost for material or psychological benefits that may be forfeited by leaving one's job. It concerns what one has to give up if they were to break the links on and off the job following a decision of leaving or relocation. The more one has to give up, the more difficult it is to break from the current links. Some examples of job-related sacrifice are salary, benefits, non-portable benefits, switching cost, job advancement opportunities, and stability. Community sacrifice may contain conveniences that come along with the particular community one lives in (e.g., an easy commute, good day care). It seems relocation makes community sacrifice more important because a change of job without relocation may not influence one's off-the-job embeddedness factors as much.

CONSTRUCT DIFFERENTIATION

In the previous section, we cite research that supports ideas incorporated into our six job embeddedness dimensions. However, it is also important that we differentiate job embeddedness from specific similar constructs and measures already in the literature at the following three levels: the overall embeddedness level, the two-factor level (on and off-the-job), and the six-factor level (i.e., Fit-Organization, Fit-Community, Links-Organization, Links-Community, Sacrifice-Organization, Sacrifice-Community). We proceed by presenting the definition, measure,[1] and specific comparison with JE for each similar construct. Tables 7.1 and 7.2 summarize our discussion.

Job Embeddedness: Unified Level

Job embeddedness is an overall construct conceptualized as the forces that keep a person from leaving his or her job. It reflects an overall stuckness or the reasons why someone cannot leave a job. The only other main use of the word, embeddedness, comes from the sociological and economic research on social networks.

Granovetter (1985) describes embeddedness with an emphasis on the economic behavior of individuals and institutions that is constrained by ongoing social relations. Uzzi (1996, 1997, p. 35) says that, "embeddedness is a concept that has been used to refer broadly to the contingent nature of economic action with respect to cognition, social structure, institutions, and culture." This definition focuses broadly on the relationships between individuals and institutions and the influence of these relationships on a broad array of economic actions. In that sense, it is very different from our explicit focus on one behavior, leaving one's job. On the other hand, the social network's idea of embeddedness incorporates the notion that social

Table 7.1. Construct Differentiation: Unified and Two-Factor Level

Level	JE and its Dimensions	Similar Construct(s)	Construct Differentiation
Unified Level	**Job Embeddedness** An overall construct conceptualized as the forces (i.e. a net or web) that keep a person from leaving his or her job.	**Social Networks Embeddedness** Economic behavior of individuals and institutions that is constrained by ongoing social relations (Granovetter, 1985).	**Similarity** Both contain the idea of social relationships constraining action. **Difference** Social network embeddedness is broader (economic actions) while JE is specific (individual behavior).
Two Factor Level	**Links-Community** **Fit-Community** **Sacrifice-Community**	**Off-the-Job Factors*** • Nonwork Influences (Steers & Mowday, 1981) • Individual nonwork variables (Mobley, 1982) • Antecedents to Commitment (Hom & Griffeth, 1995).	**Similarity** Nonwork factors are informative to JE development. **Difference** Nonwork factors are not thoroughly treated in the empirical studies except for content in relation to Links-Community, which makes JE unique.

*Lack of a standard, validated or widely used measure.

relationships constrain or inhibit economic actions. Since turnover clearly has economic implications, both the social network's idea of embeddedness and our idea of job embeddedness include the idea of social relationships constraining action.

On and Off-the-Job: Two Factor Level

Most of the major theories of turnover have multiple on-the-job factors that are seen as causes of turnover. However, it is important to note that these theories (e.g., Hom & Griffeth, 1995; Mobley, 1982; Steers & Mowday, 1981) also have an overall aggregated construct that reflects off-the-job factors. These off-the-job factors are usually grouped into two broad categories. One is a "job alternatives" or "market forces" factor, which is a construct not comparable to job embeddedness. The second is a sort of catchall "other" factor, which is described below.

Steers and Mowday (1981) refer to "Non-work Influences," and they consider things like spouses' alternatives, central life interests outside of work and family considerations. Mobley (1982) discusses "individual non-work variables" and includes family responsibilities, dual careers and conflicts between work and non-work roles. Hom and Griffeth (1995) label their factor "antecedents to commitment" and include organizational loyalties, and time and behavioral conflicts with work. Some studies have used idiosyncratic measures for these factors, but there is no one standard, validated or widely used measure that has been developed to cover these off-the-job factors.

Some of the ideas suggested by these theorists were helpful for our construct development of job embeddedness. However, these off-the-job factors are not thoroughly treated (except for one of our six composites, Links-Community, which we will review in a moment) in the empirical literature. Steers and Mowday (1981) said, "current models ignore a host of nonwork influences on staying or leaving" (p. 240). Similarly, Mobley (1982) says that these variables are "often neglected" and "prediction and understanding of turnover will require inclusion of such nonwork variables." The only non-work factor included in the Griffeth, Hom, and Gaertner (2000) meta analysis is perceived alternatives. There were not enough studies to analyze any other "non-work" factors. While previous literature discusses outside life interests and family responsibilities, ideas that are informative in developing job embeddedness, the overall job embeddedness construct, which captures the totality of these non-work forces, is clearly unique.

Table 7.2. Construct Differentiation: Six-factor Level

JE and its Dimensions	Similar Constructs	Construct Differentiation
Sacrifice-Organization The perceived cost of material or psychological benefits that may be forfeited by leaving one's job.	**Side Bets** The investments an employee makes in an organization, such as time, job effort, and the development of work friendships, organization-specific skills, and political deals (Jaros, Jermier, Koehler & Sincich, 1993; Becker, 1960). **Measure** Age and experience (Hrebiniak & Alutto, 1972; Ritzer & Trice, 1969)	**Similarity** Both contain an idea of sunk cost that makes one stuck at the job. **Difference** Side Bets is broader than S-O and was meant to reflect overall organizational commitment.
	Continuance Commitment "The magnitude and/or number of investments (or side-bets) individuals make and a perceived lack of alternatives" (Allen & Meyer, 1990, p. 4). Part of the three-factor model of organizational commitment. **Measure** Include "hard to leave" items and items about alternatives (Allen & Meyer, 1990).	**Similarity** They share notions of "sunk cost" and reluctance to give up things by leaving. **Difference** S-O does not include availability of alternatives and the items for difficulty of leaving is more specific.
	Cost of Quitting "The cost of quitting would include such considerations as loss of seniority, loss of vested benefits, and the like" (Mobley, 1977, p.238). Expected utility of search is included. **Measure** Bipolar responses asking one's feeling for leaving with items about the cost and ease of leaving (Hom, Griffeth & Sellaro, 1984; Hom & Hulin, 1981). They are combined with a cost of searching variable in subsequent studies.	**Similarity** They share notions of "sunk cost." **Difference** S-O does not include perceived alternative ideas (cost of searching) and the items for difficulty of leaving is more specific.

Table 7.2. Construct Differentiation: Six-factor Level (Cont.)

JE and its Dimensions	Similar Constructs	Construct Differentiation
	Job Investments Investments in a job may consist of resources that are intrinsic to the job or resources that are extrinsic, but inextricably connected to the job (Rusbult & Farrell, 1983, p.431). Part of the job investment model (Farrell & Rusbult, 1981). **Measure** Both general and specific items about the resources related to the job have been used (e.g., Rusbult & Farrell, 1983).	**Similarity** Share the idea of resources spent related to the job are the obstacle to one's leaving. **Difference** S-O or JE does not claim to influence turnover via commitment; measure for Job Investments contains items included in other dimensions of JE; general measure for Job Investments contains an equity comparison item not present in JE.
Fit-Organization Employee's perceived compatibility with an organization.	**Person-Organization Fit** Compatibility between a person and organization (Kristof, 1996). "The congruence of the personality traits, beliefs and values of individual persons with the culture, strategic needs, norms, and values of organizations" (Netemeyer, Boles, McKee & McMurrian, 1997, p.88). **Person-Job Fit** The match of knowledge, skills and abilities (KSA) with one's job (Saks & Ashforth, 1997). **Measure** Fit-Organization, P-O Fit and P-J Fit measures are all perceptual and supplemental (e.g., Cable & Judge, 1996; Saks & Ashforth, 1997).	**Similarity** Both are about fit with the organization. **Difference** F-O is broader than other fit construct as it aims at capturing perception of fit at a global level.

Table 7.2. Construct Differentiation: Six-factor Level (Cont.)

JE and its Dimensions	Similar Constructs	Construct Differentiation
	Organization Identity "A perceived oneness with an organization and the experience of the organization's success and failures as one's own" (Mael & Ashforth, 1992, p. 103). **Measure** Micro level measure about one's feelings and behaviors towards the organization (Mael & Ashforth, 1992).	**Similarity** Contain idea of compatibility. **Difference** At the micro-level, Organizational Identity is related to self concept, while F-O is only about perceived fit or match, hence bear less significance for the self; Fit-Organization involves broader levels (organization, group, and job).
Links-Organization Discernable connections people have on the job.	**Constituency Commitment** "Commitment is a process of identification with the goals of an organization's multiple constituencies" (Reichers, 1985, p. 465). Such constituencies include top management, customers, unions and/or the public at large. **Measure** How attached are you to the following people and groups? Top management, supervisor and work group (Becker, 1992).	**Difference** L-O is a non-affective measure assessing one's connections with other entities in the organization that decrease one's mobility; constituency commitment implies attachment, which may or may not be affective
Links-Community Discernable connections people have off the job.	**Kinship Responsibility** "The degree of an individual's obligations to relatives in the community in which the individual resides" (Blegen, Mueller & Price, 1988, p. 402). **Measure** Marital status and counts of relatives living in the community. Direct measure includes attitude towards responsibilities for family and relatives.	**Similarity** A sense of obligation. **Difference** Obligation in Kinship Responsibility bears an ethical or normative sense.

Table 7.2. Construct Differentiation: Six-factor Level (Cont.)

JE and its Dimensions	Similar Constructs	Construct Differentiation
	Relocation Take a job in another city from the same company. **Repatriation** Quitting a job overseas to return within the same company. **Measure** Simple measures like those of Kinship Responsibility as well as measures for adjustment to move (Turban, Campion & Eyring, 1992) **Subjective Norm** "An individual's perception of whether or not most people who are important to him or her think he or she should perform the behavior" (Hom, Katerberg & Hulin, 1979, p. 281). **Measure** Either one item asking about important others' opinions on leaving, or, several items for each group of important others are used.	**Similarity** Focus on family and spouse. **Difference** Like Kinship Responsibility, links to the community in relocation and repatriation are related to concerns from family and spouse rather than detached account of connections. **Difference** Subjective Norm is about pressure from important others, while L-C only contains assessment of amount of responsibilities and obligations; Subjective Norm is broader since it pertains to people both on and off-the-job.

163

Sacrifice-Organization: Six Factor Level

By far, the part of job embeddedness that is most like other constructs in the field is the sacrifice-organization composite. There are four other similar ideas: Side Bets; Continuance Commitment; Cost of Quitting and Job Investments. Each is discussed below.

Side Bets. Becker (1960) originally introduced side bets as a way of thinking about organizational commitment. He saw side bets occurring when the employee "staked something of value to him, something originally unrelated to his present line of activity" (p. 35). In other work, he suggests it reflects "other sets of rewards than income and working conditions." A more recent definition of this idea is "the investments or side bets, an employee makes in an organization, such as time, job effort, and the development of work friendships, organization-specific skills, and political deals" (Jaros, Jermier, Koehler, & Sincich, 1993). Ritzer and Trice (1969) simply used age as a surrogate for side bets while Hrebiniak and Alutto (1972) used age and experience to reflect side bets. In both studies, these measures predicted another measure of organizational commitment that asked whether an employee would leave because of better pay, freedom, status or friendlier people.

The idea of side bets as "sunk costs" is similar to our idea that job embeddedness reflects how "stuck" one feels. However, the idea for side bets was far broader than our sacrifice-organization factor and was originally meant to reflect overall organization commitment. Currently, the side bet notion is reflected in the continuance commitment construct articulated by Meyer and Allen (1997) in their overall theory of organizational commitment.

Continuance Commitment. This construct is part of the three-factor model of organizational commitment developed by Allen and Meyer (1990, p. 4). They define it as "the magnitude and/or number of investments (or side-bets) individuals make and a perceived lack of alternatives." It incorporates the ideas of stuckness through a lack of options and the idea that by staying, other "side bets" (like investments in training or projects or friends) will pay off. It is a sort of status quo bias or inertia. Items for continuance commitment include questions on if it is hard for one to leave and perceived options. Subsequent research (e.g., Meyer, Allen, & Smith, 1993) has used similar questions although Jaros, Jermier, Koehler, and Sincich (1993) used only three of the general "hard to leave" questions and omit the alternatives and options items.

Our sacrifice-organization factor and the continuance commitment ideas clearly share the notions of "sunk cost" and reluctance to give up things by leaving. However, the original continuance commitment construct combined the availability of alternatives with these ideas. We do not.

Also, even where the alternative items are omitted, our measure of sacrifice-organization includes specific items referring to perks, respect, compensation, benefits (retirement and health care), and promotional opportunities which are not included in continuance commitment. Thus, our measure omits the "alternatives" idea and offers more detail in terms of the topics involved.

Cost of quitting.   In 1977, Mobley introduced the idea of cost of quitting as a reflection of March and Simon's (1958) perceived ease of movement concept. Mobley (1977) states that "the cost of quitting would include such considerations as loss of seniority, loss of vested benefits, and the like" (p. 238). Also included as part of this "block" was the expected utility of search. Thus, similar to the continuance commitment idea, cost of quitting and perceived alternatives were combined.

Hom and Hulin (1981) and Hom, Griffeth, and Sellaro (1984) measured cost of quitting. They had three items that used bipolar responses (e.g., good-bad, pleasant-unpleasant) to the question of how it would feel to leave their job during the present year. These bipolar items were combined with three other items. It should be noted that this cost of quitting was combined with a cost of searching variable in all subsequent analysis.

Again, similar to continuance commitment, there is a combination of the stuckness or sunk cost ideas with a perceived alternatives (cost of search) idea. While job embeddedness is similar to the former, it excludes the latter. In addition, as with continuance commitment, sacrifice-organization measures many more specific attributes that one would have to give up if they left (e.g., perks, promotions, respect, benefits)

Job investments.   Based on early equity and exchange ideas, Farrell and Rusbult (1981) developed their job investment model. According to Rusbult and Farrell (1983, p. 431), "Investments in a job may consist of resources that are intrinsic to the job (e.g., years of service, nonportable training, nonvested portions of retirement programs) or resources that are extrinsic, but inextricably connected to the job (e.g., housing arrangements that facilitate travel to and from work, friends at work, extraneous benefits uniquely associated with a particular job"). In their model, commitment was seen as the antecedent to turnover and "commitment is said to increase with increases in job rewards, decreases in job costs, increases in investment size and decreases in alternative quality" (Rusbult & Farrell, 1983, p. 430).

Rusbult and Farrell have used both specific and general items to measure job investments. For example, in the 1983 article they specifically measure each of the following: length of service, job tenure, vested and nonvested retirement programs, specific or nonportable training, friendship involvement, spousal employment, home ownership, and religious and community ties. In subsequent analyses, however, only the general items were used.

Although the general idea of job-investment is similar to sacrifice-organization, it is operationalized and analyzed differently. First, Rusbult and Farrell (1983) conceive of investment as acting on turnover through commitment. We make no mediation claim for sacrifice-organization or for job embeddedness. Second, their specific measures include items that we would place in either fit-organization (e.g., friendship involvement) or links-community (e.g., home ownership, community ties). Third, their general measure includes a relative comparison or equity type judgment.

In summary, the four constructs reviewed above all have some similarities with our construct. However, the side bets, continuance commitment and cost of quitting ideas are more general than ours and include some sort of assessment of the evaluation of alternatives. Job investment is defined similarly to sacrifice-organization but measured in ways that are either broader or more inclusive than our construct.

Fit-Organization: Six Factor Level

There are two streams of research that include ideas similar to notions of fit-organization. The literature on fit, including person-organization (P-O) and person-job (P-J) fit, and research on organizational identity (OI) are both relevant to the examination of JE.

Person-organization fit.   This literature is vast and heterogeneous. The early work of Schneider (1987) and Chatman (1989) set the stage and Kristof (1996) provided the best comprehensive review to date of the person-organization fit research. The person-job fit construct, while historically present in the selection literature, has been measured and tested far less frequently (Saks & Ashforth, 1997; Werbel & Gilliland, 1999). Kristof (1996) and others simply use the idea of compatibility between a person and organization to describe fit because of the many different ways person-organization fit is defined. For example, Netemeyer, Boles, McKee, and McMurrian (1997, p. 88) say it is "the congruence of the personality traits, beliefs and values of individual persons with the culture, strategic needs, norms, and values of organizations." This definition is essentially the same for person-organization fit by O'Reilly, Chatman, and Caldwell (1991). Person-job fit is focused more on the match of knowledge, skills and abilities (KSA) with one's job (Saks & Ashforth, 1997).

Our measure of Job Embeddedness is perceptual fit (not actual fit) and supplementary (not complementary). Kristof (1996) divides the measures based on these two distinctions. In addition, the content of the person-organization fit measures varies, with values being the most prevalent, followed by goals, needs and personality.

Our goal was to measure perceptions of fit at a global, summary level. We ask how people perceive they fit with their coworkers and work group, and if they believe they are a good match with their job, company and culture. We were attempting to assess an overall fit with numerous organization factors. Our construct is therefore broader than the other constructs in the fit literature.

Organizational identity. In their outstanding edited volume *Identity in Organizations*, Whetten and Godfrey (1998) document the confusion surrounding this construct. It is described as a vague construct for which there is little agreement and that it may defy formal definitions (Albert, 1998). However, we will focus on the research that is most similar to our fit-organization factor. Mael and Ashforth (1992, p. 103) define organization identity as "a perceived oneness with an organization and the experience of the organization's success and failures as one's own." In other words, "the individual defines him or herself in terms of the organization(s) in which he or she is a member" (p. 104). It comes from the literature on social identity theory where people classify themselves as belonging or not belonging to a group and their self-esteem and work are attached to these classifications. Gioia (1998, p. 17) says, "identity is arguably more fundamental to the conception of humanity than any other notion." Again, there are macro (organization level construct) and micro definitions of organizational identity and we will focus on the latter. Mael and Ashforth (1992) used items describing how one thinks and feels about the organization (the school) as reflected in their language and belief as well as in reaction to others' behavior toward the organization.

The construct of organizational identity is fundamentally different from fit-organization. Organizational identity at the personal level is involved with self-definition; Ashforth (1998) says it involves the fusion of self and organization. Fit-organization focuses on the job, group and organization level (broader than organizational identity in that sense), but organizational identity only focuses on the idea of perceived fit or match. Job Embeddedness is a less intrusive concept than organizational identity. In summary, the person-organization and person-job fit constructs are more similar to fit-organization than the organizational identity literature. However, fit-organization is more general in that it focuses on the fit idea across one's job, work group and organization.

Links-Organization: Six Factor Level

Constituency commitment. There is only one construct specifically similar to our links-organizations factor. It is contained in the work of Reichers' (1985) notion of constituency commitment. More specifically, she proposes a redefinition of the organizational commitment construct into multiple commitments depending upon the constituency. Reichers (1985, p. 465) says that "commitment is a process of identification with the goals of an organization's multiple constituencies." She includes top management, customers, unions and/or the public at large. Becker (1992) tested the Reichers model using the following question: How attached are you to the following people and groups (top management, supervisor and work group)?

Links-organization simply assesses the number of attachments people had in terms of their length of time in a job or organization and the number of coworkers, teams and committees with which they are involved. It is a completely non-affective measure. In contrast, constituency commitment implies goal identification (more like fit in that sense) and attachment to these groups, which may or may not be affective in nature. Our rationale for links was that links make one more "stuck" independent of how positive one felt about the links.

Links-Community: Six Factor Level

Job embeddedness has three off-the-job factors assessing community links, fit and sacrifice. In our discussion of more general conceptualizations of off-the-job factors (two factor level), we mentioned that many theorists group numerous variables into "non-work factors." However, there are a couple of constructs that focus directly on links with the community. In addition, there are whole areas of research on the topics of transfers (relocation) and repatriation. This work focuses on the idea that significant pressure to stay or leave a particular job assignment can be brought to bear on an individual by friends and family off-the-job.

Kinship responsibility. In their theory of turnover, Price and Mueller (1981) suggest that kinship responsibilities may be an important reason why people stay on a job. Blegen, Mueller, and Price (1988, p. 402) define kinship responsibility as "the degree of an individual's obligations to relatives in the community in which the individual resides." They used simple indicators such as marital status and number of relatives in the community to measure kinship responsibility. Later work (e.g., Price & Kim, 1993) suggested dissatisfaction with this measure and adopted items directly asking one's belief about their responsibilities.

Price and Mueller's (1981) early idea of kinship responsibility, as a sense of obligation or responsibility, is similar to our idea of links—community. Our initial measures included information about marital state, but other items about children were dropped (low alpha). Our latest studies included items that more fully assessed this construct by asking about the presence of family and friends residing in the same community. However,

Price and Kim's (1993) ideas of kinship responsibility, which are reflected in the items adopted in later studies (e.g., looking after sick parents, divorce), focuses on family obligations in a more ethical or normative sense, which is absent in our conceptualization of links-community.

Relocation and repatriation.   The literature on relocation and repatriation also focuses on links to the community, especially one's spouse, as determinants of job related decisions. For example, Miller (1976), Spitz (1986) and Turban, Campion, and Eyring (1992) suggest that relocation (taking a job in another city but staying with the company) is severely hindered if a spouse doesn't want to move. Turban et al. (1992) use a measure that is very much like the Price and Mueller (1981) kinship responsibility measure. In addition, they measured adjustment to the move.

For repatriation, the issue is a little different. It involves who stays and who comes home early. Still, these are essentially relocation decisions. They involve quitting an assignment overseas to return to one's job in the home country but usually do not involve quitting the organization. Black (1988) and Shaffer and Harrison (1998) provide good reviews of this literature. Again, the relationship with one's spouse and family is seen as important. Black (1988) and Shaffer and Harrison (1998), for example, use the kinship responsibility measure of Blegen, Mueller, and Price (1988) and some additional items to assess spouses' adjustment. They also asked some questions about one's satisfaction with their living conditions. These ideas are very similar to our links—community factor—but are different in the same ways that kinship responsibility was shown to be different from links-community.

Subjective norm.   Based on Fishbein (1967) and Ajzen and Fishbein's (1977) attitude model, a number of researchers have used a construct called, "subjective norm" to predict turnover (Hom & Hulin, 1981; Parker & Dyer, 1976). Hom, Katerberg, and Hulin (1979, p. 281) define subjective norm as "an individual's perception of whether or not most people who are important to him or her think he or she should perform the behavior." This subjective norm is weighted by the extent to which the person feels that these others are "important" (described as motivation to comply). As defined, this notion could include people on and off-the-job. In terms of measurement, sometimes a single measure is used; other times a score is aggregated across reference groups (e.g., friends, family, employer). For example, Newman (1974) used the item: Most of the people, whose opinion I respect, think I should leave my present job within the next two months; in contrast, Hom et al. (1984) used: "People who are important to me and whose opinion I value think I should quit my present job before the end of the year."

The subjective norm research focuses directly on the perceived pressure brought to bear on an individual to stay on or to leave a job. In contrast, links-community is more focused on the sheer number of links, obligations and responsibilities one has off-the-job, not whether these people want or don't want one to leave. In addition, subjective norm researchers often assess and combine both on and off-the-job pressure brought to bear by others.

In summary, the work by Price and Mueller (1981) on kinship responsibility is fairly similar conceptually and empirically (in terms of measurement) to our links-community factor. Studies on relocation and repatriation share such similarity due to the same concern of responsibility toward the family and adoption of kinship responsibility measures. In contrast, subjective norm conveys a greater sense of social pressure and is broader than links-community as it incorporates both on and off-the-job pressure.

METHODOLOGICAL ISSUES

The first and foremost concern for new construct development is to begin the ongoing process of construct validation. Through an iterative process of modifying the items in the measures and establishing relationships between the focal construct and other constructs in the theoretical and nomological network, we can better understand the phenomenon of interest and fine-tune relevant measures.

The items for each dimension of JE are based on our initial and revised conceptualizations of the construct. They reflect issues brought up in interviews and discussions with the subjects as well as focus group meetings with employees from participating organizations. In addition, items from similar constructs were used. Thus, the items are intended to cover the content within each dimension and at the same time capture issues raised in our literature review and over discussion with the research participants. All these procedures ensure content validity of the JE measure.

JE summarizes and integrates the many forces that pull or keep a person in a job. The forces represented by the measure of JE are fairly heterogeneous, and the items are formative rather than reflective. In other words, JE is formed or induced by its indicators (i.e., the items cause job embeddedness but not the reverse) (Edwards & Bagozzi, 2000). Items under each dimension aggregate to form on-the-job and off-the-job aspects of one's current state, and the dimensions in turn combine to become "job embeddedness." Consequently, the reliability coefficient need not be high because various forces are not expected to relate to one another. They may come from very different sources (e.g., the weather of the place one lives, the friendliness of the neighbors, one's favorite activity offered by the community or the culture of one's organization). This notion applies to both the within-dimension and the between-dimension alpha reliability.

To date, the alpha reliability for the six dimensions reported by Mitchell et al. (2001) and Lee et al. (forthcoming) ranges from .50 to .86. It should be noted that items were modified across studies. At the overall level, alpha for JE is quite stable at the .85–.87 level, which may be due in part to the large number of items.

Mitchell et al. (2001) and Lee et al. (forthcoming) provide evidence for the concurrent and predictive validity of JE. Both studies found JE to be negatively related to intent to leave measured at the same point of time. In other words, those who are more embedded are less likely to think of leaving. JE predicted later voluntary turnover (over a period of 12 months after the measurement of JE). In addition, JE also predicted subsequent voluntary absences and job performance and correlated with concurrently measured OCB.

Mitchell et al. (2001) and Lee et al. (forthcoming) also reported evidence on convergent and discriminant validity. Consistent with the conception of fit-organization as a dimension closely related to work-related attitudinal measures, fit-organization is positively and significantly associated with job satisfaction and organizational commitment. In addition, we expected people who are highly embedded to search less and perceive fewer job alternatives. These hypotheses are supported by the negative and significant correlations between JE, and job search and job alternatives. As evidence for discriminant validity, non-affective dimensions of JE should be weakly related to other affective constructs. For example, links-organization is weakly correlated with job satisfaction and organizational commitment. Furthermore, off-the-job factors should be weakly related to on-the-job factors, or other on-the-job affective and attitudinal variables. The correlations between on and off-the-job factors are .26 and .36 ($p < .01$) for the grocery and hospital samples, respectively (Mitchell et al., 2001). Off-the-job factors in aggregate correlate weakly with job satisfaction and organizational commitment.

In our previous section, we cite research that supports ideas incorporated into our six job embeddedness dimensions. Further evidence for convergent and discriminant validity can be gathered based on correlations between JE and other theoretically similar constructs. For example, we can examine the correlation between continuance commitment (Allen & Meyer, 1990) and Sacrifice-Organization; between person-organization (Kristof, 1996), person-job fit (Saks & Ashforth, 1997) and Fit-Organization. We expect these correlations to be moderate to high.

For discriminant validity, we expect to find weak and non-significant correlations between dissimilar constructs such as: organization identity (Mael & Ashforth, 1992) and Fit-Organization; constituency commitment (Reichers, 1985) and Links-Organization; and subjective norm (Hom et al., 1979) and Links-Community.

CURRENT RESEARCH EVIDENCE

To date, there are two studies addressing issues of measurement and the nomological network in which JE resides. Mitchell et al. (2001) first developed the construct and its measure. Using two samples of grocery clerks and hospital employees, they demonstrated: (1) high reliability of the measure with alpha ranges from .80 to .90; (2) JE was negatively related to intent to leave and subsequent voluntary turnover; and (3) JE contributed to the prediction of voluntary turnover over and beyond that of gender, perceived desirability of movement (job satisfaction and organizational commitment), and perceived ease of movement (job alternatives and job search).

Recently, Lee et al. (forthcoming) replicated the previous finding of the predictability of job embeddedness on intent to leave and voluntary turnover with a third sample. Furthermore, they extended the nomological network for job embeddedness. They found that job embeddedness also predicted incremental variance in voluntary absences, OCB and job performance over and beyond job satisfaction. This finding serves as evidence for linking the "decision to perform" with the "decision to participate" (March & Simon, 1958) and supports Hulin and colleagues' broad withdrawal construct that incorporates both variables directly concerning leaving and those reflecting a tendency of decreased involvement (e.g., absenteeism). A third important issue examined in the study was the joint effect of job embeddedness and shock on the general withdrawal construct measures. Lee and Mitchell (1994) developed the shock construct as part of their unfolding model of turnover. A shock is a very distinguishable event that jars people toward deliberate judgments about their jobs and possibly leads to voluntary turnover. An individual can perceive shocks to be positive or negative, expected or unexpected, family or organization-centered, and internal or external to the person. Results from Lee et al.'s (forthcoming) show that certain types of shocks, as pushing forces, have opposite effects to job embeddedness on quitting and absences, and a slightly different set of shocks compete with the pulling forces contained in job embeddedness to affect OCB and job performance.

FUTURE RESEARCH DIRECTIONS

Structure of JE

The current operationalization of JE combines each item and six dimensions using equal weights. However, the combination of number and strength of one's relationships with other entities in the network may differ by person. Put differently, people may have the same JE score, but the structure of the formation for JE can be different. Some may have many weaker connections; others may have a few very strong connections; and still others may have a mixture of weak and strong connections that affect one's perception of JE. For example, individual A can score high on the organizational dimensions, but low on community factors; individual B can score in the opposite direction, high on community factors and low on organizational ones. In other words, individual A may really like the job, get along well with coworkers, find the compensation and other benefits of the job very desirable, but does not like the community atmosphere, the weather, or has few family members living nearby. Individual B may enjoy all the outdoor activities offered by the community, befriend the neighbors, but does not find the job particularly appealing. B may have been on the job only for a relatively short period of time, and have few on-the-job links. Thus, this person may not feel strongly about the compatibility between him/herself and the organization. Because we currently use averaged score for JE, it is very likely that A and B have comparable scores of JE. We will not be able to know why they are embedded unless we analyze how they score on specific dimensions.

How can we use this information of JE composition? Theoretically, we may be able to identify critical factors, rather than the overall JE, related to outcome variables. Empirically, it helps with prediction and intervention. If the organization wants to know what keeps their people on the job or if the management wants to "embed" employees, it is necessary to find out the key dimensions that are operating. The importance of different aspects depend on characteristics of the group of people under investigation. It can also be determined by investigators' interests. Some potential variables for distinguishing groups of people who may have different JE structures are: industry, job complexity, general self-efficacy, need for achievement, personality (e.g., conscientiousness), and so forth. For instance, in industries with good job opportunities, one may want to know if the community factors help to predict which individual is embedded. On the contrary, people with a high need for achievement may value more the on-the-job aspects of embeddedness. Opportunities to move on can be critical for them. In this case, greater weights should be given to on-the-job factors.

Development of JE

Research on job embeddedness can be extended through investigating developmental issues. By examining how one becomes embedded in the job and their community, we can further understand the relationship between job embeddedness and variables of interest over time.

Research on realistic job previews (RJPs) (e.g., Phillips, 1998) and realistic socialization (e.g., Wanous & Colella, 1989) indicates that the turnover rate is lower and job satisfaction is higher if people have the opportunity to learn what they will actually do on the job or if they lower their expectation for the job through socialization soon after entering the organization. As individuals get used to their daily routine, establish plans for long-term development, and become more committed. They come to realize that their life revolves around a certain number of important activities and individuals either at work or outside work. Any planning beyond what they are already occupied with seems to be unrealistic or unworthy of the effort. In ways similar to RJPS, this process can be thought of as "lowering expectations" for alternative jobs and activities. Therefore, people may be willing to become "embedded" and proactively seek to get involved in the activities that extend their "web" both on and off the job. A related question is to ask which of the six dimensions occur first. That is, is there an order of the formation of each factor? This timing issue can inform both the researchers and practitioners on how to predict the state of embeddedness and how and when to intervene.

How may JE evolve over time? An individual can become more embedded in a set of unique conditions due to accumulation of relationships, financial and psychological investment in various types of activities, and a sense of growing comfortableness and content with the surroundings. In addition, development of JE may stop after one reaches a ceiling of embeddedness. That is, unless some critical events take place (e.g., a sick spouse who requires stable income, constant care-taking, etc.), one does not get more embedded when a certain level has been reached.

Implicit in the development of JE is the prediction of JE. Because JE is considered an outcome of the various forces on and off the job, we expect factors that increase links, sacrifice and fit to predict the degree of embeddedness. Links on the job is closely related to the connections one has with other entities, which can result from the design of one's job. For example, people tend to have more links with other people when working in a group/team setting than working individually. For those working in a group/team environment, greater task interdependence tends to result in more ties with other group members. However, we can think of people who stay detached despite working in a group environment and those who cultivate their relationships with others despite working independently. Hence, individual differences such as need for affiliation may determine whether one is susceptible to embeddedness with respect to group membership. Links in the community are strengthened by events such as family members and relatives moving to the same community, a major league team being brought into the city or the city having built a new opera house.

Years living in the same community can represent links in the community as well.

In a similar way, factors that contribute to increasing Sacrifice-Organization, Sacrifice-Community, Fit-Organization, and Fit-Community can also predict JE. For instance, future research can explore the possibility of selection and socialization as predictors of JE based on their potential to promote person-organization fit (Kristof, 1996).

JE and Justice

There are different types of organizational justice: distributive, procedural, and interactional. Distributive justice is the fairness of the outcome from a decision, whereas procedural justice is the fairness of the processes taken to make decisions in an organization. There exists disagreement as to whether interactional justice (including interpersonal and informational justice) is part of procedural justice or a third type of justice (Cropanzano & Greenberg, 1997; Mitchell & Daniels, 2001). In this chapter, we conceptualize interactional justice as the social aspect of procedural justice (Cropanzano & Greenberg, 1997).

Organizational justice, especially procedural justice, has been found to be related to job satisfaction, organizational commitment, turnover and OCBs (e.g., Mowday, 1991). People are particularly sensitive to procedural injustice: if they believe that they are treated unfairly, it is much easier for them to generate negative reactions to inequitable outcomes; but if the treatment appears to be fair, the effect of inequitable outcomes is less detrimental. For example, work-related attitudes have shown to be influenced by a distributive-procedural justice interaction such that one's reaction to an unfair outcome is greater when the procedure is perceived to be unfair (Cropanzano & Folger, 1991; Cropanzano & Greenberg, 1997).

In the same vein, distributive and procedural justice may also interact to affect JE. People may be more likely to be embedded when they perceive the procedure of decision-making is fair although the outcome is unfair. Hence a perception of fair treatment (e.g., the supervisor shows respect for them, or they are well informed of decision processes) adds up as a benefit from the organization. If people choose to leave the organization, they run the risk of entering a new organization with less satisfying justice procedures, which means that they will have to sacrifice this fair environment should they leave. However, if individuals receive an unfair outcome under the impression of an unfair procedure, they may feel that there is a bad fit with the organization (low Fit-Organization), or, they don't sacrifice too much should they exert less effort or leave the organization (low Sacrifice-Organization). These aspects contribute to lowered JE.

If we treat justice and JE as predictors for criteria related to withdrawal behaviors such as absence, lack of OCBs, and lowered performance, we may expect an interaction effect. It is possible that there exists a three-way interaction among distributive justice, procedural justice and JE such that in the presence of unfair procedures and/or unfair outcomes, people's justice perceptions become a shock (see more discussion in the following section). We apply the same "shock" idea from the unfolding model (Lee & Mitchell, 1994), for example, unfair procedures used to determine performance appraisal can be a negative, unexpected, organization-centered shock. The consequence of a shock of injustice may trigger employees' withdrawal behavior, voluntary turnover being one of them, which JE tends to fend off (Lee et al., forthcoming).

In sum, we suspect that unfair outcomes, procedures and treatments all contribute to undermining JE or generating withdrawal behaviors through negative effect on one of the six dimensions.

JE as a Moderator

We are particularly interested in how one will react to negative shocks at high versus low level of JE. As noted earlier, shocks resemble the pushing forces that jerk one out of the current position in life; while JE works in the opposite direction, pulling people back. Hence JE may have a buffering effect for shock experiences. Highly embedded people may not change easily in response to a shock. They can have a greater tolerance for shocks, particularly negative. They may be quite conscious about the various aspects in ones life that embed them, and they make decisions with respect to preservation of those factors. On the other hand, continuous small shocks can possibly accrue and breach the limit of JE so that high JE individuals can only resist shocks to a certain point, after which the effects of shocks will dominate.

Brockner, Tyler, and Cooper-Schneider (1992) argued that if individuals are guided by relational concerns, then those who are most committed to their institutions will be the most upset by violations of procedural justice. This interaction between commitment and procedural justice suggests that procedural justice is more strongly related to various outcomes when commitment is high. When commitment is low, however, the effects of procedural justice should be weaker. In a similar way, JE may also moderate one's reaction to procedural justice such that a highly embedded individual may react more negatively than someone with a low level of embeddedness. Because the person is "stuck" with the current situation, willingly or unwillingly, procedural justice violations regarding an unfavorable working environment such as compensation, participation, and recognition, etc., are what the person has to bear. Thus, people who are less flexible to move away are more likely to display greater affective, attitudinal or behavioral reactions to a shock involving procedural injustice. People with low JE may not care how the organization is doing or how people are treated, hence have weaker reactions.

These previous two accounts give different predictions about how one will react to a (negative) shock. It would be an empirical issue for researchers to find out the exact direction for moderation in the future. Here we only discuss procedural justice as one type of shock. There could be other types of shocks inducing people's reactions such as different changes occurring in the organization. We think that the moderating effect of JE still applies to those various changes.

It is also possible that rather than the overall level of JE, one or more of the JE dimensions serve as a moderator. For instance, someone heavily embedded due to on-the-job factors is greatly affected by procedural injustice, while other highly embedded individuals with respect to community life may not care as much as long as it does not affect their off-the-job enjoyment.

JE and Outcome Variables

Preliminary evidence showed that JE is related to withdrawal behaviors (Lee et al., forthcoming). There are several possibilities how this may happen. Since people are embedded through both on-the-job and off-the-job forces, it is possible that forces from these two "camps" may compete with each other. If someone is embedded more off the job through family obligations, hobbies, community activities, and the like, the person may not put adequate time in the job. Thus, off-the-job forces may erode job performance, lower OCBs and increase absenteeism. Another possible reason why people may withdraw (i.e., declining performance, fewer OCBs, and attendance) from their work is that they are neither motivated to change their embedded situation nor motivated to perform at work. Awareness of embeddedness, then, does not necessarily result in people's working harder. They may simply lack motivation in general. A third situation may be that the individual wants to move, but feels "stuck," perhaps due to great sacrifice at work or in the community leaving. She or he is not satisfied with this type of "embeddedness" and decides to withhold effort at work.

Although the construct of JE grew out of studies on withdrawal behavior, the outcome of being embedded may be more than withdrawal. Psychological well-being is another criterion worth studying. The relation between JE and well-being is probably more complex than a simple positive or negative correlation, such as the positive, significant and moderate-sized correlations found between JE and work-related attitudes (Lee et al., forthcoming; Mitchell et al., 2001). JE conveys the idea of a stable structure of life, but it does not necessarily refer to the consistency of the "content" a person experiences. For instance, one may have to deal with a lot of uncertainty and stressful situations at work. Likewise, one's family life may be full of turbulence. However, the individual is unable to escape such situations if heavily embedded. Here JE seems to be an annoying state trapping people at an unpleasant stage. Contrary to that, one may be happily embedded because of challenging work, congenial coworkers, exciting activities in the community. All these combined with a stable structure should contribute to one's psychological well-being. Therefore, there could be some moderating factors that need to be identified before the relationship can be further pursued.

JE and Change

Organizations are constantly experiencing change: downsizing, reengineering, restructuring, layoffs, new technologies, so on and so forth. Despite the fact that JE grew out of a time when the labor market was tight and retention is the major concern for most organizations, it is also important during a time of change. Change means drastic alteration to one's present state of embeddedness. For those who are heavily embedded, it is a "collapse" of the web built both on and off the job. At this point, the possible affective, cognitive, and behavioral reactions one has as related to JE do not appear to be a simple one. The reactions not only depend on the individual's previous attitude toward the embedded state (positive, negative, or neutral), the nature of the change, but also his/her interpretation of the change. One scenario can be that the embedded person embraces reengineering in the organization because of the opportunities that rise from the change. Another heavily embedded person may feel threatened and dislike any changes in the pace of life. A third person with low JE may become more embedded as a result of change. Developing and test a comprehensive model will then help us understand better how people change in response to external change.

CONCLUSION

Mitchell, Lee and their colleagues have taken a step in examining retention issues by including off-the-job factors long neglected in most studies. The outgrowth of this perspective, job embeddedness, informs us not only on the more traditional turnover inquiries, but also on people's day-to-day behaviors at work. In this paper, we go through the theoretical threads leading to the construct of job embeddedness. We show evidence from empirical work supporting our conceptualization of people being "entrapped" in a network of relationships, investments and benefits. We also try to describe possible ties between JE and other constructs under different circumstances. The introduction of job embeddedness to our understanding of psychological and behavioral processes brings promising descriptive and explanatory power for work-related attitudes, decisions and behaviors.

NOTE

1.   Please see the Appendix for measures of JE and related constructs.

REFERENCES

Ajzen, I., & Fishbein, M. (1977). Attitude-behavior relations: A theoretical analysis and review of empirical research. *Psychological Bulletin, 84*, 888–918.

Albert, S. (1998). The definition and meta definitions of identity. In D.A. Whetton & P.C. Godfrey (Eds.), *Identity in organizations: Building theory through conversations* (pp. 1–16). Thousand Oaks, CA. Sage.

Allen, N.J., & Myer, J.P. (1990). The measurement and antecedents of affective, continuance, and normative commitment to the organization. *Journal of Occupational Psychology, 63*, 1–18.

Ashforth, B.E. (1998). Epilogue: What does the concept of identity add to organization science. In D.A. Whetten & P.C. Godfrey (Eds.), *Identity in Organizations: Building theory through conversations* (pp. 273–294). Thousand Oaks, CA. Sage.

Becker, H. (1960). Notes on the concept of commitment. *American Journal of Sociology, 66*, 32–42.

Becker, T.E. (1992). Foci and bases of commitment: Are there distinctions worth making. *Academy of Management Journal, 35*, 232–244.

Black, J.S. (1988). Work role transitions: A study of American expatriate managers in Japan. *Journal of International Business Studies, 19*, 277–294.

Blegen, M.A., Mueller, C.W., & Price, J.L. (1988). Measurement of kinship responsibility for organizational research. *Journal of Applied Psychology, 73*, 402–409.

Brockner, J., Tyler, T.R., & Cooper-Schneider, R. (1992). The influence of prior commitment to an institution on reactions to perceived unfairness: The higher they are, the harder they fall. *Administrative Science Quarterly, 37*, 241–261.

Cable, D., & Judge, T.A. (1996). Person-organization fit, job choice decision and organizational entry. *Organizational Behavior and Human Decision Processes, 67*, 294–311.

Cable, D.M., & Parsons, C.K. (1999). *Establishing person-organization fit during organizational entry*. Paper presented at the Annual Meetings of the Academy of Management, Chicago.

Chan, D. (1996). Cognitive misfit of problem-solving style at work: A facet of person-organization fit. *Organizational Behavior and Human Decision Processes, 68*, 194–207.

Chatman, J.A. (1989). Improving interactional organizational research: A model of person-organization fit. *Academy of Management Review, 14*, 333–349.

Cohen, A. (1995). An examination of the relationships between work commitment and nonwork domains. *Human Relations, 48*, 239–263.

Cohen, S.G., & Bailey, D.E. (1997). What makes teams work: Group effectiveness research from the shop floor to the executive suite. *Journal of Management, 23*, 239–290.

Cropanzano, R., & Folger, R. (1991). Procedural justice and worker motivation. In R.M. Steers & L.W. Porter (Eds.), *Motivation and work behavior* (pp. 72–83). New York: McGraw Hill.

Cropanzano, R., & Greenberg, J. (1997). Progress in organizational justice: Tunneling through the maze. In C.L. Cooper & I.T. Robertson (Eds.), *International review of industrial and organizational psychology*. New York: Wiley Publishers.

Edwards, J.R., & Bagozzi, R.P. (2000). On the nature and direction of relationships between constructs and measures. *Psychological Methods, 5*, 155–174.

Farrell, E., & Rusbult, C.E. (1981). Exchange variables as predictors of job satisfaction, job commitment, and turnover: The impact of rewards, costs, alternatives, and investments. *Organizational Behavior and Human Performance, 28*, 78–95

Fishbein, M. (1967). Attitude and the prediction of behavior. In M. Fishbein (Ed.), *Readings in attitude theory and measurement*. New York; Wiley.

Gioia, D.A. (1998). From individual to organizational identity. In D.A. Whetton & P.C. Godfrey (Eds.), *Identity in organizations: Building theory through conversations* (pp. 17–32). Thousand Oaks, CA: Sage.

Granovetter, M. (1985). Economic action and social structure: The problems of embeddedness. *American Journal of Sociology, 91*, 481–510.

Griffeth, R.W., Hom, P.W., & Gaertner, S. (2000). A meta-analysis of antecedents and correlates of employee turnover: Update, moderator tests, and research implications for the millennium. *Journal of Management, 26*, 463–488.

Hom, P.W., & Griffeth, R. W. (1995). *Employee turnover*. Cincinnati, OH: South-Western College Publishing.

Hom, P.W., Griffeth, R.W., & Sellaro, C.L. (1984). The validity of Mobley's 1977 model of employee turnover. *Organizational Behavior and Human Performance, 34*, 141–174.

Hom, P.W., & Hulin, C.L. (1981). A competitive test of the prediction of reenlistment by several models. *Journal of Applied Psychology, 66*, 23–39.

Hom, P., Katerberg, R., & Hulin, C. (1979). A comparative examination of three approaches to the prediction of turnover. *Journal of Applied Psychology, 64*, 280–290.

Hulin, C.L. (1991). Adaptation, persistence and commitment in organizations. In M. Dunnette & L. Hough (Eds.), *Handbook of industrial and organizational psychology* (2nd ed., pp. 445–507). Palo Alto, CA: Consulting Psychologists Press.

Hrebiniak, L.G., & Alutto, J.A. (1972). Personal and role-related factors in the development of organizational commitment. *Administrative Science Quarterly, 17*, 555–573.

Jaros, S.J. (1997). An assessment of Meyer and Allen's (1991) three-component model of organizational commitment and turnover intentions. *Journal of Vocational Behavior, 51*, 319–337.

Jaros, S.J., Jermier, J.M., Koehler, J.W., & Sincich, T. (1993). Effects of continuance, affective, and moral commitment on the withdrawal process: An evaluation of eight structural equation models. *Academy of Management Journal, 36*, 951–995.

Kristoff, A.L. (1996). Person-organization fit: An integrative review of its conceptualizations, measurement and implications. *Personnel Psychology, 48*, 1–49.

Lee, T.W., & Mitchell, T.R. (1994). An alternative approach: The unfolding model of voluntary employee turnover. *Academy of Management Review, 19*, 51–89.

Lee, T.W., Mitchell, T.R., Holtom, B.C., McDaniel, L., & Hill, J.W. (1999). Theoretical development and extension of the unfolding model of voluntary turnover. *Academy of Management Journal, 42*, 450–462.

Lee, T.W., Mitchell, T.R., Sablynski, C.J., Burton, J.P. & Holtom, B.C. (forthcoming). The effects of job embeddedness on organization citizenship, job performance, volitional absences and voluntary turnover. *Academy of Management Journal.*

Mael, F., & Ashforth, B.E. (1992). Alumni and their alma mater: A partial test of the reformulated model of organizational identification. *Journal of Organizational Behavior, 13*, 103–123.

Maertz, C.P., Stevens, M.J., Campion, M.A., & Fernandez, A. (1996). *Worker turnover in Mexican factories: A qualitative investigation and model development.* Paper presented at the Annual Meetings of the Academy of Management, Cincinnati, OH.

March, J.G., & Simon, H.A. (1958). *Organizations.* New York: John Wiley.

Marshall, C.M., Chadwick, B.A. & Marshall, B.C. (1992). The influence of employment on family interaction, well-being, and happiness. In S.J. Bahr (Ed.), *Family research: A six-year review, 1930–1990* (vol. 2, pp. 167–229). San Francisco: The New Lexington Press.

Meyer, J.P., & Allen, N.J. (1997). *Commitment in the workplace.* Thousand Oaks, CA: Sage.

Meyer, J.P., Allen, N.J., & Smith, C.A. (1993). Commitment to organizations and occupations: Extension and test of a three-component conceptualization. *Journal of Applied Psychology, 78*, 538–551.

Miller, S.J. (1976). Family life cycle, extended family orientations, and aspirations as factors in the propensity to migrate. *The Sociological Quarterly, 17*, 323–335.

Mitchell, T.R., & Daniels, D. (2001). Motivation. In W.C. Borman, D.R. Ilgen, & R.J. Klimoski (Eds.), *Comprehensive handbook of psychology, Vol. 12: Industrial and organizational psychology.* New York: John Wiley & Sons, Inc.

Mitchell, T.R., Holtom, B.C., Lee, T.W., Sablynski, C.J., & Erez, M. (2001). Why people stay: Using job embeddedness to predict voluntary turnover. *Academy of Management Journal.*

Mobley, W.H. (1977). Intermediate linkages in the relationship between job satisfaction and employee turnover. *Journal of Applied Psychology, 62,* 237–240.

Mobley, W.H. (1982). *Employee turnover: Causes, consequences, and control.* Menlo Park, CA: Addison-Wesley.

Mowday, R.T. (1991). Equity theory predictions of behavior in organizations. In R.M. Steers & L.W. Porter (Eds.), *Motivation and work behavior* (5th ed., pp. 111–130). New York: McGraw-Hill.

Netemeyer, R.G., Boles, J.S., McKee, D.O., & McMurrian, R. (1997). An investigation into the antecedents of organizational citizenship behaviors in a personal selling context. *Journal of Marketing, 61,* 85–98.

Newman, J.E. (1974). Predicting absenteeism and turnover: A field comparison of Fishbein's model and traditional job attitude measures. *Journal of Applied Psychology, 59,* 610–615.

O'Reilly, C.W., Chatman, J., & Caldwell, D.F. (1991). People and organizational culture: A profile comparison approach to person-organization fit. *Academy of Management Journal, 34,* 487–516.

Parker, D.F., & Dyer, L. (1976). Expectancy theory as a within-person behavioral choice model: An empirical test of some conceptual and methodological refinements. *Organizational Behavior and Human Decision Processes, 17,* 97–117.

Phillips, J.M. (1998). Effects of realistic job previews on multiple organizational outcomes: A meta-analysis. *Academy of Management Journal, 41,* 673–690.

Prestholdt, P.H., Lane, I.M. & Mathews, R.C. (1987). Nurse turnover as reasoned action: Development of a process model. *Journal of Applied Psychology, 72,* 221–227.

Price, J.L., & Kim, S. W. (1993). The relationship between demographic variables and intent to stay in the military: Medical personnel in a U.S. Airforce hospital. *Armed Forces and Society, 20,* 125–144.

Price, J.L., & Mueller, C.W. (1981). A causal model of turnover for nurses. *Academy of Management Journal, 24,* 543–565.

Reichers, A. (1985). A review and reconceptualization of organizational commitment. *Academy of Management Review, 10,* 465–476.

Ritzer, G., & Trice, H.M. (1969). An empirical study of Howard Becker's side-bet theory. *Social Forces, 47,* 475–479.

Rusbult, C.E., & Farrell, D. (1983). A longitudinal test of the investment model: The impact on job satisfaction, job commitment, and turnover of variations in rewards, costs, alternatives, and investments. *Journal of Applied Psychology, 68,* 429–438.

Saks, A.M., & Ashforth, B.E. (1997). A longitudinal investigation of the relationships between job information sources, applicant perceptions of fit, and work outcomes. *Personnel Psychology, 50,* 395–426.

Schneider, B. (1987). The people make the place. *Personnel Psychology, 40,* 437–453.

Shaffer, M.A., & Harrison, D.A. (1998). Expatriates' psychological withdrawal from international assignments: Work, nonwork, and family influences. *Personnel Psychology, 51,* 87–118.

Spitz, G. (1986). Family migration largely unresponsive to wife's employment: Across age groups. *Sociology and Social Research, 70*, 231–234.

Steers, R.M., & Mowday, R.T. (1981). Employee turnover and post-decision justification. In L.L. Cummings & B.M. Staw (Eds.), *Research in organizational behavior* (Vol. 3, pp. 235–282). Greenwich, CT: JAI Press.

Turban, D.B., Campion, J.E., & Eyring, A.R. 1992. Factors relating to relocation decisions of research and development employees. *Journal of Vocational Behavior, 41*, 183–199.

Uzzi, B. (1996). The sources and consequences of embeddedness for the economic performance of organizations. The network effect. *American Sociological Review, 61*, 674–698.

Uzzi, B. (1997). Social structure and competition in interfirm networks: The paradox of embeddedness. *Administrative Science Quarterly, 42*, 33–67.

Wanous, J.P., & Colella, A. (1989). Organizational entry research: Current status and future directions. In K.M. Rowland & G.R. Ferris (Eds.), *Research in personnel and human resources management* (Vol. 7, pp. 59–120). Greenwich, CT: JAI Press.

Whetten, D.A., & Godfrey, P.C. (1998). *Identity in organizations: Building theory through conversations.* Thousand Oaks, CA: Sage Publications, Inc.

Werbel, J.D., & Gilliland, S.W. (1999). The use of person-environment fit in the selection process. In G. Ferris (Ed.), *Research in Personnel and Human Resources Management* (Vol. 17). Greenwich, CT: JAI Press.

APPENDIX
MEASURES FOR JOB EMBEDDEDNESS AND SIMILAR CONSTRUCTS

Job Embeddedness
(Mitchell, Holtom, Lee, Sablynski & Erez, 2001)

Fit—Community

1. I really love the place where I live.
2. The weather where I live is suitable for me.
3. This community is a good match for me.
4. I think of the community where I live as home.
5. The area where I live offers the leisure activities that I like.

Fit—Organization

1. I like the members of my work group.
2. My coworkers are similar to me.
3. My job utilizes my skills and talents well.
4. I feel like I am a good match for this company.

5. I fit with the company's culture.

6. I like the authority and responsibility I have at this company.

* Additional items in hospital sample.

7. My values are compatible with the organization's values.

8. I can reach my professional goals working for this organization.

9. I feel good about my professional growth and development.

Links—Community

1. Are you currently married?

2. If you are married, does your spouse work outside the home?

3. Do you own the home you live in?

* Additional items in hospital sample.

4. My family roots are in this community.

5. How many family members live nearby?

6. How many of your close friends live nearby?

Links—Organization

1. How long have you been in your present position?

2. How long have you worked for this company?

3. How long have you worked in the grocery industry?

4. How many coworkers do you interact with regularly?

5. How many coworkers are highly dependent on you?

6. How many work teams are you on?

7. How many work committees are you on?

Sacrifice—Community

1. Leaving this community would be very hard.

2. People respect me a lot in my community.

3. My neighborhood is safe.

Sacrifice—Organization

1. I have a lot of freedom on this job to decide how to pursue my goals.

2. The perks on this job are outstanding.

3. I feel that people at work respect me a great deal.

4. I would sacrifice a lot if I left this job.

5. My promotional opportunities are excellent here.

6. I am well compensated for my level of performance.

7. The benefits are good on this job.
8. The health-care benefits provided by this organization are excellent.
9. The retirement benefits provided by this organization are excellent.
10. The prospects for continuing employment with this company are excellent.

Continuance Commitment

(Allen & Meyer, 1990)

1. I am not afraid of what might happen if I quit my job without having another one lined up.
2. It would be very hard for me to leave my organization right now, even if I wanted to.
3. Too much in my life would be disrupted if I decided I wanted to leave my organization now.
4. It wouldn't be too costly for me to leave my organization now.
5. Right now, staying with my organization is a matter of necessity as much as desire.
6. I feel that I have too few options to consider leaving my organization.
7. One of the few serious consequences of leaving my organization would be the scarcity of available alternatives.
8. One of the major reasons I continue to work for my organizations is that leaving would require considerable personal sacrifice—another organization may not match the overall benefits I have there.

Cost of Quitting

(Part of the combined items in Hom, Griffeth & Sellaro, 1984; and Hom and Hulin, 1981)

1. How costly would it be for you to quit your present job?
2. It is easy for me to leave my present job.
3. My investment in my job is too great for me to think of quitting.

Job Investment

(General items in Rusbult & Farrell, 1983)

1. In general, how much have you invested in this job?
2. All things considered, to what extent are there activities/events/persons/objects associated with your job that you would lose if you were to leave?
3. How much does your investment in this job compare to what most people have invested in their jobs?

Person-Organization Fit

(Cable & Judge, 1996)

1. To what degree do you feel your values 'match' or fit this organization and the current employees in this organization?
2. My values match those of current employees in this organization
3. Do you think the values and 'personality' of this organization reflect your own values and personality?

Person-Organization Fit

(Saks & Ashforth, 1997)

1. To what extent does your new organization measure up to the kind of organization you were seeking?
2. To what extent are the values of the organization similar to your own values?
3. To what extent does your personality match the personality or image of the organization?
4. To what extent does the organization fulfill your needs?
5. To what extent is the organization a good match for you?

Person-Job Fit

(Saks and Ashforth, 1997)

1. To what extent do your knowledge, skills and abilities match the requirements of the job?
2. To what extent does the job fulfill your needs?
3. To what extent is the job a good match for you?
4. To what extent does the job enable you to do the kind of work you want to do?

Organizational Identity

(Mael and Ashforth, 1992)

1. When someone criticizes (name of school), it feels like a personal insult.
2. I am very interested in what others think about (name of school).
3. When I talk about this school, I usually say "we" rather then "they."
4. This school's successes are my successes.
5. When someone praises this school, it feels like a personal compliment.
6. If a story in the media criticized the school, I would feel embarrassed.

Kinship Responsibility

(Blegan et al., 1988)

1. Marital status (0 of not married at present, 1 if married)
2. Number of children (0 if not children, 1 if 1 child, 2 if more than 1 child)
3. Relatives in community (0 if no relatives in community, 1 if relatives in community)
4. Spouse's relatives in community (0 if no spouse's relatives in community, 1 if spouse's relatives in community)

Later work suggests use of more direct scaled items like:

1. Children should look after their old and/or sick parents, even if the children have to make some sacrifices.
2. It is almost unthinkable to obtain a divorce

Relocation

(Turban, Campion & Eyring, 1992)

1. Marital status
2. Whether spouse is employed
3. Number and ages of children at home (ultimately coded to 1 = children ages 15-18 [high school age] and 0 = no children under 15 or over 18)
4. Number of years they had lived in the general area

Additional measure on adjustment to move

1. My family encouraged me to accept the new job
2. Moving provides excellent career opportunities for my spouse
3. My children would adjust easily to the move

CHAPTER 8

DYNAMIC SYSTEMS IN HUMAN RESOURCE MANAGEMENT

Chaos Theory and Employee Turnover

Reidar Hagtvedt, Gregory Todd Jones, Stefan Gaertner, and Rodger Griffeth

ABSTRACT

The employee turnover process is highly complex and dynamic. One reason why traditional, linear models of turnover do not explain more than 20% of the variation of turnover may be due to this complexity, specifically the chaotic nature of the process. If this is the case, chaos theory will help to understand and control turnover. The empirical study of chaos in turnover presents certain challenges, but through simulation we may shed light on chaotic aspects of employee turnover and expose dynamic aspects of human resource management that warrant further investigation.

Innovative Theory and Empirical Research on Employee Turnover, pages 189–208

INTRODUCTION

Research related to employee turnover has focused on explaining the behavior of individuals who voluntarily terminate their relationship with an organization that had previously offered compensation in exchange for that individual's participation within the organization (Hom & Griffeth, 1995; Lee & Mitchell, 1994; March & Simon, 1958; Mobley, 1977; Price, 1977). Previous theoretical models of employee turnover have followed two basic approaches. One group, consisting largely of quantitative models, has attempted to identify the psychological constructs that are determinants to the turnover behavior (Farrell & Rusbult, 1981; Hom & Griffeth, 1995; Hom, Griffeth, & Sellaro, 1984; Hulin, Roznowski, & Hachiya, 1985; March & Simon, 1958; Mobley, 1977; Mobley, Griffeth, Hand, & Meglino, 1979; Muchinsky & Morrow, 1980; Porter & Steers, 1973; Price, 1977). A second group of qualitative models has sought to identify decision theoretic antecedents to the turnover behavior (Lee & Mitchell, 1994; Steers & Mowday, 1981).

An alternative to these viewpoints is one that recognizes that the turnover process may be dynamic. Not that there have not been previous turnover modeling efforts that have included dynamic components. Hom and Griffeth (1995) describe a number of models that are dynamic over time, including feedback effects between job satisfaction and intention to quit (Mobley, 1977) and between role conflict and role ambiguity (Kemery et al., 1985). The time series aspect of turnover is explicitly recognized in Rosse (1988), in which the conditional probability of turnover is estimated following multiple episodes of lateness. Finally, nonlinear effects are postulated in Sheridan and Abelson's Cusp Catastrophe Model of Employee Turnover (1983). In sum, the literature does not insist upon the linear models that have become prevalent empirically. Instead, these models are better regarded as first order Taylor approximations to the true turnover function. One symptom of this may be that linear models have trouble explaining more than 20% of the variation in turnover (Griffeth et al., 2000).

One possible explanation for the remaining 80% can be found in stochastic noise; however, there is the possibility that this noise may also be deterministic. Dynamic systems that exhibit deterministic noise are known as chaotic. What is chaos? Lorenz (1993) used the pinball machine to elucidate chaos theory as it applies to weather. As Lorenz pointed out, like a pinball in play, the weather is never quite stable and small changes in initial conditions can have tremendous consequences. Small changes in the pinball's weight, surface characteristics, initial velocity, and starting position will lead to substantially different trajectories. Likewise, small differences in meteorological conditions, most famously illustrated by Lorenz's butterfly flapping its wings across the ocean in the Brazilian jungle, can have enormous influence on the path of a hurricane that seems to randomly choose between coming ashore in Texas and coming ashore in Florida. In fact, chaos may be defined by dynamic systems that are sensitive to initial conditions and do not seem to settle down to an equilibrium. This may seem irrelevant to systems with a great deal of stochastic noise, but this is precisely why chaos theory may be useful. How can a researcher be certain that noise is due to random shocks rather than the result of a dynamic system without an equilibrium?

In the sequel we argue that the turnover literature, especially Sheridan and Abelson (1983), calls for an exploration of the more complex dynamics of turnover models. We illustrate and explain how chaos may have an impact and then indicate how we can address the difficult issue of applying chaos theory empirically. The chapter begins with a brief look at other disciplines in business and economics that have applied chaos to models where noise had previously been assumed to be stochastic. We then attempt an intuitive illustration of chaos using the logistic map. Employee turnover is examined from a chaos theoretic point of view and limits on predictability are considered. We next discuss the difficulties associated with empirical examination of a chaotic system and propose simulation as a solution to extracting meaning out of methodologies so data hungry as to render traditional empiricism intractable. Finally, we consider the implications of our proposals for the future of turnover research.

A BRIEF LOOK AT OTHER APPLICATIONS OF CHAOS

Naturally, the first applications of chaos theory were in the hard sciences where data is plentiful, especially physics, but studies in the social sciences have been published in the last two decades. Work has been done in both finance (see, e.g., Mandelbrot, 1999; Scheinkman & LeBaron, 1989) and economics (see, e.g., Whitby, Parker, & Tobias, 2001). An overview of what complexity has to offer the social sciences is given in Mathews et al. (1999), in which one emphasis is that the chaotic viewpoint may serve as an invaluable tool to break apart the linear paradigm that exists today. While admitting that it is very difficult to use the tools of chaos on social dynamics, the authors argue that social systems are inherently nonlinear and exhibit feedback. It is therefore highly unlikely that human systems do not exhibit chaos. The difficulty in studying the phenomenon is no excuse for avoiding the implications dynamical systems have for social interaction.

In fact the applications have been many. Whitby et al. (2001) explicate the nonlinear dynamics of duopolistic competition and apply simulation modeling to shed light on the interactions. Hayward and Preston (1999) apply chaos theory to information economics. Panas and Ninni (2000) examine the oil markets and find evidence for chaos using the BDS statistic and the Lyapunov exponent. Another example from economics is Serletis and Gogas (2000), who apply the NEGM LENNS test to find chaos in real exchange rates. More theoretical papers in economics include Bohm and Kaas (2000), who find chaos in a neoclassical one-sector economy, Goeree and Hommes (2000) who find that given general and reasonable assumptions on supply and demand, the evolutionary dynamics of the economy may exhibit chaos, and Larsen, Morecroft, and Thomsen (1999) who use simulation to demonstrate the potential for chaos in a production-distribution model.

The above examples come from the more traditionally mathematical areas of the social sciences, such as economics, management science or operations research. However, given that social systems are prime candidates for being chaotic, it would be unreasonable to state categorically that applying chaos to human interactions would be fruitless. In fact, since Dechert, Sprott, and Albers (1999) showed that most dynamical systems with even slightly unstable parameters may exhibit chaos, we may even argue that the burden of proof should be on those who would insist any given dynamic system is not chaotic.

To round out this brief overview of relevant literature, an article by van Staveren (1999) is particularly apt. The author argues that even if simulation modeling is only a metaphor, applications of chaos may still be useful. In other words, although simulations cannot provide the explanatory power of explicit models with precise functional form, unreasonable adherence to linear effects may halt true understanding of a phenomenon. After all, if a dynamical system is chaotic, it is mathematically impossible to provide a reasonable model using linear algebra.

AN ILLUSTRATION OF CHAOS USING THE LOGISTIC MAP

The logistic map is an excellent example of a potentially chaotic system because it is a simple, yet reasonable, model for an observable dynamic system. Population dynamics are often modeled using the logistic equation (Lorenz, 1993). The equation itself is quite short:

$$X_{t+1} = \alpha[X_t(1 - X_t)]$$

where X takes on values between zero and one. Therefore, typically in a population dynamics model, one would represent 100% of a maximum population, and zero would represent extinction. α is a parameter greater than zero but less than four. It does not have an interpretation per se, but the value of α determines the behavior of the logistic map. In general, a higher value of α corresponds to a greater change in X as t increases. Simulation allows us to study the behavior of the system over many iterations. From a given starting point, a value for X at time t, the simulation calculates a value for X at time t+1. Then the value of X at time t+2 is calculated based on the value of X at time t+1, and so on. We retain the entire list of values of X.

Returning to our logistic example, notice that if X is very large, then (1–X) becomes quite small. A biological interpretation of a large X in a given time period is that in the subsequent time period there are insufficient resources to sustain the population in this period due to the heavy taxing of the system. Conversely, if X initially is small, the next period's population will also be small, given a small population inability to propagate as well as a larger population, provided that the resources are available. For many values of the parameter, the model behaves very nicely, and rapidly settles down to an equilibrium value. For instance, if alpha is equal to one (1), only five hundred iterations of the logistic map for quite disparate starting points are illustrated in Figure 8.1.

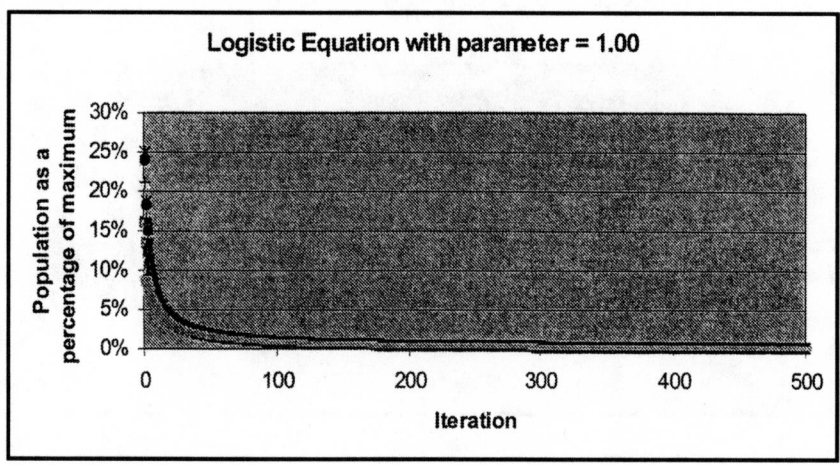

Figure 8.1.   Alpha = 1.00

As we increase alpha to a value of three (3), we see the less stable behavior illustrated in Figure 8.2.

The system slowly settles down to an equilibrium value of about 67.57% of the maximum size of the population. It is interesting to note that even after 65,530 iterations, the model had not yet reached equilibrium. For greater values of alpha, the behavior is stranger still. With an alpha equal to 3.5, the dynamic system fairly quickly settles down to jump between only four levels, in a predictable cycle (see Figure 8.3).

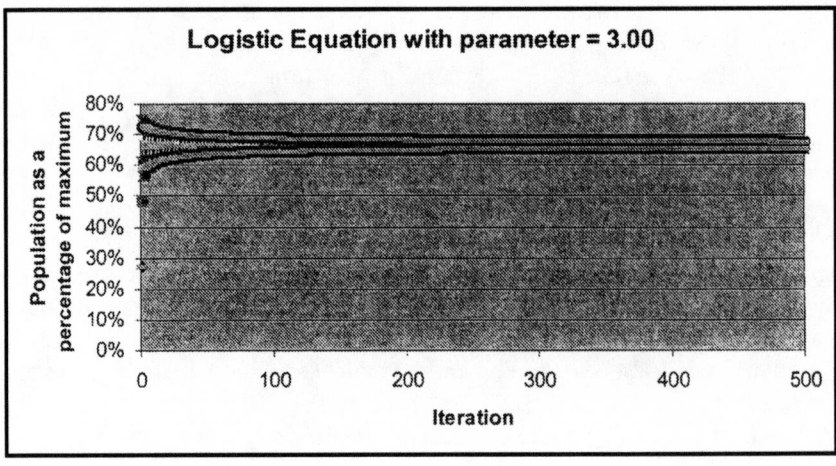

Figure 8.2.   Alpha = 3.00

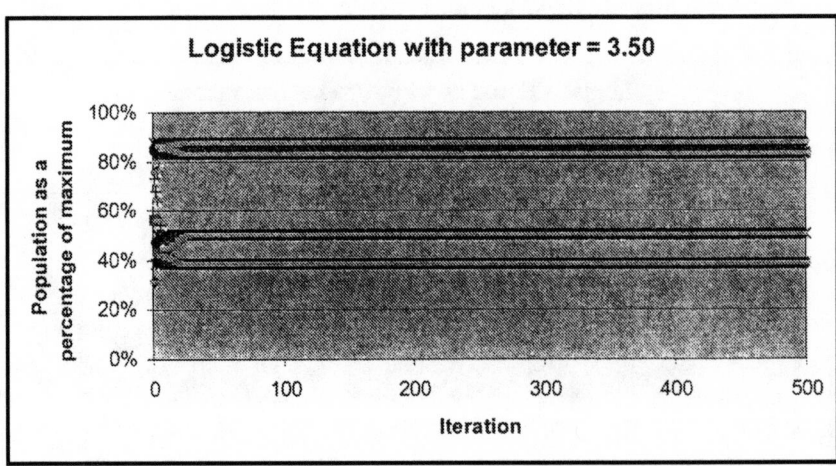

Figure 8.3.   Alpha = 3.50

If the parameter is even greater, e.g., with alpha equal to 3.90 (see Figure 8.4), there is chaos. The process does not settle down to any equilibrium at all, but moves about from close to zero to close to one, seemingly at random. Yet the system is completely deterministic, so the behavior of the population level is not the result of any random shock.

Perhaps the most interesting situation is in situations where there exist bands within which the deterministic system remains, while it is impossible to say just where within the band the system will be for any given iteration. An example of this is for alpha equal to 3.6 (see Figure 8.5).

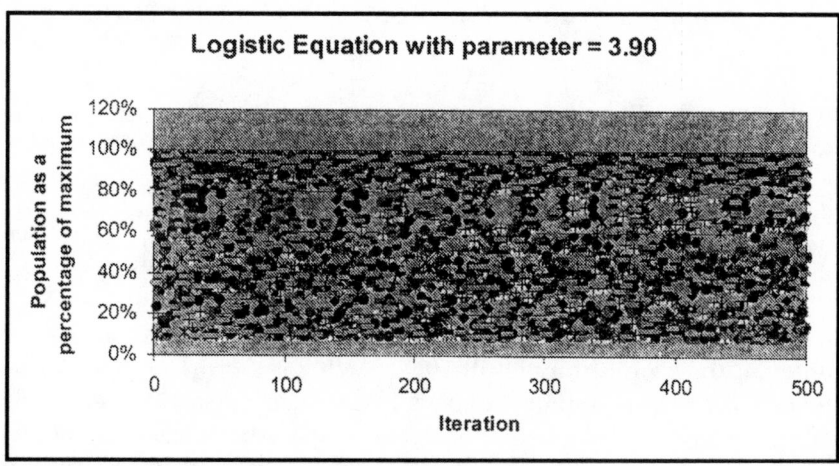

Figure 8.4.   Alpha = 3.90

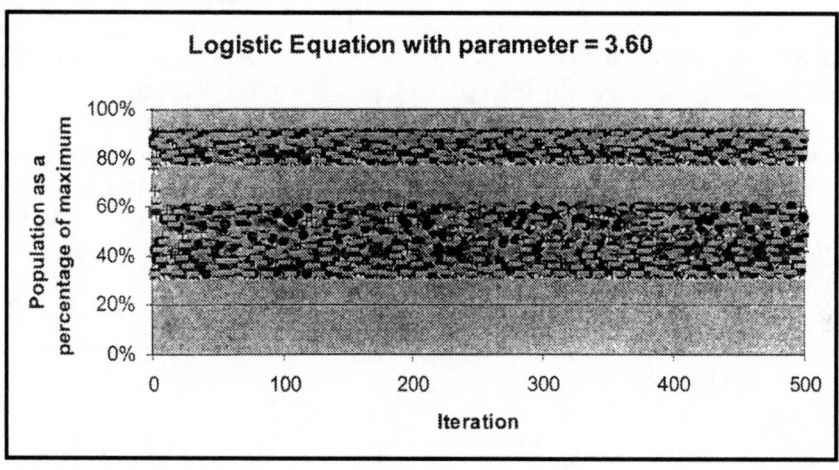

Figure 8.5.   Alpha = 3.60

In this model the population value will jump from band to band, as well as anywhere within the two bands. Naturally, this makes prediction challenging, but *not if the level of precision is to within the two bands*. In fact, we know with certainty that the system will remain within the bands. If we expand the definition of equilibrium to include such bands and call them "attractors," we find that many chaotic systems have such attractors. Most often the geometry of such attractors is very complex and if an attractor has a fractal shape, it is dubbed a "strange attractor." A fractal is an object that exhibits self-similarity. This term again means that if we examine a small part of a fractal, the part exhibits as much detail as the whole (Oliver 1992).

EMPLOYEE TURNOVER FROM A CHAOS THEORETIC
POINT OF VIEW

In modeling employee turnover, simple models with linear effects leading to a probabilistic outcome may not adequately model reality (Mathews et al., 1999). Here, we continue with Lorenz's pinball machine model, described above, to illustrate the complexity of turnover. The path of the ball is used as an analogy for the trajectory of an employee in a firm, with the final exit as leaving the firm. In pinball, an entirely deterministic input, the initial velocity of the ball, yields an extremely complex outcome. Similarly, in employee turnover, very similar starting points may yield radically different trajectories through the firm. Such a sensitivity to initial conditions is the very definition of chaos in a dynamic system (Ruelle 1989, 1991). In a dynamical system, it is necessary to have feedback and nonlinear effects in order for chaos to arise, and in the complicated world of human employment, we would expect both requirements to be met.

A more difficult hurdle is the similarity of stochastic disturbance to deterministic noise, which is another term for the presence of chaos. Given a system that exhibits chaos, the addition of stochastic noise can make it difficult to decompose the effects. In empirical studies of chaos, the sample size requirements are extreme when noise is present in systems of high dimension. This makes quantitative modeling, particularly prediction and identification of a specific functional form, infeasible. Fortunately, tools have been developed to allow us to qualitatively describe chaos, even in the presence of stochastic noise (Ellner et al., 1992; Sugihara & May, 1991).

In the case of turnover models, it has been suggested that a number of variables cause employee quit behavior (Kim et al., 1996). It is a small step to consider an employee a vector of such variables, where the values of the variables change over time.

$$
V_t = \begin{bmatrix} JobMotivation_t \\ Stress_t \\ JobSatisfaction_t \\ OrganizationalCommitment_t \end{bmatrix} = v(V_{t-1})
$$

We have left out most of the relevant variables, but the idea is that an employee's situation, as captured by the vector V_t is driven in part by V_{t-1}. In addition, of course, changes in parameters, both with regards to work and other responsibilities, as well as random shocks to the system, will also have an impact on an employee's tendency to quit voluntarily. We can imagine a function T_t for turnover such that the function takes on the value zero as long as the employee remains with the employer, and one if the employee quits:

$$T_t = T_t(V_{t-1}, u_t)$$

where u_t is the only variable undefined, and it is assumed to be a vector of random shocks.

Describing turnover in such a general functional form allows a number of important deviations from the linear structural models that have become the norm in turnover research. First, the impact from the previous period may be nonlinear. In other words, for some values of OrganizationalCommitment, an employee will remain regardless of stress level. If the OrganizationalCommitment decreases, stress levels that would otherwise be unimportant may be enough to cause turnover. In addition to such interaction effects, the direct impact of inputs such as stress may also have nonlinear effects. Perhaps a little stress is actually helpful; a wide band of different stress levels has no impact on turnover, but once a threshold is crossed, stress alone may drive turnover. Second, the level of JobSatisfaction and other variables from one period directly impact the variables in the future. This means there exists feedback in the system. Third, the noise vector, u_t, is an independent variable of the function for turnover. This means that noise is not assumed to be of the simplest possible form, i.e., linear, but may be multiplicative, it may interact with other variables, or perturb the system in a number of ways.

The main purpose of this notation is to point out that it is an extremely strong assumption to assert that the effects of antecedents on turnover are purely linear and the effect of noise is additive. While it is true that there is an enormous amount of noise in the linear statistical models, to decide that the model must be so simply because we do not have the data to test it is to ignore very real potential to elucidate phenomena in the social sciences. At best, it is convenient to assume linear effects with additive noise. At worst, such assumptions obscure the issues and hinder progress. This is not to say that empirical testing of models in the social sciences is easy, but it is possible to posit reasonable models, and simulate. The resulting data sets, like the simulated data sets derived from the logistic equation described above, are clearly amenable to analysis.

LIMITS OF PREDICTABILITY

In a stochastic system, confidence intervals for predictions grow exponentially larger. In a model with deterministic chaos, the system will typically converge to what is called a *strange attractor* (Mullin, 1993) (recall the bands in the logistic illustration above) and remain in that region indefinitely. This means short-term predictability may be awful, but it also implies that long-term predictability may be quite good, provided that knowing that the system will remain within the strange attractor is useful information.

We can illustrate a strange attractor using a phase diagram. The value of X_t is graphed as a function of X_{t-1} rather than over time. Surprisingly, even with a parameter equal to 3.60 and the systems seeming to wander over much of the map, we find that such a phase diagram reveals a great deal of order (see Figure 8.6).

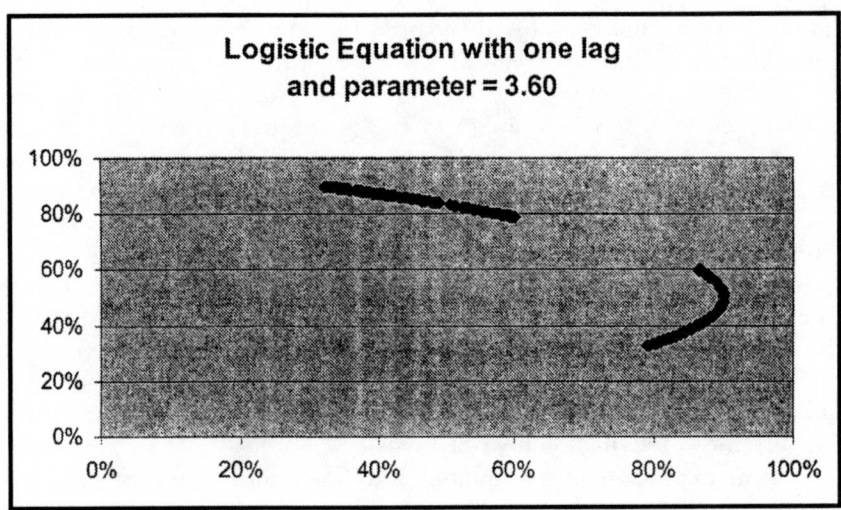

Figure 8.6.

Even if we increase the parameter to 3.9, when the system truly does seem to have no structure at all, a very similar order appears in the phase diagram (see Figure 8.7).

This is a picture of the strange attractor. No matter what, the system will not leave this area. The difficulty is that only with infinite precision will one be able to predict very far into the future, since every point is arbitrarily close to another that will lead to any other part of the strange attractor. This seeming breakdown in common sense and continuity may be the reason why chaos theory is so difficult to grasp. The fact that it was impossible to experiment with thousands of iterations before the advent of computers also slowed development. In examining any chaotic system, it is therefore important to study two characteristics. The first characteristic is the unpredictability of a system in the short run, and the second is the dimensionality of the strange attractor. Measuring these qualities of dynamical systems requires unusual tools.

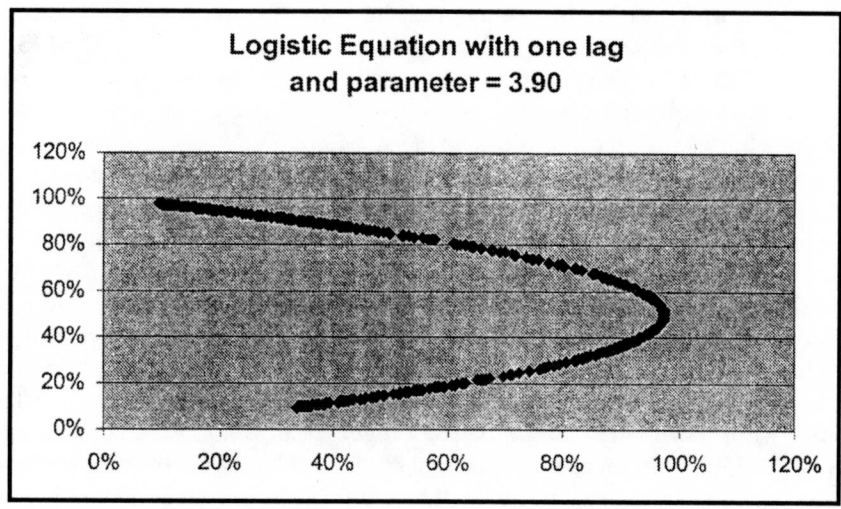

Figure 8.7.

EXAMINING A CHAOTIC SYSTEM

It may seem paradoxical that a fully deterministic system of equations could exhibit behavior so difficult to predict that quantitative descriptions, and especially predictions, have to be given up as impossible. Instead, qualitative measures that indicate the degree to which the system is unpredictable or how large a space the system inhabits are what must be relied upon to characterize the model. However, such satisficing is not alien to analytic decision making. These measures are similar in kind to a sample standard deviation, which, after all, is a measure of the quality of variability in a system with stochastic noise.

In the presence of only deterministic noise, it is critical to remember that there is no stochastic component. Therefore, given infinite precision, predictions infinitely far into the future are not only possible, they are trivial. But if a system is chaotic, arbitrarily close starting points will relatively quickly produce completely divergent trajectories. The *Lyapunov Exponent* (Frøyland, 1992) is a measure of how quickly two points that are indistinguishable will diverge completely. This measure is directly linked to "the rate at which information is lost."

The other main type of qualitative measure characterizes the space a process moves through. As mentioned above, if a process has entered a strange attractor, it will remain there. The link between chaos and fractals is that the shape of the attractor will typically be a fractal (Mullin, 1993), i.e., have non-integer dimension. Fractals were discovered and explored by

Mandelbrot in a series of papers published after computers made it possible to experiment with long-running algorithms (Mandelbrot, 1977, 1982, 1985, 1999). Fractals became very interesting to the public as it was discovered that familiar objects such as the coastline of Britain or the outline of clouds have a fractal dimension.

This perhaps begs the question of what is meant by dimension. The Euclidean dimension is the common idea behind a room being three-dimensional. A shoelace twisted about in a room would also be imbedded in a three-dimensional Euclidean space, but if the shoelace had no width and was stretched out, it would form a line segment. Such a line segment is of course one-dimensional. A dimensional measure of an object that is "stretched out" is referred to as its topological dimension. It is between these two dimensions where one will find various definitions of fractal dimension (Peitgen & Saupe, 1988; Peitgen et al., 1992). The idea is that both the extreme measures of dimension, Euclidean and Topological, say something about the amount of space an object occupies, yet neither is wholly satisfactory. A common substitute is the *correlation dimension* (Grass-berger & Procaccia, 1983), which is one measure of fractal dimension. We can readily imagine a fractional dimension. Take for example a sheet of paper that most people would define to be two-dimensional. Fold the paper in half, but leave it folded so that the creasing angle is ninety degrees. Then the paper is more than two-dimensional, but it does not really fill three-dimensional space either. Strange attractors, as it turns out, have fractal dimension.

To return to the pinball metaphor for turnover, we envision an employee's path through a company or career to be driven by stochastic and deterministic noise, in addition to the conventional drivers. The basins of attraction for a person's path may have fractal dimension and be a strange attractor. In addition, similar paths may diverge explosively after a very short time. Thus, a career path may be considered chaotic. The logical next question is whether or not it is possible to separate this chaos from simple random noise.

DETERMINISTIC NOISE, STOCHASTIC NOISE, AND SIMULATION

In stark contrast to a chaotic system, the moon travels around the earth in a predictable, stable, orbit. The orbit is a simple attractor and prediction is straightforward. In this situation there is neither chaos nor stochastic noise. With a purely chaotic system, by comparison, extreme short-term prediction will be possible, but in the long run all we can say is that the system will remain within the strange attractor. A system with only stochastic noise, on the other hand, can be predicted with a certain amount of confidence, but the predictability decreases exponentially the further into the future we attempt to predict. The worst possible scenario for prediction is when both deterministic and stochastic noise are present.

If a stochastic noise term is added to a chaotic system, naturally it becomes even more difficult to predict future paths that may be taken (Ellner et al., 1992). Yet the most natural case for a deterministic system would be to have some component of randomness. This has implications for the predictability of the system. Provided the stochastic component is not so large as to drive the chaotic system completely away from the strange attractor, little is lost in terms of prediction. The best possible prediction will still be that the process will remain somewhere within the basin of attraction. If the disturbance may be so great that the process ceases to be chaotic, then little predictability is lost due to the additive noise.

Similarly, since a chaotic system can only be controlled up to a limit, little control is lost by adding a stochastic noise term. There are two methods we can imagine controlling a chaotic system. Either the parameters of the system can be changed to move the process into a non-chaotic orbit, or we can nudge the trajectory of the path itself (Kapitaniak, 1996; Pyragas, 1992). In a human resources context, examples would be changing the benefits package that all employees have access to, and insisting that a given employee serve a term overseas, respectively.

In this way, the qualities of dynamical systems are useful for theoretically characterizing a nonlinear system. However, without empirical testing the usefulness of chaos theory to the sciences is extremely limited. We therefore turn now to the data needed to study chaos and the measures we can calculate from the data.

SIMULATION AS A SOLUTION FOR EMPIRICALLY MODELING CHAOS

The qualitative concepts briefly described above may be useful in the sense that they shed metaphorical light on chaotic aspects of turnover. However, empirical study of chaos is significantly more difficult and has, in fact, evolved into a sub-discipline of its own (Abarbanel, 1996; Tsonis, 1992). In order to study chaotic aspects of turnover we would need both sample statistics and an appropriate data set. The problem with data is perhaps obvious: in order to tease out the necessary nonlinear relationships, we would need prohibitively large data sets. As an example, for consistent estimates of some measures of fractal dimension, 200,000 observations or more are needed (Scheinkman & LeBaron, 1989). A fortunate simplification is provided by Takens, who showed that if a large enough number of lags are included in the calculations, lagged data will exhibit the same dynamical invariants as the output variable with inputs (Takens, 1981).

The alternative approach is to assume certain functional forms and simulate. As with the logistic equation described above, this means iterating an equation a large number of times and observing the characteristics of the resulting data set. Such simulations were pioneered by Mandelbrot (1977). Based on such simulations, we can calculate qualitative measures that will help identify regions of parameter space that may be called chaotic. This appears to be a more promising approach for the social sciences, where extremely large data sets are few and far between. The measures of dimension and sensitivity to initial conditions can then be calculated based on the simulated data.

Simulation is used quite often in the physical sciences, and it is not surprising that the tool may shed light on social scientific phenomena as well. Yet, many researchers in the social sciences appear to feel that chaos theory has little to contribute based on simulations. Such researchers argue that stochastic noise, even in a simple additive form, adequately models disturbance. The prevalence of ordinary least squares regression is excellent testimony to this perceived success of the general linear model with additive noise. Nevertheless, the study of dynamic systems may shed light on some phenomena that exhibit nonlinear effects and feedback. Importantly, the conclusions we may draw using chaos theory are qualitatively different from the type of conclusions we may reach using linear statistical models. In particular, it may surprise a researcher in the social sciences that many posited models exhibit chaos for certain values of the parameters (Dendrinos & Sonis, 1990; Frøyland, 1992; Trippi, 1995). In such a situation a feasible next step is to simulate and note whether or not the dynamic model approaches equilibrium, appears to be completely unstable, or orbits within some limited space, even though it may be difficult to adequately describe that space.

In the following we will assume that we have a possible functional form with a specified vector of variables:

$$X_t = \begin{bmatrix} x_{1,t} \\ x_{2,t} \\ \dots \\ x_{n,t} \end{bmatrix}$$

We will further assume that X_t is a function of X_{t-1}, in a nonlinear way. When a model is nonlinear and exhibits feedback, there is the potential for chaos. A particularly relevant example is Sheridan and Abelson's Cusp model of employee turnover (Sheridan & Abelson, 1983):

$$W_t = \beta_0 + \beta_1 W_{t-1}^3 + \beta_2 W_{t-1}^2 + \beta_3 (T_{t-1} W_{t-1}) + \beta_4 C_{t-1} + \beta_5 T_{t-1}$$

where W = Withdrawal Behavior, T = Job Tension and C = Group Cohesion.

The purpose of this model is to suggest there may be a bifurcation in the response surface to the drivers: Job Tension and Organizational Commitment. However, the suggested function for withdrawal may exhibit chaos because there are both feedback and nonlinearity in the model. One possible way to assess the degree to which there may be chaos in the model would be to simulate.

Once a data set has been simulated with a large number of iterations, it remains to check if the trajectory of the model exhibits chaos. Simply graphing the models is often instructive, as for the logistic map example above. A graph of X_t with itself one lag prior is called a phase plot. Another graphical approach is to construct a Poincare section (Frøyland, 1992). This is especially useful if the vector we are observing has more than one dimension. A Poincare section is a plot of the points of the trajectory along only two of the variables' dimensions. If the resulting plot has a pattern, this is evidence of something more orderly that stochastic noise. For instance, if we imagine a large piece of paper with the Earth in the middle and let the Moon make a hole in the paper each time its orbit intersected our graph, we would rapidly note that the Moon essentially goes through the same two holes in each orbit around the Earth. Hence, we can conclude that the Moon's position is neither stochastic nor chaotic.

However, it is also of interest to develop more formal methods, for those instances where there is doubt. There are two steps, both of which are empirically tested in Barnett et al. (1997). One approach the authors recommended after testing the different methods was to first use the BDS test, in which the null hypothesis is that the process is linear. This test is based on Grassberger and Procaccia's correlation dimension (Grassberger & Procaccia, 1983) and developed by Brock et al. (1987) and Brock and Baek (1991). The correlation dimension is one measure of the dimension of the space a process moves through. Although it is true that chaotic processes tend to move within strange attractors with non-integer dimensions, the test itself can only be used to reject the null hypothesis of linearity. Barnett et al. (1997) nevertheless recommended beginning with the BDS test because it is much more straightforward to use than a method that directly tests for the presence of chaos.

It is useful to keep in mind the definition of chaos: sensitivity to initial conditions. In words, this means that even infinitesimally different starting points quickly lead to paths that seem to be totally unrelated. This is obviously not true when someone throws a baseball. If the speed, angle or weight of the ball is changed only slightly, then the divergence of paths will be very slight, as well. In fact, if this were not true, it would be impossible to play the game. The logistic map, however, shows that there exist systems in which arbitrarily small differences in starting conditions lead to completely different trajectories. How quickly two paths diverge is one measure of chaos. Wolf et al. (1985) developed the first algorithm to measure what is called the maximal Lyapunov exponent. This Lyapunov exponent measures the speed at which two processes converge or diverge, and it is scaled so that a positive exponent indicates chaos.

Unfortunately, Wolf's algorithm is sensitive to stochastic noise, so Nychka et al. (1992) developed the Lyapunov Exponent for Noisy Nonlinear Series test (LENNS). This test not only allows for additive noise, but non-additive noise within the function and changing levels of noise. Barnett et al. (1997) recommend that researchers apply LENNS to those series that the BDS test first found to be nonlinear because of the tremendous computing resources LENNS requires.

If LENNS indicates that the simulated series is based on a chaotic model, clearly this has implications for the research. For one thing, long-term predictability is difficult. Second, traditional comparative statics or comparative dynamics based on derivatives become almost meaningless. This is because such comparative dynamics indicate what would happen if the process continued for one more infinitesimal moment. However, the assumption is that this moment may be fruitfully expanded to, e.g., one time period, perhaps a day or a month. In a chaotic system one could use comparative dynamics with validity for only an infinitesimal period of time, which clearly would limit applicability.

On the other hand, the presence of chaos would show that there are limits to how useful a statistical model could possibly be. In spite of a perfect model and limited stochastic noise, it may be impossible to model turnover so that more than, e.g., 20% of the variation is explained. If the parameter space is adequately mapped for chaos, however, and chaos is something to be avoided, then a simulation that maps "pockets of chaos" may be helpful in selecting parameters that avoid chaos. In the human resources context, such parameters may be pay, length of vacation, benefits, etc. In fact, it may not be that more pay or more vacation days will bring a seemingly chaotic system into a stable orbit—perhaps the opposite is true. Regardless of the direction of the effect, mapping the potential of chaos to erupt in turnover models may be useful.

It is clear that chaotic systems pose a difficult challenge for empirical research in the social sciences. The sample size requirements alone almost preclude meaningful analysis of data-sets (Abarbanel, 1996). However, when models are simulated an extremely large data set is available at the cost of some computer time. Hence it would be useful to consider the following steps when assessing the potential for chaos:

1. Examine the functional form to see if there are nonlinear effects and if feedback loops are present. If so, there is at least the potential for chaos. Conversely, if not, the proposed model cannot be chaotic.

2. Simulate the proposed model and graph the trajectories. If the trajectories settle into a region of the state space that is difficult to describe, perhaps a strange attractor, there is a possibility that the system is chaotic.

3. Use the BDS test to see if the model is truly nonlinear if the data is empirical. This is clearly not necessary if the data is simulated based on a nonlinear model. If the model is nonlinear, apply the LENNS test for chaos.

The results from the LENNS test have implications to the qualitative as well as the quantitative conclusions drawn. In particular, comparative dynamics are suspect in the presence of chaos.

IMPLICATIONS

Given the complexity of human interactions, it would be arrogant to assume that chaos could not arise in the dynamical system that is constitutes employees and firms. Given that we have nonlinear effects and feedback, some instances of deterministic chaos are virtually guaranteed. The difficulty is in identifying and handling the chaos.

Since very large sample sizes are needed in order to reliably estimate the BDS statistic and the Lyapunov Exponent, a far more reasonable approach is to take simpler models of interaction and simulate. If the simulations indicate that for some ranges of the parameter values chaotic effects may occur, there are implications to decisions regarding the parameters and monitoring of the process. There are several ways to address such a challenge.

Assuming that better predictability is desirable, the firm can take steps to avoid the type of system that exhibits chaos. In terms of turnover, this may mean altering salary or benefits packages so that there is more predictability in the system as a whole. Another method for handling chaos would be to move employees that exhibit unpredictable behavior to another, more stable, location. The implications of chaos to turnover naturally must come after identification of the chaotic aspects of turnover, if indeed there are any to be discovered.

REFERENCES

Abarbanel, H.D.I. (1996). *Analysis of observed chaotic data.* New York: Springer.

Barnett, W.A., Gallant, A.R., Hinich, M.J., Jungeilges, J.A., Kaplan, D.T., & Jensen, M.J. (1997). A single-blind controlled competition among tests for nonlinearity and chaos. *Journal of Econometrics, 82,* 157–192.

Bohm, V., & Kaas, L. (2000). Differential savings, factor shares, and endogenous growth cycles. *Journal of Economic Dynamics & Control, 24*(5–7), 965–980.

Brock, W.A., & Baek, E.G. (1991). Some theory of statistical inference for nonlinear science. *Review of Economics Studies, 58,* 697–716.

Brock, W.A., Dechert, W.D., & Scheinkman, J.A. (1987). *A test for independence based on the correlation dimension.* Madison: University of Wisconsin.

Dechert, W.D., Sprott, J.C., & Albers, D.J. (1999). On the probability of chaos in large dynamical systems: A Monte Carlo study. *Journal of Economic Dynamics & Control, 23*(8), 1197–1206.

Dendrinos, D.S., & Sonis, M., (1990). *Chaos and socio-spatial dynamics.* New York: Springer.

Ellner, S., Nychka, D.W., & Gallant, A.R. (1992). *LENNS, a program to estimate the dominant Lyapunov exponent of noisy nonlinear systems from time series data.* Raleigh: North Carolina State University.

Farrell, A.D. & Rusbult, C.E. (1981). Exchange variables as predictors of job satisfaction, job commitment, and turnover: The impact of rewards, costs, alternatives, and investments. *Organizational Behavior and Human Performance, 28,* 78–95.

Frøyland, J. (1992). *Introduction to chaos and coherence.* New York: Institute of Physics Publishing.

Goeree, J., K. & Hommes, C.H. (2000). Heterogeneous beliefs and the non-linear cobweb model. *Journal of Economic Dynamics & Control, 24*(5–7), 761–798.

Grassberger, P., & Procaccia, I. (1983). Characterization of strange attractors. *Phys.Rev.Lett., 50,* 346–349.

Griffeth, R.W., Hom, P.W., & Gaertner, S. (2000). A meta-analysis of antecedents and correlates of employee turnover: Update, moderator tests, and research implications for the next millennium. *Journal of Management, 26*(3), 463–488.

Hayward, T., & Preston, J. (1999). Chaos theory, economics and information: The implications for strategic decision-making, *Journal of Information Science, 25*(3), 173–182.

Hom, P.W., & Griffeth, R.W. (1995). *Employee turnover.* Cincinnati, OH: South-Western.

Hom, P.W., Griffeth, R.W., & Sellaro, C.L. (1984). The validity of Mobley's 1977 model of employee turnover. *Organizational Behavior and Human Performance, 34,* 141–174.

Hulin, C.L., Roznowski, M., & Hachiya, D. (1985). Alternative opportunities and withdrawal decisions: empirical and theoretical discrepancies and an integration. *Psychological Bulletin, 97,* 233–250.

Kapitaniak, T. (1996). *Controlling chaos.* San Diego, CA: Academic Press.

Kemery, E.R., Bedeian, A.G., Mossholder, K.W., & Touliatos, J. (1985). Outcomes of role stress: A multisample constructive replication. *Academy of Management Journal, 28*(2), 363–75.

Kim, S., Price, J.L., Mueller, C.W., & Watson, T.W. (1996). The determinants of career intent among physicians at a U.S. Air Force hospital. *Human Relations, 49*, 947–975.

Larsen, E.R., Morecroft, J.D.W., & Thomsen, J.S. (1999), Complex behavior in a production-distribution model. *European Journal of Operational Research, 119*(1), 61–74.

Lee, T.W., & Mitchell, T.R. (1994). An alternative approach: The unfolding model of voluntary employee turnover. *Academy of Management Review, 19*, 51–89.

Lorenz, E. (1993). *The essence of chaos.* Seattle: University of Washington Press.

Mandelbrot, B.B. (1977). *Fractals, form, chance, and dimension.* San Francisco: W.H. Freeman.

Mandelbrot, B.B. (1982). *The fractal geometry of nature.* San Francisco: W.H. Freeman.

Mandelbrot, B.B. (1985). Self-affine fractals and fractal dimension. *Physica Scripta, 32*, 257–260.

Mandelbrot, B.B. (1999, February). A multifractal walk down Wall Street. *Scientific American*, 70–73.

March, J.G., & Simon, H.A. (1958). *Organizations.* New York: Wiley.

Mathews, K.M., White, M.C., & Long, R.G. (1999). Why study the complexity sciences in the social sciences? *Organization Theory Studies, 52*(4), 439–462.

Mobley, W.H. (1977). Intermediate linkages in the realtionhsip between job satisfaction and employee turnover. *Journal of Applied Psychology, 62*, 237–240.

Mobley, W.H., Griffeth, R.W., Hand, H.H., & Meglino, B.M. (1979). Review and conceptual analysis of the employee turnover process. *Psychological Bulletin, 86*, 493–522.

Mobley, W.H., Horner, S.O., & Hollingsworth, A.T. (1978). An evaluation of precursors or hospital employee turnover. *Journal of Applied Psychology, 63*(4), 408.

Muchlinsky, P.M., & Morrow, P.C. (1980). A multidisciplinary model of voluntary employee turnover. *Journal of Vocational Behavior, 17*(3), 263–290.

Mullin, T. (1993). A dynamical systems approach to times series. In T. Mullins (Ed.), *The nature of chaos* (pp. 23–50). Oxford: Clarendon Press.

Nychka, D., Ellner, S., Gallant, A.R., & McCaffrey, D. (1992). Finding chaos in noisy systems. *Journal of the Royal Statistical Society (B), 54*(2), 399–426.

Oliver, D. (1992). *FractalVision: Put fractals to work for you.* Carmel, IN: Sams Publishing.

Panas, E., & Ninni, V. (2000), Are oil markets chaotic? A non-linear dynamic analysis. *Energy Economics, 22*(5), 549–568.

Peitgen, H.O., Jurgens, H., & Saupe, D. (1992). *Chaos.* New York: Springer-Verlag.

Peitgen, H.O., & Saupe, D. (Eds.). (1988). *The science of fractal images.* New York: Springer-Verlag.

Porter, L.W., & Steers, R.M. (1973). Organizational, work, and personal factors in employee turnover and absenteeism. *Psychological Bulletin, 80*, 151–76.

Price, J.L. (1977). *The study of turnover.* Ames: Iowa State University Press.

Pyragas, K. (1992). Continuous control of chaos by self-controlling feedback. *Physics Letters A, 170*, 421–428.

Rosse, J.G. (1988). Relations among lateness, absence, and turnover: Is there a progression of withdrawal? *Human Relations, 41*, 517–31.

Ruelle, D. (1989). *Chaotic evolution and strange attractors: The statistical analysis of time series for deterministic nonlinear systems.* Cambridge: Cambridge University Press.

Ruelle, D. (1991). *Chance and chaos.* Princeton, NJ: Princeton University Press.

Scheinkman, J., & LeBaron, B. (1989). Nonlinear dynamics and stock returns. *Journal of Business, 62*(3), 311–338.

Serletis, A., & Gogas, P. (2000), Purchasing power parity, nonlinearity and chaos, *Applied Financial Economics, 10*(6), 615–622.

Sheridan, J.E., & Abelson, M.A. (1983). Cusp catastrophe model of employee turnover. *Academy of Management Journal, 26*, 418–36.

Staveren, I.(1999). Chaos theory and institutional economics: Metaphor or model. *Journal of Economic Issues, 33*(1),141–167.

Steers, R.M., & Mowday, R.T. (1981). Employe turnover and postdecision accommodation processes. In L.L. Cummings & B.M. Staw (Eds.), *Research in organizational behavior* (Vol. 3, pp. 235–281). Greenwich, CT: JAI Press.

Sugihara, G., & May, R.M. (1991). Nonlinear forecasting as a way of distinguishing chaos from measurement error in time series. *Nature, 344*, 737–741.

Takens, F. (1981). Dynamical systems and turbulence. *Lecture notes in mathematics* (Vol. 898). New York: Springer.

Trippi, R.R. (Ed.). (1995). *Chaos & nonlinear dynamics in the financial markets.* Chicago: Irwin Professional Publishing.

Tsonis, A.A. (1992). *Chaos: From theory to applications.* New York: Plenum Press.

Whitby, S., Parker, D., & Tobias, A. (2001). Non-linear dynamics and duopolistic competetion: A R&D model and simulation. *Journal of Business Research, 51*(3),179–191.

Wolf, A., Swift, J., Swinney, H., & Vastano, J. (1985). Determining Lyapunov exponents from a time series. *Physica D, 16.*

part IV

GENERALIZING TURNOVER THEORY AND RESEARCH TO NEGLECTED POPULATIONS

CHAPTER 9

ON THE RELATIONSHIP BETWEEN RACE AND TURNOVER

Loriann Roberson

ABSTRACT

Prevailing theoretical models in OB suggest that turnover will be higher for racioethnic minorities than for whites, but empirical evidence regarding this relationship is sparse and inconclusive. This chapter considers five potential moderators of the race-turnover link: job level, demographic composition of the work group, tenure and career stage, ethnicity and racial identity attitudes, and organizational climate for diversity. Implications for future research are discussed.

INTRODUCTION

Although widely discussed, the relationship between racioethnicity and turnover has not been extensively studied by organizational scholars (Nkomo, 1992). However, prevailing theoretical views in Organizational Behavior (OB) assert that because of discrimination, either real or per-

Innovative Theory and Empirical Research on Employee Turnover, pages 211–229

ceived, members of racioethnic minority groups are more likely to quit their jobs than their white majority counterparts. This belief is commonly found in discussions of diversity and diversity management (e.g., Arvey, Azevedo, Ostgaard, & Raghuram, 1996; Gomez-Mejia, Balkin, & Cardy, 2001; Robinson & Dechant, 1997). Given the belief in their higher quit rates, organizational scientists have speculated about the various contributions to minority turnover. Hom and Griffeth (1995) summarized popular speculations in a model depicted in Figure 9.1. These factors are generally believed to influence turnover through decreased job satisfaction and organizational commitment, leading to turnover intentions (Valentine, 2001). Because dissatisfying working conditions are hypothesized as more prevalent for minorities than whites, turnover for the former group is also expected to be higher.

Although the direct race-turnover link has not often been examined empirically, racioethnic group differences in turnover determinants have nonetheless received research attention. Research for the last 10–15 years on the antecedents listed in the Hom-Griffeth model has revealed racioethnic differences in experienced antecedent levels and such differences translate into group differences in job performance and career advancement (Roberson & Block, 2001). Compared to quit rates, statistics demonstrating racioethnic group differences on promotions, position levels, and salaries are widely available.

But do these factors also result in racioethnic group differences in turnover rates? Several influential articles published in the 1990s argued that they do. The Federal Glass Ceiling Commission (1995) named turnover costs as one of the important consequences of the glass ceiling for minorities, citing a report from Corning Glass, who for the period 1980–1987 found turnover rates for African Americans to be two and one-half times that for whites. Interviews with CEOs conducted for the report revealed

Figure 9.1.   Model of potential causes of turnover among minorities.
Source: Adapted from P. Hom & R. Griffeth (1996). Employee turnover. Cincinnatti, OH: Southwestern.

their concerns with retaining Black male managers. The report concluded that for Black males, "the attrition rate at the executive-trainee and middle management levels is high" (p. 66). In addition, the loss of Asian and Pacific Islander Americans to overseas enterprises and independent entrepreneurs (especially in electronics) was noted. However, this report failed to furnish data to support these conclusions, although this report documented the existence of glass ceiling effects by demonstrating group differences in earnings and in the percentages of different racioethnic groups in management positions. Similarly, Cox (1994) argued that turnover was higher for minorities than for whites, citing a 1968 study as well as the aforementioned Corning Glass report. These actual same figures were repeated by Cox and Blake (1991), who have been commonly cited by others to support the statement that turnover is higher among minorities than whites (Gomez-Mejia et al., 2001; Valentine, 2001).

Other evidence of a higher turnover rate for racioethnic minorities is anecdotal. Jones (1986) gave several examples of African American managers who had resigned due to frustration over biased evaluations and lack of advancement. Case studies of organizations who developed diversity programs as a response to concerns over minority retention are provided by Jamison and O'Mara (1991) and Thomas (1990). And still other authors mention problems with retention of racioethnic minorities, with no supporting data or citation (e.g., Arvey et al., 1996; Harris & DeSimone, 1994; Kram & Hall, 1996).

Thus, empirical evidence for racioethnic group differences in turnover appears to be sparce, and fails to indicate a strong relationship between race and quit behavior. To illustrate, Griffeth, Hom, and Gaertner (2000), in their meta-analysis of the antecedents of turnover, found only seven out of more than 50 organizational studies conducted in the 1990s that investigated race-turnover links (this meta-analysis included only studies yielding race-turnover correlations for aggregation and thus excluded tests omitting correlations.) No significant relationship was found; the corrected correlation between race (coded as white/nonwhite) and turnover was .01. A literature search for studies conducted since Griffeth et al. revealed four studies that examined racioethnic differences in either actual turnover or intent to leave. In line with Griffeth et al.'s findings, the results of these studies were evenly split in the direction of group differences found. Baldwin (2000) found higher turnover for minority than white Air Force officers. Likewise, Valentine (2001) reported higher intent to search among nonwhite than white workers. By contrast, Sightler and Adams (1999) reported higher turnover among white than nonwhite part time workers. Higher turnover among whites than nonwhites was also found by Ghiselli, Lopa, and Bai (2001) among food service managers. Thus, supportive evidence in favor of the prevailing beliefs about higher quit rates among racioethnic minorities remains unclear.

Apart from ambiguous findings, other theoretical perspectives from labor economics challenge dominant OB models of turnover that presume racioethnic minorities are prone to leave due to their higher job dissatisfaction or weaker organizational commitment. These economic models of turnover predict the opposite effect: that turnover rates of whites exceed those of nonwhites. These theories propose that if racial discrimination occurs in hiring, employees of color must search not only for a typical job match, but also for a racial job match (i.e., a nondiscriminatory employer). As there are fewer of these acceptable jobs, the costs of job search increase and the probability of finding an acceptable alternative job decreases. Thus, prospective leavers must search more firms. As a result, such costly job searches reduce the propensity for minority employees to quit (Black, 1995; Whatley & Sedo, 1998). In support of this model, Whatley and Sedo (1998) analyzed employment data from 1913–1944 and found that African American males, particularly married men, were less likely to turnover than white workers. The Sightler and Adams (1999) and Ghiselli et al. (2001) studies cited above also support this model's predictions.

All the same, if the Griffeth et al. (2000) meta-analysis represents the most accurate estimate of the race-turnover relationship, then neither the economic nor organizational behavior models have clear-cut support. Yet the results of Griffeth et al. also revealed significant variance in the correlations that was not explained by sampling error and scale unreliability. In other words, moderators of the race-turnover link were possible. Although the small number of studies precluded empirical estimation of moderator effects, Griffeth et al. (2000) suggested two variables: specific racioethnic group membership and the demographic composition of the work group that might moderate the race-turnover link. The purpose of this chapter is to explore these and other moderators suggested by both the OB and economic models. In this chapter, five potential moderators of the race-turnover link are considered: job level, demographic composition of the work group, tenure and career stage, ethnicity and racial identity attitudes, and organizational climate for diversity.

JOB LEVEL

Both OB and economic models suggest that job level may function as a moderator of the race-turnover link. Perceived job alternatives and economic opportunities are pivotal explanatory constructs in leading OB and economic models of turnover (Hom & Griffeth, 1995). Because most turnover models are derived from March and Simon's (1958) earliest formulation, these perspectives presume that job dissatisfaction (perceived desirability of movement) and perceived employment opportunities (perceived ease of movement) jointly determine turnover (cf. Lee & Mitchell, 1994). Given their demographic scarcity in the labor market, racioethnic minority managers and professionals are often heavily recruited by other firms to support corporate diversity initiatives or comply with affirmative action edicts. Such superior job opportunities allow dissatisfied incumbents to readily translate their dissatisfaction into exits. In addition, those at higher levels may be likely to receive more unsolicited job offers via their more extensive professional networks. According to the unfolding model of turnover (Mitchell & Lee, 2001), such unsolicited job offers can constitute a "shock" that may prompt thoughts of quitting and evaluations of the utility of leaving the current job even in the absence of job dissatisfaction.

Unfortunately, there is no clear evidence of an interaction between race and job level on turnover, although the two variables are rarely studied together. Whatley and Sedo (1998), Light and Ureta (1992) and Sightler and Adams (1999) all studied lower level jobs, finding higher turnover for whites than minorities. However, in a sample of food service managers (whose job levels varied), Ghiselli et al. (2001) also found higher turnover for whites than minorities. As expected, job level was negatively related to turnover, but joint effects of race and level were not reported. Lankau and Scandura (1996) directly tested the interaction of race and level (position) on intentions to leave in a sample of nurses but uncovered no interaction. Level was significantly negatively correlated with turnover intentions, but race was not related to intent to leave. Griffeth et al. (2000) did not examine moderators of the race-turnover link, due to the small number of studies that coded race (7).

While direct evidence is nonexistent, theory and other research nonetheless suggest job level as a moderator, with higher turnover for nonwhites at higher levels. For example, career blocks and perceptions of a glass ceiling, often cited as prime reasons for minority turnover (Gomez-Mejia et al., 2001; Hom & Griffeth, 1995), are largely seen as problems facing minority managers and professionals. Pettiigrew and Martin (1987) theorized that the effect of biased performance evaluations on retention of Blacks is greatest among "those with specialized skills or extensive experience in high ranking positions" (p. 65). Moreover, statistical evidence of blocked promotions and the glass ceiling comes from studies of upper level managers, and it is at this job level that race differentials are most dramatic (Federal Glass Ceiling Commission, 1995). Further, case studies such as Jones (1986) have also focused on minority turnover at upper levels of management.

Theoretically, the impact of career blocks on turnover may be greatest among incumbents in higher job levels, who have higher expectations of advancement and more job alternatives. For those at lower levels, career blocks may result in less quit behavior, given that fewer alternatives are available and there are shorter career ladders in those jobs (that depress mobility aspirations). Empirical studies are suggestive, for race differences in promotion rates have been found at all job levels but demonstrations that promotional differences result in differential rates of turnover are absent. For instance, James (2000) studied four levels of management at a Fortune 500 financial services firm. Race had an impact on promotions, with blacks reporting slower rates than whites. Turnover was not reported. Baldwin (2000) reported racial differences in early promotion rates of officers over an 18-year period (1978–1995) in the Air Force. Baldwin also found that the quit rate for minorities was almost twice that of whites. Pergamit and Veum (1999) examined young workers at lower job levels. Although whites were more likely to be promoted than black or Hispanic workers, no race differences in voluntary turnover were observed. They found that promotions have a positive impact on wages and job satisfaction, but not on organizational commitment or retention.

Other studies have examined how career blocks impact turnover intentions and search behavior. Foley, Kidder, and Powell (2002) found that Hispanic law associates who perceived a glass ceiling formed stronger intentions to leave. Parsons (1991) and Keith and Williams (2002) reported, again among young workers, that blacks were more likely than whites to search for a new job while employed. Keith and Williams (2002) found that this was due in part to black workers perceiving fewer opportunities for promotion. In addition to examining job search among the employed, Parsons (1991) examined those who quit their jobs to search for new ones. Significant race differences were not observed on quits to search, although rates were slightly higher for whites than blacks. These findings are consistent with the notion that job level, which proxies greater job opportunities, may moderate the extent to which limited promotion opportunities translate into quit behavior.

WORK GROUP COMPOSITION

Griffeth et al. (2000) suggested the demographic diversity of the work group as a possible moderator of the relationship between race and turnover. Recent work on organizational diversity and demography has found that variations in group composition on a various demographic traits including racioethnicity, age, gender, and tenure, influence group functioning (Riordan, 2001; Williams & O'Reilly, 1998). These studies have generally found that increasing workgroup diversity has negative effects on conflict and communication, consistent with similarity-attraction (Byrne, 1971) and social categorization (Tajfel & Turner, 1986) frameworks. Those who are different from the majority are more likely to have lower commitment, satisfaction, and are more likely to leave the work group. Regarding ethnicity specifically, several studies have reported that as racioethnic diversity increases in work groups, the satisfaction and commitment of whites decreases, and turnover increases (Tsui, Egan, & O'Reilly, 1992; Riordan & Shore, 1997). For example, Cordero, DiTomaso, and Farris (1996) found a linear positive relationship between the percentage of whites in the work group and intent to remain, among white scientists and engineers.

For racioethnic minorities, relationships between work group diversity and outcomes have been less clear, but evidence suggests that the results found for whites are not the same for other racioethnic groups. Whites tend to react more negatively to increasing workgroup diversity than do minorities. For example, in Cordero et al. (1996), there was no relationship between the percentage of minorities in the work group and intent to remain for Asians or Hispanics. For African Americans, a curvilinear, U shaped relationship was reported, with lowest intent to remain in equally mixed (approximately 50%) groups.

One exception to the relatively weak relationship between group racial composition and outcomes for minorities is the work on tokenism and solo status, which suggests that being in the extreme minority (less than 15%) has negative effects and may increase turnover. Kanter (1977) proposed that token or solo status in the work group results in heightened visibility for minorities in terms of their group membership, and in three forms of stress: stereotyping, performance pressures, and boundary heightening resulting in exclusion from social networks. These are predicted to have adverse effects on job attitudes and performance. Available studies suggest that token and solo status do have negative effects on racioethnic minorities. Niemann and Dovidio (1998) studied academics at universities, finding that for African Americans and Hispanics, solo status in the department increased feelings of distinctiveness (the belief that others viewed them in terms of their race) and decreased job satisfaction. Solo minorities were significantly less satisfied than non-solos. Roberson, Deitch, Brief, and Block (2003) studied managers and executives at utilities firms, finding that solo status resulted in greater perceived stereotype threat (the belief that others judged them by racial stereotypes) and job stress. Although neither of these studies included turnover as a dependent variable, they imply that group composition may moderate the relationship of racioethnicity to turnover. When work groups are predominantly minority or relatively mixed, whites may be more likely than nonwhites to quit. When groups are extremely white dominant, nonwhites may be more likely than whites to leave.

TENURE AND CAREER STAGE

Recent work by Thomas (2001; Thomas & Gabarro, 1999) points to job tenure or career stage as another potential moderator of the race-turnover link. Thomas and Gabarro studied the career paths of minority and white professionals at three large corporations. Striking and consistent differences were found not merely in the numbers of minorities and whites who reached upper management levels, but also in the nature of the career paths experienced by these two groups. Focusing solely on those who eventually reached upper levels, successful white executives tended to progress quickly in their careers, entering a fast track that propelled them from entry, into middle and then upper management within about eight years. In contrast, successful minority executives had slower initial career progress, rising in the organization more gradually. After approximately five years of slow advancement, the careers of the successful minority executives took off, rapidly advancing until they caught up with the white executives. Promotion paths of the two groups converged after about ten years. After this point, there were no group differences in rates of advancement toward executive suites.

This research suggests that career blocks—and perceived blocks—vary with one's career stage. Thomas and Gabarro (1999) found that during the first career stage (a period of about five years), which covered the move from entry to middle management, high potential minorities were most likely to feel frustration and discouragement as they watched similarly qualified white colleagues jump ahead. Members of minority groups might be most likely to search for new employment during this period rather than during later years when differential advancement rates are less likely or apparent. Thus, job tenure is likely to moderate the race-turnover relationship for managerial and professional employees.

Tenure may also interact with performance to influence race-turnover linkages. Thomas argues that although both successful white and minority executives were initial high performers, only whites were rewarded with fast promotions to middle management. The minority winners received less visible recognition of their worth, such as expanded responsibilities or challenging assignments rather than promotions. Given such treatment, we might expect that the highest minority performers would be the most demotivated and discouraged and thus most likely to leave. Thomas (2001) encourages mentors of minority professionals to be aware of these differential reward patterns so that they can prevent discouragement and such dysfunctional turnover.

Apart from slower promotional progress during the early career stage, racioethnic minorities who are superior performers may also feel more impelled to quit if they do not receive other kinds of rewards, such as incentives and training opportunities. Specifically, Thomas and Gabarro's (1999) work indicated a feeble relationship between performance and tangible rewards for minority managers in their early careers. Because high performers tend to resign when deprived of merit-based incentives (Jackofsky, 1984; Williams & Livingstone, 1994), high performing minorities may be likely to quit during the early career stage when racial disparities in the distribution of other performance-contingent rewards (besides promotions) is are greater. A positive relationship between performance and turnover for African American managers was also proposed by Pettigrew and Martin (1987). They argued that biased performance evaluations will result in inadequate rewards and recognition for superior performing Black managers. Underreward inequity will thus increase turnover for superior performers. To summarize, minority professionals and managers may be more prone to quit during initial career stages than their white counterparts and this trend is likely to be more pronounced for high performers. Despite Jackofsky and Slocum's (1987) finding that high performers are usually satisfied and optimistic about advancement, Thomas and Gabarro (1999) showed that young minority professionals face a different workplace reality where their accomplishments are inadequately recognized and rewarded.

RACE/ETHNICITY AND RACIAL/ETHNIC IDENTITY ATTITUDES

A second potential moderator of the relationship of race to turnover suggested by Griffeth et al. (2001) was racioethnicity itself. In their meta-analysis, the turnover rates of different racioethnic minority groups were pooled together and then compared with the rates for whites. The practice of grouping all people of color together for analysis is common in the OB literature, but obscures differential turnover rates for different racioethnic groups. Although pooling different minorities increases sample sizes, it also reflects and reinforces a view of people of color as an undifferentiated "other" and fails to recognize each group's unique sociohistorical experiences in the United States (Nkomo, 1992). Yet these unique group experiences may affect treatment and experiences at work, thereby influencing quit propensities. For example, Ogbu (1986) distinguished between immigrant and caste minorities, arguing that these two groups have differing experiences, world views, and perceptions of opportunity in US society. Immigrant minorities, of which Asian Americans are a prime example, have largely come to the US voluntarily to improve their economic, political, or social status (Ogbu, 1986). Members of these groups see American society as holding opportunities and achievement as a route to success. They view existing differentials between their status and that of the majority as temporary and reducible through hard work. In contrast, caste minorities such as African Americans and Native Americans have been incorporated into the US society more or less involuntarily and subsequently relegated to low status positions through legal and societal means (Ogbu, 1986). Because of their history, caste minorities view society as oppressive and fail to believe that personal efforts can lead to advancement. Rather, they view status differences between themselves and the majority as permanent. Outcome differences for all minorities, both immigrant and caste, result from social system inequities which favor the dominant group according to Ogbu (1986). However, caste minorities distrust the inherent fairness of the dominant culture and thus reject it.

Oghu's analysis raises the possibility that the effects of perceived discrimination on job attitudes and turnover may be stronger for caste than for immigrant minorities, due to their different interpretations of discrimination. Consistent with this, Major and Schmader (1998) reported that African American and Hispanic students are less likely than Asian Americans to believe that the American system was just and fair. Foley et al. (2002) found that the link between a perceived glass ceiling and turnover intentions was mediated by justice perceptions in a sample of Hispanic law associates. If, in general, justice beliefs mediate the relationship of perceived discrimination to turnover, then the stronger system fairness beliefs of immigrant minorities may reduce turnover for such groups. Higher turnover rates would be expected for caste minorities.

Another way in which racioethnicity could function as a moderator of a race-turnover link is if different racioethnic groups experience different levels of the types of discrimination shown in Figure 9.1 that are believed to be the causes of higher turnover. There is mixed evidence regarding this possibility. In general, whites tend to experience more favorable job outcomes in terms of promotions and wages than do any other racioethnic group (African Americans, Asian Americans, Hispanics, and Native Americans) (Federal Glass Ceiling Commission, 1995; Morrison & Von Glinow, 1990). Crocker and Quinn (1998), in a study of college students, found that African American and Asian American students did not differ in levels of perceived discrimination. However, others have reported group differences. Major and Schmader (1998), who also studied college students, reported that African American, Hispanic, and Asian students differed in experienced discrimination with Asians reporting less discrimination than members of the other groups.

Crocker and Quinn (1998) argued that the effects of perceived discrimination and prejudice depend on the meaning of the disadvantaged status of one's social group. Ogbu's work offers one attempt to outline how different racioethnic groups interpret their group's experiences. Another theoretical framework is provided by work on racial and ethnic identity attitudes. Racial/ethnic identity attitudes are generally conceived as having two components: one's feelings toward one's own group, and one's feelings toward the dominant group (Leong & Chou, 1994; Thomas, Phillips, & Brown, 1998). Group identity attitudes influence both perceptions of and responses to discrimination. For example, several studies have found that those who identify more strongly with their own group are more likely to perceive discrimination toward their group and to attribute negative actions by members of the dominant group to discrimination (Button, 2001; Jefferson & Caldwell, 2002; Pinel, 1999; Stewart, 2001; Watts & Carter, 1991). In addition, Button (2001) studied a sample of gay and lesbian employees and found that perceived discrimination was more strongly related to job dissatisfaction for highly identified gays/lesbians. Leong and Chou (1994) have made similar hypotheses regarding Asian Americans' responses to discrimination. This points to racial/ethnic identity attitudes as a more meaningful predictor of reactions to discrimination than a demographic racioethnicity classification. In short, discrimination may be more likely to influence job attitudes and result in job turnover for those highly identified with their racioethnic group.

ORGANIZATIONAL CLIMATE FOR DIVERSITY

Recent work on diversity climates and cultures suggests that organizational or work group perspectives on diversity may moderate the race-turnover relationship. Thomas and Ely (1996) define three different perspectives on diversity that organizations may hold. By perspective, they refer to managerial perceptions and beliefs about why diversity is important and how it is related to the work of the firm. These beliefs influence the meaning and significance of race (as well as other identity group memberships, such as gender) in the organization, the quality of intergroup relations, and the degree to which minority members feel valued and respected. Ely and Thomas proposed that through its influence on these three intervening variables, diversity perspective moderates the relationship of diversity to work group functioning. One perspective labeled "fairness and discrimination," views diversity as existing in the organization as a way to right past wrongs. This rationale for increasing diversity is based on the belief that prejudice and discrimination have unfairly kept women and people of color out of the workforce, and so to be fair, organizations should become more diverse. With a "discrimination and fairness" perspective, the focus of diversity efforts is primarily to educate members of the majority about other cultures and to mentor minorities so that they will fit in with the existing organizational culture. Thus, an assimilationist strategy is dominant within this approach. The success of diversity efforts is seen as a function of recruitment and retention of minorities, which is often achieved. However, Roberson and Block (2001) argued that the psychological engagement (Kahn, 1990) of minority employees in an organization characterized by a fairness and discrimination perspective will be limited. With assimilation as a goal, the organization does not view diversity as a resource.

A second perspective described by Thomas and Ely is "access and legitimacy," where diversity is seen as instrumental for helping the organization reach a broader clientele. This rationale is one of the well-known "business cases" that is often made for diversity (Cox & Blake, 1991), that an organization needs to diversify demographically to gain access to different market segments and to increase its legitimacy in those markets. The result of this organizational perspective is that minority employees usually end up serving those niche markets where they are seen as having local expertise. However, minorities are not given the opportunity to move into other parts of the business because their experience is seen as only applying in that given niche (Roberson & Block, 2001). This increases perceptions of glass ceilings and segregation. Thus, members of minority groups in organizations characterized by "access and legitimacy" perspectives feel exploited when they realize that other parts of the business are not open to them. The organization fails to diversify how the work gets done, rather it diversifies certain segments of the organization.

In the third organizational perspective described by Thomas and Ely (1996), "integration and learning" diversity is seen as a resource to the organization that can improve organizational performance by facilitating the learning of new approaches to work. This approach, defined by Cox (1994) as pluralistic, enables the organization to incorporate employees' different perspectives, experiences, and ways of working into the organization's functioning and enhances work by rethinking tasks, strategies, and culture. Thomas and Ely (1996) presented a case study of a law firm that initially hired racioethnic minorities for access and legitimacy reasons. But over time, the mission of the organization, and the strategies used to pursue it changed as a result of increased workforce diversity.

Ely and Thomas (2001) further examined the relationship between organizational perspective on diversity and individual and organizational outcomes. They found that diversity perspective influenced the impact of diversity. When the access and legitimacy and the discrimination and fairness perspectives prevailed in organizations, there were greater levels of unresolved intergroup conflict and people of color felt undervalued and disrespected (Ely & Thomas 2001). Organizations adopting the integration and learning perspective realized more positive outcomes of diversity.

Ely and Thomas did not include turnover or retention as dependent variables in their study of diversity perspectives. However, the results of Gilbert and Ivancevich (2000) suggest that diversity perspectives may influence turnover rates. Their study of two organizations with differing philosophies of diversity management found that a philosophy of diversity similar to the integration and learning perspective was superior to a discrimination and fairness (focus on equal opportunity compliance) perspective in terms of employee turnover, the percentage of minorities in management, and workforce attitudes toward diversity. Specifically, minority turnover was lower in the organization characterized by an integration and learning perspective.

Although the two studies discussed above found that diversity perspectives were related to outcomes, Thomas and Gabarro (1999) found that diversity strategy of the organization (assimilationist vs. pluralistic) did not predict the advancement of minorities into upper management levels. However, they noted that the assimilationist, color-blind approach characterizing a discrimination and fairness perspective resulted in unwritten norms not to mention race as a variable affecting job experiences. The minority executives employed in such firms stressed, in formal interviews, that "I never felt anything about being black at Acme" (p. 207); and "I don't think race ever held me back." However, when the tape recorder was turned off, they were willing to discuss incidents of discrimination. Thomas and Gabarro noted that for success in such organizations, minorities may have needed to assume a personal stance on race that mirrored the organizational stance. This implicit agreement on the invisibility of race may have constituted part of the psychological contract between employees and the firm. In his previous work on cross-race mentoring, Thomas (1993) made a similar point. He argued that symmetry between mentor and protégé on the best strategy for managing and discussing race influences the success of the relationship. In addition, he proposed that different strategies (such as avoidance, or direct engagement of the topic) are more or less acceptable and desired depending on the parties' racial identity attitudes. This suggests that racial identity attitudes may interact with organizational diversity perspective in its effects on turnover. The organizational strategy for handling race may be a climate variable on which people of color assess their "fit" (Weaver, 2002). Fit perceptions have been associated with turnover intentions (Lovelace & Rosen, 1996).

SUMMARY AND CONCLUSIONS

A consistent relationship between race and turnover, with higher quit rates for people of color, is widely believed to be true, and this "fact" can be commonly found in the human resource and management literature. However, empirical evidence has failed to consistently support this commonly held view. Results of meta-analyses instead point to the existence of moderators of any race-turnover relationship. Past reviews of research on race in OB have stressed the importance of examining the meaning of race in particular situations to understand its impact on behavior and attitudes (Nkomo, 1992; Roberson & Block, 2001; Thomas et al., 1998). This perspective can also aid research on race and turnover. We suggested as potential moderators, several variables that reflect the meaning of race to the individual (e.g., racial identity attitudes) and the meaning of race in the organization (e.g., workgroup composition, climate for diversity). We also suggested other moderators that have theoretical support (e.g., level, career stage).

Based on this review, a revised model of the reasons for turnover among racioethnic minorities is shown in Figure 9.2. This model retains the aspects of the work experience that are typically hypothesized to vary as a function of race, and on which group differences have been found. In addition, in this model the overall relationship between race and turnover has been separated into three linkages, and potential moderators placed at points where they may impact the process.

The first linkage, of race to aspects of work experience, may be moderated by both individual and organizational factors. Some studies, for example, have found differences in the extent of reported discrimination by specific racioethnic groups. Others have found that racial identity attitudes are related to perceptions of the work environment. Token status, a context variable, is also hypothesized to heighten experienced stereotyping and pressures for members of minority groups. The organizational climate for diversity may also determine the extent to which race is linked to the work experience (Gilbert & Ivancevich, 2000), and other aspects of the organization may be relevant as well. For example, Konrad and Linnehan (1995) found that the number of identity conscious human resource policies in the organization predicted the employment status of women and minorities in the organization.

The second link is between the work experience and job attitudes. Some of the potential moderators discussed may operate here. For example, Ogbu's (1986) work suggests that immigrant and caste minorities, while both experiencing discrimination, interpret these experiences differently. Other studies have found that racial identity attitudes moderate the relationship between experienced discrimination and job attitudes. The last relationship is between job attitudes and actual quits, where employee level is likely to function as a moderator.

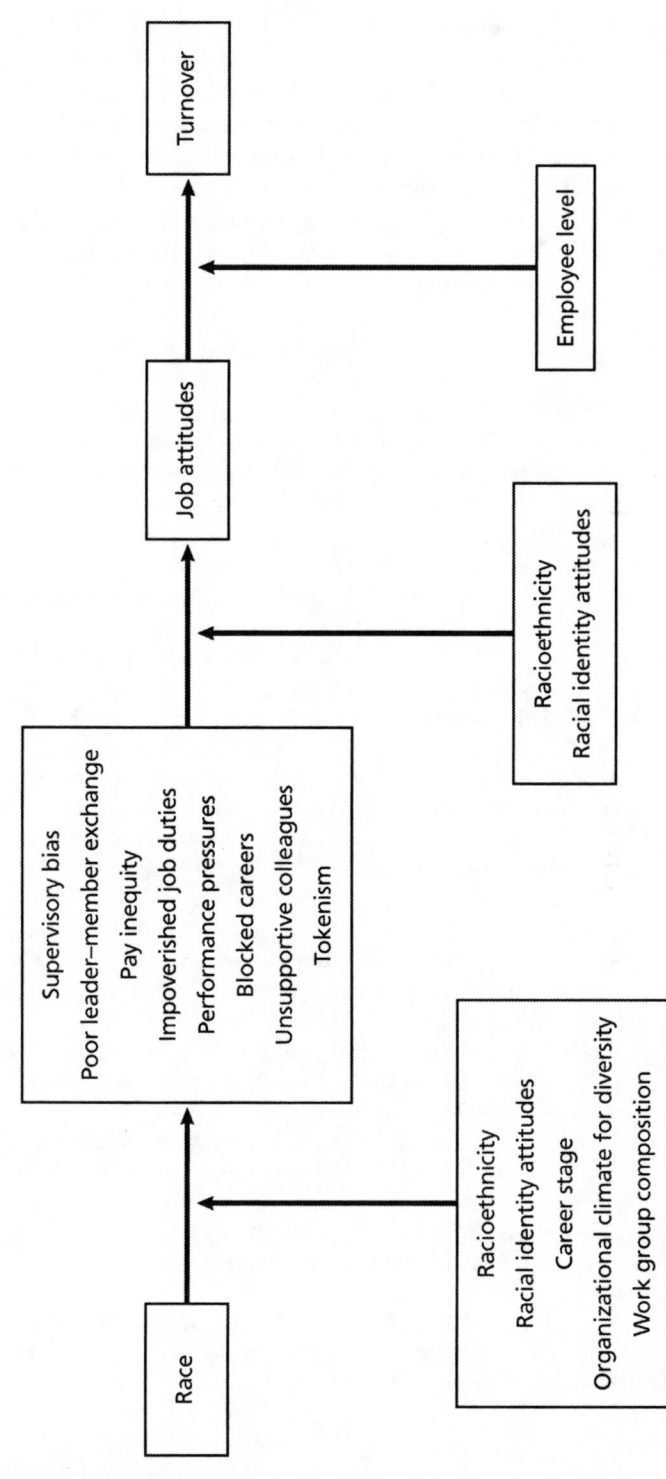

Figure 9.2. Revised model of the potential causes of turnover among minorities.

In closing, although it has been criticized here, the OB model of the relationship between race and turnover has had some positive impact. It has focused research attention on factors that may not directly influence quit rates, but do influence job attitudes, performance, and advancement. It has guided organizations in the design of programs and interventions to increase retention of minorities. Hopefully the revised model will also guide research to improve our understanding of the meaning of race for the work experience and stimulate organizational efforts for managing diversity.

REFERENCES

Arvey, R.D., Azevedo, R.E., Ostgaard, D.J., & Raghuram, S. (1996). The implications of a diverse labor market on human resource planning. In E.E. Kossek & S.A. Lobel, (Eds.), *Managing diversity: Human resource strategies for transforming the workplace* (pp. 51–73). Cambridge, MA: Blackwell.

Baldwin, J.N. (2000). Early promotions of women and minorities in the United States Air Force. *Journal of Political and Military Sociology, 28,* 109–130.

Black, D.A. (1995). Discrimination in an equilibrium search model. *Journal of Labor Economics, 13,* 309–334.

Button, S.B. (2001). Organizational efforts to affirm sexual diversity: A cross-level examination. *Journal of Applied Psychology, 86,* 17–28.

Byrne, D. (1971). *The attraction paradigm.* New York: Academic Press.

Cordero, R., DiTomaso, N., & Farris, G.F. (1997). Gender and race/ethnic composition of technical work groups: Relationship to creative productivity and morale. *Journal of Engineering and Technology Management, 13,* 205–221.

Cox, T. (1994). *Cultural diversity in organizations: Theory, research, and practice.* San Francisco: Berrett-Koehler.

Cox, T., & Blake, S..(1991). Managing cultural diversity: Implications for organizational competitiveness. *Academy of Management Executive, 5,* 45–56.

Crocker, J., & Quinn, D. (1998). Racism and self esteem. In J.L. Eberhardt & S.T. Fiske, (Eds.), *Confronting racism: The problem and the response* (pp. 169–187). Thousand Oaks, CA: Sage.

Ely, R.J., & Thomas, D.A. (2001). Cultural diversity at work: The effects of diversity perspectives on work group processes and outcomes. *Administrative Science Quarterly, 46,* 229–273.

Federal Glass Ceiling Commission. (1995). *Good for business: Making full use of the nation's human capital* (Glass Ceiling Reports). Washington, DC: U.S.Government Printing Office.

Foley, S., Kidder, D.L., & Powell, G.N. (2002). The perceived glass ceiling and justice perceptions: An investigation of Hispanic law associates. *Journal of Management, 28,* 471–496.

Ghiselli, R.F., La Lopa, J.M., & Bai, B. (2001). Job satisfaction, life satisfaction, and turnover intent among food service managers. *Cornell Hotel and Restaurant Administration Quarterly, 42,* 28–37.

Gilbert, J.A., & Ivancevich, J.M. (2000). Valuing diversity: A tale of two organizations. *Academy of Management Executive, 14*, 93–105.

Gomez-Mejia, L.R., Balkin, D.B., & Cardy, R.L. (2001) *Managing human resources* (3rd ed.). Upper Saddle River, NJ: Prentice-Hall.

Griffeth, R.W., Hom, P.W., & Gaertner, S. (2000). A meta-analysis of antecedents and correlates of employee turnover: Update, moderator tests, and research implications for the next millennium. *Journal of Management, 26*, 463–488.

Harris, D.M., & DeSimone, R.L. (1994). *Human resource development*. Fort Worth, TX: Dryden Press.

Hom, P.W., & Griffeth, R.W. (1995). *Employee turnover*. Cincinnati, OH: South-Western.

Jackofsky, E.F. (1984). Turnover and job performance: An integrated process model. *Academy of Management Review, 9*, 74–83.

Jackofsky, E.F., & Slocum, J.W. (1987). A causal analysis of the impact of job performance on the voluntary turnover process. *Journal of Occupational Behavior, 8*, 263–270.

James, E.H. (2000). Race-related differences in promotions and support: Underlying effects of human and social capital. *Organization Science, 11*, 493–508.

Jamieson, D., & O'Mara, J. (1991). *Managing workforce 2000: Gaining the diversity advantage*. San Francisco; Jossey-Bass.

Jefferson, S.D., & Caldwell, R. (2002). An exploration of the relationship between racial identity attitudes and the perception of racial bias. *Journal of Black Psychology, 28*, 174–192.

Jones, E.W. (1986, May-June). Black managers: The dream deferred. *Harvard Business Review*.

Kahn, W.A. (1990). Psychological conditions of personal engagement and disengagement at work. *Academy of Management Journal, 33*, 692–724.

Kanter, R.M. (1977). *Men and women of the corporation*. New York: Basic Books.

Keith, K., & Williams, D.R. (2002). A note on racial differences in employed male job search. *Industrial Relations, 41*, 422–429,

Konrad, A.M., & Linnehan, F. (1995). Formalized HRM structures: Coordinating equal employment opportunity or concealing organizational practices? *Academy of Management Journal, 38*, 787–820.

Kram, K.E., & Hall, D.T. (1996). Mentoring in a context of diversity and turbulence. In E.E. Kossek & S.A. Lobel, (Eds.), *Managing diversity: Human resource strategies for transforming the workplace* (pp. 108–136). Cambridge, MA: Blackwell.

Lankau, M.J., & Scandura, T.A. (1996). An examination of job attitudes of white, black, and Hispanic nurses in a public hospital. *International Journal of Public Administration, 19*, 377–398.

Lee, T.W., & Mitchell, T.R. (1994). An alternative approach: The unfolding model of voluntary employee turnover. *Academy of Management Review, 19*, 51–89.

Leong, F.T.L., & Chou, E.L. (1994). The role of ethnic identity and acculturation in the vocational behavior of Asian Americans: An integrative review. *Journal of Vocational Behavior, 44*, 155–172.

Light, A., & Ureta, M. (1992). Panel estimates of male and female job turnover behavior: Can female nonquitters be identified? *Journal of Labor Economics, 10*, 156–181.

Lovelace, K., & Rosen, B. (1996). Differences in achieving person-organization fit among diverse groups of managers. *Journal of Management, 22,* 703–722.

Major, B., & Schmader, T. (1998). Coping with stigma through psychological disengagement. In J.K. Swim & C. Stangor (Eds.), *Prejudice: The target's perspective* (pp. 219–241). San Diego, CA: Academic Press.

March, J. & Simon, H.A. (1958). *Organizations.* New York: Wiley.

Mitchell, T.R., & Lee, T.W. (2001). The unfolding model of voluntary turnover and job embeddedness: Foundations for a comprehensive theory of attachment. In B. Staw (Ed.), *Research in organizational behavior* (Vol. 23, pp. 189–246). Greenwich, CT: JAI Press.

Morrison, A.M., & VonGlinow, M.A. (1990). Women and minorities in management. *American Psychologist, 45,* 200–208.

Niemann, Y.F., & Dovidio, J.F. (1998). Relationship of solo status, academic rank, and perceived distinctiveness to job satisfaction of racial/ethnic minorities. *Journal of Applied Psychology, 83,* 55–71.

Nkomo, S.M. (1992). The emperor has no clothes: Rewriting "race in organizations". *Academy of Management Review, 17,* 487–513.

Ogbu, J.U. (1986). The consequences of the American caste system. In U.Neisser, (Ed.), *The school achievement of minority children: New perspectives* (pp. 19–56). Hillsdale, NJ: Erlbaum.

Parsons, D.O. (1991). The job search behavior of employed youth. *The Review of Economics and Statistics, 73,* 597–604.

Pergamit, M.R., & Veum, J.R. (1999). What is a promotion? *Industrial and Labor Relations Review, 52,* 581–601.

Pettigrew, T.F., & Martin, J. (1987). Shaping the organizational context for Black American inclusion. *Journal of Social Issues, 43,* 41–78.

Pinel, E.C. (1999). Stigma consciousness: The psychological legacy of social stereotypes. *Journal of Personality and Social Psychology, 76,* 114–128.

Riordan, C. (2001). Relational demography within groups: Past developments, contradictions, and new directions. *Research in Personnel and Human Resource Management, 19,* 131–173.

Riordan, C., & Shore, L. (1997). Demographic diversity and employee attitudes: Examination of relational demography within work units. *Journal of Applied Psychology, 82,* 342–358.

Roberson, L., & Block, C.J. (2001). Racioethnicity and job performance: A review and critique of theoretical perspectives on the causes of group differences. In B.M. Staw (Ed.), *Research in organizational behavior* (Vol. 23, pp. 247–325). Greenwich, CT: JAI Press.

Roberson, L., Deitch, E., Brief, A.P., & Block, C.J. (2003). Stereotype threat and feedback seeking in the workplace. *Journal of Vocational Behavior, 62,* 176–188.

Robinson, G., & Dechant, K. (1997). Building a business case for diversity. *Academy of Management Executive, 11,* 21–31.

Sightler, K.W., & Adams, J.S. (1999). Differences between stayers and leavers among part-time workers. *Journal of Managerial Issues, 11,* 110–125.

Stewart, M.M. (2001). I'll take your word for it, but not his . . . : An examination of minority recipient reactions to negative feedback. *Dissertation Abstracts International (Section A: Humanities and Social Sciences), 61,* 4460.

Tajfel, H., & Turner, J. (1986). The social identity of intergroup behavior. In S. Worchel & W. Austin (Eds.), *Psychology and intergroup relations* (pp. 7–24). Chicago: Nelson-Hall.

Thomas, D.A. (2001, April). The truth about mentoring minorities: Race matters. *Harvard Business Review,* 99–107.

Thomas, D.A. (1993). Racial dynamics in cross-race developmental relationships. *Administrative Science Quarterly, 38,* 169–194.

Thomas, D.A., & Ely, R.J. (1996, September-October). Making differences matter: A new paradigm for managing diversity. *Harvard Business Review,* 79–90.

Thomas, D.A., & Gabarro, J.J. (1999). *Breaking through: The making of minority executives in corporate America.* Boston: Harvard Business School Press.

Thomas, K.M., Phillips, L.D., & Brown, S. (1998). Redefining race in the workplace: Insights from ethnic identity theory. *Journal of Black Psychology, 24,* 76–92.

Thomas, R.R. (1990). From affirmative action to affirming diversity. In M.C. Gentile (Ed.), *Differences that work: Organizational excellence through diversity* (pp. 27–48) Boston: Harvard Business School Press.

Tsui, A., Egan, T., & O'Reilly, C. (1992). Being different: Relational demography and organizational attachment. *Administrative Science Quarterly, 37,* 549–579.

Valentine, S.R. (2001). A path analysis of gender, race, and job complexity as determinants of intention to look for work. *Employee Relations, 23,* 130–145.

Watts, R.J., & Carter, R.C. (1991). Psychological aspects of racism. *Group and Organizational Studies, 16,* 328–344.

Weaver, V.J. (2002). If your organization values diversity, why are *they* leaving? *Employment Management Today, 5*(4).

Whatley, W.C., & Sedo, S. (1998). Quit behavior as a measure of worker opportunity: Black workers in the interwar industrial north. *The American Economic Review, 88,* 363–367.

Williams, C.R., & Livingston, L.P. (1994). Another look at the relationship between performance and voluntary turnover. *Academy of Management Journal, 37,* 269–298.

Williams, K.Y., & O'Reilly, C.A. (1998). Demography and diversity in organizations: A review of 40 years of research. In B.M. Staw (Ed.), *Research in organizational behavior* (Vol. 20, pp. 77–140). Greenwich, CT: JAI Press.

CHAPTER 10

INVESTIGATING TURNOVER IN THE INTERNATIONAL CONTEXT

A Turnover Model for the Mexican Culture

Mindy S. West

ABSTRACT

A turnover model developed for the Mexican culture is presented. The proposed model integrates constructs from turnover theories developed in the United States and incorporates constructs that play a heightened role in the Mexican context. The model emphasizes the impact of various types of satisfaction, including job, supervisor and co-worker as factors that contribute to withdrawal cognitions. As companies in Mexico attempt to attract and retain employees with a myriad of benefits, benefit satisfaction is theorized to contribute to job satisfaction and continuance commitment. The model indicates that life events independent of a person's level of job satisfaction may contribute to withdrawal cognitions. Specific testable hypotheses are presented.

Innovative Theory and Empirical Research on Employee Turnover, pages 231–256

INTRODUCTION

Employee turnover has long been the subject of pervasive interest by scholars and practitioners. Yet despite this widespread interest, most turnover investigations have been conducted in the United States. A void exists in our knowledge about turnover in other cultures (Hom & Griffeth, 1995; Maertz, Stevens, Campion, & Fernandez, 1996). Moreover, models developed from the perspective of domestic scholars often overlook the role of culture (Boyacigiller & Adler, 1991; Hofstede, 1983; Maertz et al., 1996). The extent to which theories designed by American scholars and tested on American workers are representative of other cultures is an open question which has received little attention by academic scholars. Now researchers are beginning to investigate turnover from the perspective of cultures other than the United States to test the generalizability of the mainstream turnover theories.

One country that is apt for turnover investigation is Mexico. Many firms in Mexico have high turnover levels, and the turnover rates in Mexico may be limiting the number of high-technology firms that will establish facilities in Mexico (Lucker, 1987). Many U.S. firms have established facilities in Mexico and many others are considering operations in Mexico, and thus the results of turnover studies would have practical implications for managers from both countries (Teagarden, Butler, & Von Glinow, 1992; Teagarden & Von Glinow, 1990). Moreover, the culture of Mexico is substantially different from that of the United States (cf. Hofstede, 1980) and thus the Mexican culture would provide an appropriate context to test the generalizability of turnover models developed from the "cultural lens" of another nation (Maertz et al., 1996).

The model developed here uses the Mexican cultural lens to apply turnover constructs to the Mexican context. Knowledge of the Mexican culture and qualitative interviews provided the appropriate cultural lens. The following section reviews the turnover constructs and models derived from research in the United States that are likely relevant to turnover decisions in Mexico. The next section provides an overview of the limited turnover work that has been conducted in Mexico to highlight constructs that should be integrated into a turnover model for the Mexican context. The third section presents the proposed model and specific hypotheses for empirical testing. The final section discusses future research implications.

EMPLOYEE TURNOVER

Turnover has been the subject of widespread scholarly research and various models have been developed and empirically tested (see Hom & Griffeth, 1995 for a comprehensive review). Although there are conceptual similarities across the diverse models, different theorists emphasize different processes and explanatory constructs when looking at turnover. The traditional approach has been to investigate the intermediate linkages between job satisfaction and employee turnover (Lee & Mitchell, 1994). For example, the process model presented by Mobley (1977) proposed that there are several intermediate steps between job dissatisfaction and turnover decisions. These intermediate steps include thinking of quitting, evaluating the expected utility of withdrawal, searching for alternatives, evaluating alternatives, and finally intending to quit. The Hom and Griffeth (1995) model is representative of this tradition, emphasizing the pivotal role of job attitudes for initiating withdrawal processes while integrating constructs uncovered by contemporary research. Their model is considered to be a comprehensive integration of the turnover literature.

By comparison, newer models of turnover emphasize the impact of life events that are independent of job attitudes but nonetheless can contribute to turnover decisions. The unfolding model developed by Lee and colleagues (Lee & Mitchell, 1994; Lee, Mitchell, Wise, & Fireman, 1996; Mitchell & Lee, 2001) has pioneered this approach. This new line of turnover research investigates nonattitudinal factors that can cue turnover, including the impact of family responsibilities and unsolicited job offers (Lee et al., 1996). As traditional models of turnover have ignored the role of life events, the unfolding model represents a valuable complement to the traditional approach. The following sections will briefly review the main tenets of models that are characteristic of the traditional and new approaches to investigating turnover: the Hom and Griffeth (1995) model and the unfolding model, respectively.

The Hom and Griffeth (1995) Model

The Hom and Griffeth (1995) model integrates two preeminent turnover models: Mobley (1977) and Price and Mueller (1986). Hom and Griffeth (1995) claim that their model is consistent with meta-analyses of turnover correlates, as well as with a validation study by Griffeth and Hom (1990). In this model, job satisfaction and organizational commitment are antecedents to withdrawal cognitions (thoughts about quitting). Factors that contribute to job satisfaction include characteristics of the work itself and characteristics of the work environment, including group cohesion and compensation. Labor market perceptions also impact job satisfaction: employees who believe that superior job alternatives exist at other firms may become increasingly disenchanted with their current position. Factors that bind employees to organizations due to the economic or opportunity costs of leaving also contribute to organizational commitment. Firm-specific knowledge and seniority-based or non-transferable benefits are examples. Perceptions of fairness in reward distribution on the part of the employer foster organizational commitment, as will a work schedule that permits sufficient time to deal with family and personal interests.

Under the Hom and Griffeth (1995) framework, job satisfaction and organizational commitment are negatively related to withdrawal cognitions and the expected utility of withdrawal. Withdrawal cognitions can lead directly to turnover or may impact perceptions of the expected utility of withdrawal. In the later situation, the person will begin to investigate other job alternatives. Once he has found other job opportunities, the person will do a utility analysis to determine if the benefits of leaving the firm outweigh the costs of leaving. If the net gain of leaving to the person is positive, turnover will occur.

The Unfolding Model

In their unfolding model, Lee and colleagues (Lee & Mitchell, 1994; Lee, Mitchell, Holtom, McDaniel, & Hill, 1999; Lee et al., 1996; Mitchell & Lee, 2001) break from traditional views by indicating that many turnover decisions are independent of the level of job satisfaction. In the unfolding model, turnover decisions can be caused by jarring events, referred to as shocks, which evoke mental deliberations about current employment status. Shocks can be external or internal to the organization. Examples of external shocks would include pregnancy, illness of a family member, change in day care arrangements, or the transfer of a spouse. External life events such as these may not impact a person's level of job satisfaction, but could nonetheless trigger withdrawal cognitions or turnover decisions. By comparison, internal shocks, including the hiring of a new supervisor, being passed over for promotion, or a change in the company's strategic mission, could directly impact the person's level of job satisfaction (Lee et al., 1996; Maertz et al., 1996).

The unfolding model further specifies different types of turnover decisions and each type requires different degrees of mental deliberations. Four decision paths are proposed, which vary in regard to if the person has specific job alternatives prior to quitting, whether the person conducts an expected utility of withdrawal process prior to quitting and whether a shock has occurred, among other factors. The unfolding model framework is a promising new view on turnover decisions but has been subjected to few empirical investigations (Lee et al., 1999; Lee et al., 1996). Mexico is a perfect location to test the parameters of the unfolding model, given the high level of turnover in Mexican firms.

EMPLOYEE TURNOVER IN MEXICO

Assembly operations in Mexico, especially maquiladoras, traditionally have had high levels of employee turnover (Tiano, 1994). A maquiladora is a manufacturing or processing firm that assembles component parts from other countries and then exports the finished items to the home country for further processing or final sale (Paik & Teagarden, 1995). Maquiladoras are usually located in Mexican border towns and operate under special trade provisions that allow the plant to import the needed factors of production without having to pay import duties (Teagarden & Von Glinow, 1990). The phrase "maquiladora industry" is used to refer to firms that operate under the maquiladora regulations rather than to describe what these firms produce (Sklair, 1989). The maquiladora industry supports a variety of firm types and the principal industry sectors are electronics, transportation equipment and textiles (Vargas, 1998).

Turnover rates of 30% per month and 100% annually are common in maquiladoras (Bannister & Peña, 1993; Hecht & Morici, 1993; Teagarden & Von Glinow, 1990). Because maquiladora workers change jobs for employment at other maquiladoras with such ease, the phenomena has been labeled "musical maquilas" (Moffett, 1984). Despite widespread turnover within the maquiladoras, little systematic research investigating factors contributing to this turnover has been conducted (English, Williams, & Ibarreche, 1989; Lucker, 1987; Maertz et al., 1996). Historically, high turnover was not considered a threat to productivity because the simple and the rudimentary tasks performed by the maquiladora workers took only a few minutes to master (English et al., 1989). With workers performing simple job tasks that were easily trained and with a large supply of workers, plant managers did not worry about preventing turnover.

Today, assembly operations in Mexico are becoming more complex and more sophisticated, requiring greater use of technology and higher levels of worker skill. The more firms invest in employee training, the greater the costs associated with turnover, and thus firms are becoming more interested in reducing turnover rates (Cascio, 1991). Currently, managers in Mexico are placing a higher priority on retaining quality workers and turnover studies are now being conducted in Mexico.

Although academic inquiry about the causes of turnover in Mexico is in its infancy, some early findings are important to note. Some research has focused on the relationship between demographic variables and turnover or job tenure in Mexico. Work by Alvarez (1985) demonstrated that individuals who quit a maquiladora were more likely to be male, to be single, to be less educated, to have more children, and to be secondary wage-earners for their households. English et al.'s (1989) comparison of long-term workers (i.e., more than two years employment) versus short-term workers (i.e., less than six months employment) in one maquiladora demonstrated that long-term workers were more likely to be female and living in the same community since birth. Work by Maertz (1999) demonstrated that respondents living apart from their mothers had higher turnover rates, as did employees who had previously quit other plants.

A key determinant emerging from this demographic research stream is the place of origin of the workers. Many individuals migrate from central Mexico to the northern border towns in search of enhanced employment options. Mexico currently has an imbalance between locations of demand for labor and locations of labor supply. The maquiladora industry has created an employment boom near the Mexican-U.S. border, but border communities do not have a sufficient local labor pool to support the maquiladora industry and its increasing growth (Williams & Passé-Smith, 1989). In contrast, the interior of Mexico, where the bulk of the population lives, has few jobs in manufacturing or otherwise. The result of this imbalance of supply and demand for labor is that many Mexican workers migrate from rural and central Mexico to the border to seek employment (Young & Fort, 1994).

When migrating to the border in search of work, rural immigrants leave behind their immediate and extended families and must adjust to life in a new urban setting (Teagarden et al., 1992). Like American expatriates working abroad (Shaffer & Harrison, 1998), this separation from family and home community creates immense personal adjustment problems for teenaged workers. This adjustment process may contribute to turnover, as young migrants might find adjusting to a new way of life without family or friends to be too great and may simply return to the Mexican interior. Indeed, this demographic research has demonstrated that border migrants are more likely to quit when compared to hometown workers, and thus a migrant's level of satisfaction with his or her new community is likely to impact turnover decisions.

In addition to demographic studies, there have been ethnographic and qualitative studies into employee attitudes and the working conditions at maquiladoras, including work by Fernández-Kelly (1983), Tiano (1994), and Maertz et al. (1996). An excellent example of a qualitative investigation of the turnover causes in Mexico was conducted by Maertz et al. The researchers conducted in-depth one-on-one interviews with 47 participants in two maquiladoras in Juarez. One key finding was that excessive turnover at the maquiladoras creates an environment that fosters the belief that it would not be difficult for an employee to find a new job ("turnover culture"). The majority of the interviewees (63%) reported that it would take only five days or less to find a comparable job. This belief surely reflects the fact that maquiladora employment opportunities in the border cities far outstrip the labor supply (Williams & Passé-Smith, 1989). A maquiladora worker can quit one maquiladora with the knowledge that he or she will quickly resume employment at another. Thus, workers' perceptions about job alternatives likely impact turnover decisions in the maquiladora context.

The lack of organizational commitment among the workers was another key finding of the Maertz et al. (1996) study: Only one of the 102 responses to the question "To what or whom are you loyal?" was "to the company." In contrast, having friendly supervisors and co-workers were important bases of attachment for maquiladora respondents. Several respondents stated that they stayed at the organization due to effective relations with co-workers and supervisors, and 66% of respondents indicated they were loyal to supervisors or co-workers when asked what they were loyal to with respect to work. Having cooperative and friendly co-workers is important to Mexican workers (Bond & Wang, 1983; Stoddard, 1987; Triandis, 1989). In addition, the role of the supervisor reportedly takes on special importance in the Mexican culture, as the supervisor-worker relationship is often extremely paternalistic (Kras, 1989). Management's role is to take care of the workers and workers become a manager's "extended family" (Teagarden et al., 1992). Thus, it is likely that individuals in the Mexican context may not have loyalty to the organization as a whole, but may form strong loyalties to certain people in the organization. In line with the constituent-based theory of organizational commitment (Hunt & Morgan, 1994; Reichers, 1985), commitment to supervisors and co-workers are likely essential determinants of turnover in Mexico.

Although the Maertz et al. (1996) results indicated that employees might not feel affective commitment to the organization (Meyer & Allen, 1997), their results did show that employees can feel bound to employers through continuance commitment. Continuance commitment represents the perceived costs of leaving an organization and can be characterized as a "need" to stay (Meyer & Allen, 1997). Continuance commitment can bind workers to their employers because individuals believe that they would lose too much if they were to quit. For example, employees generally lose all bonuses based on seniority when they quit to work elsewhere, and this decreases the probability that an individual will quit. Many maquiladoras provide various seniority-based inducements (e.g., bonuses, vacation time and premiums) that are forfeited when workers seek employment elsewhere, thereby increasing the financial costs of quitting (Miller, Hom, & Gomez-Mejia, 2001). Firm-specific training or knowledge that is not transferable to other firms can also bind employees to their current employers as other employers would not offer a premium for such idiosyncratic skills (cf. Price & Mueller, 1986). Many of the tasks performed by workers in maquiladoras are unique to a specific product of a single firm, and thus skills acquired at one factory may not be readily transferred to other positions (Stoddard, 1987; Tiano, 1994). In addition, firm-specific experience and job seniority may lead to greater promotion opportunities, which are highly valued (Maertz et al., 1996). Basically, advancement prospects are also given up when maquiladora workers quit (cf. Mitchell, Holtom, Lee, Sablynski, & Erez, 2001). Maertz et al. concluded that continuance commitment is a relevant construct for reducing turnover in the Mexican context.

A key work value of Maertz et al.'s (1996) respondents was the extent to which their employer helped them deal with the conflicts between work and family responsibilities. Respondents preferred to work at places where management provided flexibility for dealing with family issues. In the Mexican culture, the family is of paramount importance and a high priority is placed on family and family responsibilities (e.g., Diaz-Guerrero, 1967; Kras & Whatley, 1990). Mexicans believe in taking care of all members of the family system, including not only small children, but also brothers and sisters, and elderly parents and relatives (Teagarden et al., 1992). Although working to meet the economic needs of their family, work demands may nonetheless conflict with workers' other family obligations, such as child-rearing or elder care, especially for female workers (Tiano, 1994). Paik and Teagarden (1995) identify family issues as one of the pivotal strategic challenges to organizational effectiveness in Mexico because work-family conflict issues often spill over to the workplace and increase absenteeism and turnover. Indeed, family reasons are a legitimate excuse for absence in the eyes of Mexican workers (Teagarden et al., 1992). Because of the extreme importance of the family in Mexico, Maertz et al. concluded that workers appreciate efforts by supervisors and organizations to reduce these conflicts, and prefer to be employed by companies that respect family interests.

West (2000) followed up Maertz et al.'s (1996) valuable insights into the turnover process in the maquiladoras with another qualitative study conducted with firms in Mexicali, Mexico. Her project included in-depth interviews with human resource managers and focus group interviews with workers. The companies involved in the project ranged from American-owned maquiladoras, to Mexican firms, to other foreign-owned companies. According to the human resource managers, the primary reasons that employees quit included conflict with family-care and work responsibilities, conflict with work and school schedules, homesickness, having to work in harsh working conditions, and poor relationships with the supervisor or co-workers. The quality of the supervisory relationship was considered to be a key factor in retaining workers. All the human resource managers emphasized the variety of benefits offered by their firm to reduce turnover, including life insurance and company saving plans, organized athletic and social activities, transportation programs and attendance and performance incentives.

The focus group interviews conducted by West (2000) included employees ranging from entry-level assembly workers to professional employees. The participants' comments highlighted the importance of salary and benefits on turnover decisions. Respondents had left previous employers for wage increases and confirmed that many of their former co-workers had quit for better wages. Satisfaction with benefits was a primary reason why employees did not leave, as those individuals with several years of seniority thought they would lose too much in seniority-based benefits to quit the company. Additionally, training and development opportunities were highly valued by the individuals. Several people acknowledged that they were staying with their current company because of the opportunities for skill acquisition and the possibility of receiving a promotion in the future. Further, respondents stated that "work atmosphere" was an important consideration for employees. If relationships with the supervisor or co-workers were not effective, this would contribute to turnover decisions, even if the company offered acceptable compensation packages.

In order to develop a more comprehensive understanding of turnover processes in Mexico, enhanced model development and testing in the Mexican context needs to be conducted. The model developed here seeks to achieve the first of these goals by integrating insights gained from the limited work that has been conducted on the topic, including the Maertz et al. (1996) and West (2000) qualitative studies, to create a model that depicts the turnover process in Mexico. In the proposed model, constructs uniquely relevant for turnover decisions in Mexico are combined with constructs and linkages supported by previous turnover research findings that are likely to hold more universally. The proposed model is presented and described in the following section.

A MODEL OF THE TURNOVER PROCESS IN MEXICO

The unfolding model (Lee & Mitchell, 1994) framework is a major new theory on turnover decisions. Nonetheless, empirical tests by Lee and colleagues (Lee et al., 1999; Lee et al., 1996) conceded that 55% of the cases "conform fairly well to processes depicted by traditional turnover models" (Lee et al., 1996, p. 32). Thus, rather than select the new approach espoused by Lee and colleagues over the traditional approach as exemplified by Hom and Griffeth (1995), it seems more appropriate for researchers to develop turnover models integrating both perspectives given their empirical support.

The current objective is to develop a comprehensive model that represents the turnover process for employees in Mexico. The integrative model presented in Figure 10.1 synthesizes constructs from the traditional and new

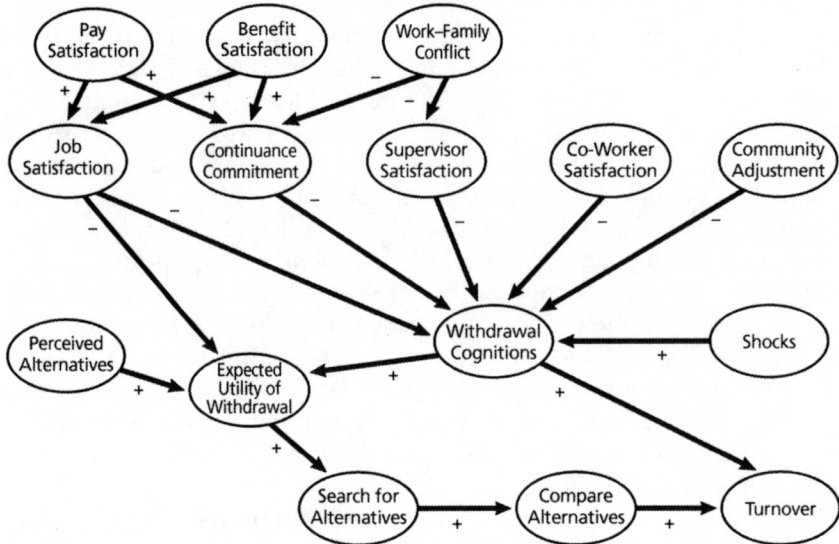

Figure 10.1.   A model of the turnover process for Mexican employees.

domestic theories to develop a framework for understanding turnover decisions in Mexico. Specifically, consistent with Hom and Griffeth's (1995) framework, the proposed model emphasizes the role of job attitudes and the factors that bind employees to their current employer. However, to be consistent with our current understanding of turnover decisions in Mexico based on available evidence, the proposed model includes continuance organizational commitment instead of affective organizational commitment. Furthermore, this model includes supervisor satisfaction and co-worker satisfaction as separate determinants that contribute to withdrawal cognitions. Borrowing from the unfolding model (Lee & Mitchell, 1994), the present framework emphasizes the role of nonwork factors that may independently contribute to withdrawal cognitions. Specifically, the notion of nonwork shocks from the unfolding model and degree of community adjustment—promulgated by Shaffer and Harrison's (1998) model of expatriate turnover—are proposed as antecedents to withdrawal cognitions. The research supporting each model linkage is presented in the sections that follow and specific hypotheses are presented after each relationship.

Pay Satisfaction ➤ Job Satisfaction

Research has indicated that pay satisfaction is an important predictor of job satisfaction (Heneman, Greenberger, & Strasser, 1988; Hom & Griffeth, 1995; Ting, 1997). Heneman et al. found a significant positive relationship between job satisfaction and pay level. Ting's results indicated that pay satisfaction and job satisfaction were significantly correlated and that pay satisfaction had significant effects on increasing job satisfaction. Brown and Peterson's (1993) meta-analysis demonstrated that the corrected correlation between pay and job satisfaction was .26 and furthermore the researchers concluded that greater job satisfaction is associated with higher pay. Work by Price and Mueller (1981, 1986) has validated the link between pay and satisfaction. The results of West (2000) indicate this relationship is likely to hold true in Mexico as well—especially given the poor standard of living faced by Mexican nationals (Miller et al., 2001), and therefore the first hypothesis is:

Hypothesis 1: *Pay satisfaction is positively related to job satisfaction.*

Pay Satisfaction ➤ Continuance Commitment

Individuals who believe that they are being paid more than they would receive at other firms are more likely to feel bound to the employer to continue to receive high wages (Farrell & Rusbult, 1981; Wallace, 1997). Mathieu and Zajac's (1990) meta-analysis indicated a corrected correlation between pay satisfaction and continuance commitment of .31. In the Maertz et al. (1996) study, 20% of responses cited pay or benefits being too low as the reason why respondents believed there is substantial turnover in the maquiladoras. Consequently, the second hypothesis in the model is:

Hypothesis 2: *Perceptions of pay satisfaction are positively related to continuance commitment.*

Benefit Satisfaction ➤ Job Satisfaction

A limited number of empirical studies have dealt specifically with how benefits impact job satisfaction, and even less is known about how benefits influence valued organizational outcomes (Dreher, Ash, & Bretz, 1988). However, satisfaction with benefits and the availability of benefits have been found to covary with job satisfaction (Heshizer, 1994). Goldberg, Greenberger, Kock-Jones, O'Neil, and Hamill (1989) determined that employee satisfaction with benefits was associated with higher levels of job satisfaction. Firms in Mexico rely on a variety of benefits to attract and retain workers (Miller et al., 2001) and benefits represent a substantial portion of total compensation in Mexico (Teagarden & Von Glinow, 1990).

Thus, benefit satisfaction is likely to increase job satisfaction, and the following relationship is proposed:

Hypothesis 3:   *Benefit satisfaction is positively related to job satisfaction.*

Benefit Satisfaction ➤ Continuance Commitment

As with satisfaction with pay, firms that provide valued benefits create situations where employees believe that they should not quit (Becker, 1960; Meyer & Allen, 1997; Mitchell et al., 2001). Certain benefits (e.g., pension, vacation time) are generally not transferable across firms and therefore can serve as deterrents to job changes (Mitchell, 1982). The loss of benefits and the forfeiting of seniority-based benefits can be perceived as potential costs of leaving a company and employees may be reluctant to quit if a particular firm offers a superior benefits package (Meyer & Allen, 1991, 1997). The fact that firms in Mexico mainly compete for employees through benefits results in some companies offering better benefits than others. Individuals will perceive the costs of quitting to be higher if they believe that the benefits they receive from their current employer are better than the benefits offered by other firms. For example, Miller et al. (2001) demonstrated that maquiladora plants that offer higher profit-sharing and company savings plans have lower turnover rates. Thus, the proposed model indicates the following relationship:

Hypothesis 4:   *Benefit satisfaction is positively related to continuance commitment.*

Work-Family Conflict ➤ Continuance Commitment

Work-family conflict has been defined as "interrole conflict in which the general demands of, time devoted to, and strain created by the job interfere with performing family-related responsibilities" (Netemeyer, Boles, & McMurrian, 1996, p. 400). Mexicans consider family to be their primary responsibility and a high priority is placed on meeting family responsibilities (Diaz-Guerrero, 1967; Kras & Whatley, 1990; Maertz et al., 1996; Selby & Murphy, 1982). However, work demands (not just hours and scheduling but also commuting distance) might conflict with a worker's care-giving duties, especially for women in the Mexican culture (Tiano, 1994). Because of the extreme importance of the family in Mexico, workers appreciate efforts by organizations to reduce these conflicts, and prefer to be employed by companies that respect family interests (Maertz et al., 1996).

If the company eases work interference with family activities, workers are likely to feel bound to a particular employer, thus creating a continuance commitment attachment (Netemeyer et al., 1996). Wallace (1997) theorizes that a person's level of nonwork responsibilities impacts an employee's continuance commitment to the organization because individuals with important nonwork responsibilities are less willing to lose the firm-specific skill investments that have been made in the firm. Respondents in the Goldberg et al. (1989) study reported that they would leave their current employer if a new employer offered better family-friendly benefits. Grover and Crooker (1995) demonstrated that employees who had access to family-responsive policies felt higher continuance commitment. In the Stoddard (1987) study, 66% of respondents indicated that they stayed at their current maquiladora because of family care reasons (p. 47). Moreover, respondents in the Maertz et al. (1996) study expressed great interest in employers who allowed them to take care of children or other family members. Based on these reasons, the following relationship is proposed:

Hypothesis 5: *Work-family conflict is negatively related to continuance commitment.*

Work-Family Conflict ➤ Supervisor Satisfaction

Thomas and Ganster (1995) note that a family-supportive work environment is a function of family-supportive organizational policies and family-supportive supervisors. Anecdotal and empirical evidence supports the notion that the relationship with the supervisor is a major influence on work-family problems and affects employees' belief that they can effectively balance their family and work responsibilities (Aryee, Luk, & Stone, 1998). Scheduling flexibility offered by the supervisor can reduce the conflict between work and family demands. Supervisors who accommodate employees' desire to balance their work and family responsibilities will contribute to employee satisfaction (Thomas & Ganster, 1995). Aryee et al. found that satisfaction with supervisor work-family support was positively related to commitment and negatively related to turnover intentions. In contrast, Tepper (2000) demonstrated that abusive supervision augmented work-family conflict.

Similarly, Mexican supervisors play a role in alleviating work-family tensions for maquiladora workers. To illustrate, Maertz et al. (1996) observed that supervisors in Mexican facilities often control work assignments and task responsibilities. Providing "easier jobs" to certain individuals is one way that supervisors can reduce work-family conflict because the individuals are not as tired when they leave work. Furthermore, supervisors can approve *permissos*, or workers' requests for time off. The Maertz et al. study indicated that loyalty was fostered when supervisors provided flexibility for care giving responsibilities. Maertz et al. concluded that Mexican workers will feel the greatest satisfaction with supervisors who generously approve permissos and assign less demanding jobs. Therefore, the following relationship is proposed:

Hypothesis 6:   *Work-family conflict is negatively related to supervisor satisfaction.*

Job Satisfaction ➤ Withdrawal Cognitions

Central to all turnover perspectives is that poor job attitudes underlie turnover decisions (Hom & Griffeth, 1995). Job satisfaction plays a pivotal role in many theories of turnover and tests of these models have indicated that job satisfaction is negatively related to withdrawal cognitions. A meta-analysis by Tett and Meyer (1993) demonstrated that job satisfaction is a strong antecedent of withdrawal cognitions. Furthermore, Hom and Griffeth (1991) found a strong negative structural relationship between job satisfaction and withdrawal cognitions. Given the consistent relationship between job satisfaction and withdrawal cognitions found in the research, the following hypothesis is offered for the Mexican context:

Hypothesis 7:   *Job satisfaction is negatively related to withdrawal cognitions.*

Continuance Commitment ➤ Withdrawal Cognitions

Meyer and Allen (1997) note that common to all commitment frameworks is the belief that commitment should be negatively correlated with employees' intentions to leave the organization. Continuance commitment is a function of employees' job investments and the perceived opportunity costs of leaving (Farrell & Rusbult, 1981). Significant negative relationships between continuance commitment and withdrawal behaviors have been noted in the literature (Allen & Meyer, 1996; Jaros, Jermier, Koehler, & Sincich, 1993; Mathieu & Zajac, 1990). The results of Jaros et al. indicated a negative correlation between continuance commitment and thinking of quitting and search intentions. Mathieu and Zajac's meta-analysis indicated a negative correlation between continuance commitment and intention to leave. Based on these research findings, the following relationship is hypothesized:

Hypothesis 8:   *Continuance commitment is negatively related to withdrawal cognitions.*

Supervisor Satisfaction ➤ Withdrawal Cognitions

Turnover and commitment research have empirically demonstrated the relationship between supervisor attachment and the desire to remain with an organization (Aquino, Griffeth, Allen, & Hom, 1997; Griffeth, Hom, & Gaertner, 2000; Hom & Griffeth, 1995; Jaros et al., 1993). Specifically, Aquino et al. demonstrated that supervisor satisfaction lowered withdrawal cognitions. Two meta-analyses conducted by Griffeth and Hom (Griffeth et al., 2000; Hom & Griffeth, 1995) indicated strong relationships between various supervisory behaviors and turnover. Given the special role of the supervisory relationship in the Mexican culture, the quality of the interaction and relationship with the supervisor is likely related to job tenure in the Mexican context (Kras & Whatley, 1990; Lawrence & Yeh, 1994). For example, respondents in Stoddard (1987) indicated that the relationship with the supervisor was one of the primary reasons they continued working for their current employer. Thus, the following hypothesis is offered:

Hypothesis 9:   *Supervisor satisfaction is negatively related to withdrawal cognitions.*

Co-Worker Satisfaction ➤ Withdrawal Cognitions

Meyer and Allen (1997) note that individuals who have strong attachments to their co-workers may experience less interest in leaving the organization. The potential to disrupt personal relations can be perceived as a cost of leaving a company (Meyer & Allen, 1991). Individuals who have effective relationships with their co-workers may choose to remain employed with the organization to avoid breaking social ties (Cohen, 2000; Mitchell et al., 2001; Randall & Cote, 1991). Previous research has found that commitment to work groups is an important determinant of intentions to quit (Becker, 1992). Moreover, research by Cohen (2000) indicated that group commitment and turnover intentions were negatively correlated.

A positive interpersonal relationship with co-workers is important to Mexican workers (Bond & Wang, 1983; Stoddard, 1987; Triandis, 1989). Respondents in the Maertz et al. (1996) study indicated that friendship with co-workers fosters attachment to employers by providing roots. The workers expressed worry about having to find new friends if they changed employers. Stoddard's (1987) research at five maquiladoras found that more than 60% of current employees reported that close co-worker relations were the reason they stayed with the company (p. 47). A negative relationship between co-worker satisfaction and withdrawal behaviors could therefore be expected in the Mexican context. Thus:

Hypothesis 10:   *Co-worker satisfaction is negatively related to withdrawal cognitions.*

Community Adjustment ➤ Withdrawal Cognitions

Steers and Mowday (1981) indicate that thoughts of quitting can be cued by affective responses to jobs and nonwork variables. Many models of turnover assume that nonwork variables remain constant, and therefore focus on affective responses to jobs (Black & Gregersen, 1990). However, nonwork variables assume more importance when workers have significant changes in their nonwork situation, such as when individuals relocate to a new community or country (Black & Gregersen, 1990; Fisher & Shaw, 1994; Shaffer & Harrison, 1998). In Black and Gregersen's study of American expatriate managers in Japan, general adjustment was the only significant predictor of intentions to leave. Furthermore, Shaffer and Harrison demonstrated that nonwork satisfaction was a direct determinate of expatriate withdrawal cognitions. These results indicate nonwork adjustment or satisfaction with a new community play a critical role in withdrawal behaviors when employees are adjusting to very different lifestyles.

As indicated earlier, there is an imbalance between local supply of labor and local demand for labor in Mexico, with the number of jobs along the border outnumbering the local workforce. Such economic forces drive immigration from the Mexican interior to fill the available positions. Although border migrants are not leaving their native country, life on the border is vastly different than life in rural Mexico, and they will experience many changes that will require a degree of adjustment (Maertz, 1999). Workers who move to the border miss their hometowns and are often unprepared for how different life is on the border. These youthful migrants will need to make new friends, adjust to costlier living in a larger metropolitan area, and deal with being separated from their family back home. If newcomers are unhappy with their new living situation, they are more likely to want to move back to their home community or else temporarily return for short visits. Individuals who have adjusted well to their new community would be less likely to quit to return to their home community (or taking temporary "vacations"; Miller et al., 2001), whereas individuals unhappy with the area would be at greater risk of quitting. How well a person has adjusted to the new community may be related to withdrawal cognitions (Maertz, 1999). Therefore, the following relationship is offered:

Hypothesis 11: *Community adjustment is negatively related to withdrawal cognitions.*

Shocks ➤ Withdrawal Cognitions

The unfolding model (Lee & Mitchell, 1994) emphasizes the impact of shocks in the decision-making process culminating in a person's decision to stay or quit. Some shocks are directly related to the work context, such as a change in supervisor or a company merger, and therefore would be reflected in the person's level of job satisfaction. In contrast, other shocks may not be directly related to the person's job nor impact the level of job satisfaction but still result in a quit decision (Lee et al., 1996). For example, an unplanned pregnancy would not impact job satisfaction, but the person may begin to think about quitting if she had planned to stay at home to raise her child when she became pregnant (i.e., matching script). Therefore, shocks can directly trigger withdrawal cognitions. The following hypothesis expresses this relationship:

Hypothesis 12: *Shocks increase withdrawal cognitions.*

Withdrawal Cognitions ➤ Expected Utility of Withdrawal

Hom and Griffeth (1991) proposed that if higher levels of withdrawal cognitions do not result in immediate turnover, they will result in the person evaluating the expected utility of withdrawal from the organization. Expected utility of withdrawal is the process of evaluating the perceived costs and benefits of quitting and searching for another job (Hom & Griffeth, 1995). Research by Hom and colleagues (Hom & Griffeth, 1991, Hom, Griffeth & Sellaro, 1984) has supported this proposed relationship between withdrawal cognitions and the expected utility of withdrawal. Hom et al. demonstrated by using hierarchical regression that the expected utility of search and quitting was accurately predicted by thoughts of quitting. Furthermore, the results of Hom and Griffeth (1991) indicated that withdrawal cognitions correlated highly with expected utility of withdrawal and the path loading between the two constructs was significant and positive. Based on these research findings, the proposed model indicates that withdrawal cognitions lead to a subjective assessment of the value of quitting by calculating the expected utility of withdrawal. This results in the following hypothesis:

Hypothesis 13: *Withdrawal cognitions are positively related to the expected utility of withdrawal.*

Job Satisfaction ➤ Expected Utility of Withdrawal

Hom and Griffeth (1991) proposed that job satisfaction was negatively related to the expected utility of withdrawal. This proposed relationship was based on their earlier finding (Hom et al., 1984) that satisfaction with the current job reduced positive beliefs about other possible jobs (perhaps because satisfied incumbents do not enter the labor market and thus form more concrete impressions of job availability). The Hom and Griffeth results supported this proposed relationship as the structural relationship between job satisfaction and expected utility of withdrawal was negative and significant. The following hypothesis is therefore proposed:

Hypothesis 14: *Job satisfaction is negatively related to expected utility of withdrawal.*

Perceived Alternatives ➤ Expected Utility of Withdrawal

Perceived alternatives refer to the perceived favorableness of different jobs and the ease with which alternate employment can be obtained (Chen, Hui, & Sego, 1998). Several preeminent models of turnover indicate that job opportunities influence turnover behaviors, including models developed by March and Simon (1958), Price (1977), and Mobley, Horner, and Hollingsworth (1978). Quit decisions are more likely when individuals perceive that they could obtain a different job that would provide them higher levels of job satisfaction (Hulin, Roznowski, & Hachiya, 1985). Thus, perceptions about the availability of jobs will directly influence beliefs about the expected utility of conducting a job search process (Hom & Griffeth, 1995).

In the Mexican labor market, education often provides workers with the necessary human capital to obtain more rewarding jobs (Tiano, 1994). Education provides workers the flexibility to look for the best jobs, and workers with more education are the most likely to switch jobs (Silvers & Lara Valencia, 1990). Similarly, relevant work experience may allow workers to progress to better jobs in the labor market (Silvers & Lara Valencia, 1990). Workers who believe that their education or work experience provides them with more job alternatives will have stronger beliefs about the expected utility of withdrawal. The following relationship is thus hypothesized:

Hypothesis 15: *A positive relationship will exist between perceived alternatives and the expected utility of withdrawal.*

Expected Utility of Withdrawal ➤ Search for Alternatives

Mobley (1977) proposed that if the expected utility of withdrawal is perceived to be positive, workers will search for other jobs. If a person believes that the costs of quitting are outweighed by the benefits and if the costs of searching for a new job are not prohibitive, the person will search for new job alternatives. Thus, the higher the perceived utility of quitting, the greater the search for alternatives. The results of Hom et al. (1984) support this relationship by demonstrating that the expected utility of searching and quitting directly impacted search intention. The results of Hom and Griffeth (1991) again support this relationship, as the structural path between expected utility of withdrawal and job search was positive and significant. Consistent with these research findings, the proposed model indicates a positive relationship between the expected utility of withdrawal and the search for alternatives. Therefore,

Hypothesis 16: *Expected utility of withdrawal is positively related to the search for alternatives.*

Search for Alternatives ➤ Compare Alternatives

Mobley (1977) proposed that if a worker is able to identify job alternatives, the individual will subsequently compare the various options. The Hom and Griffeth (1991) results support this idea with a significant path association (.58) between job search and comparison of alternatives. The proposed model therefore indicates a causal relationship between the search for alternatives and comparison of alternatives. The following hypothesis expresses this relationship:

Hypothesis 17: *Search for alternatives is positively related to the comparison of alternatives.*

Comparison of Alternatives ➤ Turnover

Under the Mobley (1977) model, if a worker is able to locate an alternative that is perceived to be better than the current position, the individual will terminate the employment relationship. Hom et al. (1984) validated this relationship by demonstrating that comparison of alternatives accounted for a significant unique variance in turnover intention. Furthermore, Hom and Griffeth (1991) demonstrated a significant negative relationship between comparison of alternatives and retention. Finally, Griffeth et al. (2000) found the corrected population correlation between comparison of alternatives and turnover was .19. The proposed model therefore indicates a causal relationship between the comparison of alternatives and turnover. This relationship is expressed in the following hypothesis:

Hypothesis 18: *Comparison of alternatives is positively related to turnover.*

Withdrawal Cognitions ➤ Turnover

Although withdrawal cognitions may trigger an evaluation of the expected utility of withdrawal as discussed with Hypothesis 13, another possible result of withdrawal cognitions is that they will lead directly to turnover (Hom & Griffeth, 1991). Individuals who follow this path to turnover do not actively seek employment prior to quitting. These individuals may plan to look for a job after quitting or may be exiting the workforce (Griffeth & Hom, 1988; Hom & Griffeth, 1991). Research supports the direct link between withdrawal cognitions and turnover (Griffeth et al., 2000; Hom et al., 1984; Mitchell & Lee, 2001; Tett & Meyer, 1993). Tett and Meyer found that withdrawal cognitions were the strongest predictor of turnover. Hom and Griffeth (1991) found that withdrawal cognitions were negatively related to retention. Sager, Griffeth, and Hom (1998) compared several models of withdrawal cognitions and found consistent positive relationships between withdrawal cognitions and turnover. The metaanalysis conducted by Griffeth et al. (2000) indicated a corrected correlation between withdrawal cognitions and turnover of .36. Thus, a strong relationship between withdrawal cognitions and turnover should be expected. Accordingly:

Hypothesis 19: *Withdrawal cognitions are positively related to turnover.*

FUTURE RESEARCH IMPLICATIONS

The premise of the model developed here is that constructs from the Hom and Griffeth (1995) turnover model and the unfolding model (Lee & Mitchell, 1994) can be modified to fit the context in Mexico and accurately explain employee turnover decisions. Previously, no model of turnover has been developed and empirically tested specifically from the perspective of the Mexican culture. Empirical research is needed to confirm or refute the proposed model linkages and the overall appropriateness of the model. The proposed model indicates that culture-specific constructs play a more important role in explaining turnover in the Mexican context, and empirical evidence is needed to support these linkages.

In order to empirically test the proposed model, it will be necessary to develop a survey instrument that is appropriate for the Mexican culture. One concern will be that the average education level in Mexico is lower than in the United States. Although many individuals complete *preparatoria*, which is comparable to high school in the United States, many maquiladoras only require completion of *secundaria* (cf. junior high), for employment. Thus, survey items must be consistent with the reading level of respondents. Moreover, scale items will need to be developed for the Spanish language. If existing English survey items are used, the scales must be translated into Spanish in a manner that results in a translation of the intended meaning of the items. The translation approach suggested by Brisling (1980) should be utilized: English scale items should be translated into Spanish by a trained individual and then other native speakers should independently conduct a back-translation process whereby the survey items are translated into English to verify translation accuracy.

In addition to developing an appropriate survey instrument, research is needed to test the proposed model linkages. It is possible that the proposed linkages do not characterize turnover decisions for all worker types in Mexico. For example, the model assumes that Mexican employees conduct job search and evaluation activities prior to quitting. It is possible though that individuals in this labor market are inclined to quit without investigating specific job alternatives beforehand because a new job can be obtained immediately with little effort (cf. Hom & Kinicki, 2001; Mitchell & Lee, 2001). Individuals with higher levels of education have more job opportunities in Mexico and thus may feel less need to actively seek and secure jobs prior to quitting. Similarly, young individuals without family responsibilities (i.e., spouses or children) may quit without a specific job alternative because no one else is impacted by their unemployment, versus those individuals with substantial family responsibilities might feel uneasy about quitting without a specific job option. Research is therefore needed to determine the extent to which Mexican employees locate and evaluate alternate employment prior to quitting.

Furthermore, the impact of gender differences on the proposed model linkages should be investigated. Although the family is important to both men and women in the Mexican culture, women still assume primary caregiving responsibilities. It is possible that the proposed model linkages for work family conflict will have greater importance for Mexican women as compared to Mexican men. In contrast, men are still regarded as the primary breadwinners for the family unit. Thus, pay adequacy and benefit satisfaction may prove to be more important to men in determining job satisfaction and continuance commitment than for women.

The proposed model should be viewed as an initial attempt to understand turnover processes in Mexico. Empirical research will likely result in modifications to the proposed linkages and contribute to greater understanding of the Mexican culture. Only by viewing turnover from the perspective of the Mexican culture and developing turnover models that are unique to this environment will we be able to fully understand turnover processes in this international context.

ACKNOWLEDGMENT

This research was funded in part by a grant from the Associated Students, the Graduate College and the Office of the Vice-Provost for Research of Arizona State University.

Correspondence concerning this article should be addressed to Mindy S. West, Imperial Valley Campus, San Diego State University, 720 Heber Avenue, Calexico, CA 92231. E-mail: mswest@mail.sdsu.edu.

REFERENCES

Allen, N.J., & Meyer, J.P. (1996). Affective, continuance, and normative commitment to the organization: An examination of construct validity. *Journal of Vocational Behavior, 49,* 252–276.

Alvarez, A.J. (1985). *Prediction of turnover in a maquiladora from demographic variables.* Unpublished master's thesis, University of Texas at El Paso.

Aquino, K., Griffeth, R.W., Allen, D.G., & Hom, P.W. (1997). Integrating justice constructs into the turnover process: A test of a referent cognitions model. *Academy of Management Journal, 40,* 1208–1227.

Aryee, S., Luk, V., & Stone, R. (1998). Family responsive variables and retention-relevant outcomes among employed parents. *Human Relations, 51,* 73–87.

Bannister, B., & Peña, L. (1993). Turnover in the maquiladora industry in Mexico: A challenge of transferring high technology production processes to developing countries. In L. Gomez-Mejia & M. Lawless (Eds.), *Advances in global high technology management* (Vol. 4, pp. 199–218). Greenwich, CT: JAI Press.

Becker, H.S. (1960). Notes on the concept of commitment. *American Journal of Sociology, 65,* 32–42.

Becker, T.E. (1992). Foci and bases of commitment: Are they distinctions worth making? *Academy of Management Journal, 35,* 232–244.

Black, J.S., & Gregersen, H.B. (1990). Expectations, satisfaction, and intention to leave of American expatriate managers in Japan. *International Journal of Intercultural Relations, 14,* 485–506.

Bond, M.H., & Wang, S.H. (1983). Aggressive behavior in Chinese society: The problem of maintaining order and harmony. In A.P. Goldstein & M. Segall (Eds.), *Global perspectives on aggression* (pp. 58–74). New York: Pergamon.

Boyacigiller, N.A., & Adler, N.J. (1991). The parochial dinosaur: Organizational science in a global context. *Academy of Management Review, 16,* 262–290.

Brown, S.P., & Peterson, R.A. (1993). Antecedents and consequences of salesperson job satisfaction. *Journal of Marketing Research, 30,* 63–77.

Cascio, W.F. (1991). *Costing human resources: The financial impact of behavior in organizations* (3rd ed.). Boston: Kent.

Chen, X., Hui, C., & Sego, D.J. (1998). The role of organizational citizenship behavior in turnover: Conceptualization and preliminary tests of key hypotheses. *Journal of Applied Psychology, 83,* 922–931.

Cohen, A. (2000). The relationship between commitment forms and work outcomes: A comparison of three models. *Human Relations, 53,* 387–417.

Diaz-Guerrero, R. (1967). *Psychology of the Mexican: Culture and personality.* Austin: University of Texas Press.

Dreher, G.F., Ash, R.A., & Bretz, R.D. (1988). Benefit coverage and employee cost: Critical factors in explaining compensation satisfaction. *Personnel Psychology, 41,* 237–254.

English, W., Williams, S., & Ibarreche, S. (1989). Employee turnover in the maquiladoras. *Journal of Borderlands Studies, 4*(2), 70–99.

Farrell, D., & Rusbult, C.E. (1981). Exchange variables as predictors of job satisfaction, job commitment, and turnover: The impact of rewards, costs, alternatives, and investments. *Organizational Behavior and Human Performance, 28,* 78–95.

Fernández-Kelly, M.P. (1983). *For we are sold, I and my people: Women in Mexico's frontier.* Albany: State University of New York Press.

Fisher, C.D., & Shaw, J.S. (1994). Relocation attitudes and adjustment: A longitudinal study. *Journal of Organizational Behavior, 15,* 209–224.

Goldberg, W.A., Greenberger, E., Kock-Jones, J., O'Neil, R., & Hamill, S. (1989). Attractiveness of child care and related employer-supported benefits and policies to married and single parents. *Child & Youth Care Quarterly, 18,* 23–37.

Griffeth, R.W., & Hom, P.W. (1988). A comparison of different conceptualizations of perceived alternatives in turnover research. *Journal of Organizational Behavior, 9,* 103–111.

Griffeth, R.W., & Hom, P.W. (1990, August). *Competitive examination of two turnover theories: A two-sample test.* Paper presented at the annual meeting of the Academy of Management, San Francisco, CA.

Griffeth, R.W., Hom, P.W, & Gaertner, S. (2000). A meta-analysis of antecedents and correlates of employee turnover: Update, moderator tests, and research implications for the next millennium. *Journal of Management, 26,* 463–488.

Grover, S.L., & Crooker, K.J. (1995). Who appreciates family-responsive human resource policies: The impact of family-friendly policies on the organizational attachment of parents and non-parents. *Personnel Psychology, 48,* 271–288.

Hecht, L., & Morici, P. (1993). Managing risks in Mexico. *Harvard Business Review, July-August,* 32–40.

Heneman, R.L., Greenberger, D.B., & Strasser, S. (1988). The relationship between pay-for-performance perceptions and pay satisfaction. *Personnel Psychology, 41,* 745–759.

Heshizer, B. (1994). The impact of flexible benefits plans on job satisfaction, organizational commitment and turnover intentions. *Benefits Quarterly, 10*(4), 84–90.

Hofstede, G. (1980). *Culture's consequences: International differences in work-related values.* Beverly Hills, CA: Sage Publications.

Hofstede, G. (1983). The cultural relativity of organizational practices and theories. *Journal of International Business Studies, 14,* 75–89.

Hom, P.W., & Griffeth, R.W. (1991). Structural equations modeling test of a turnover theory: Cross-sectional and longitudinal analyses. *Journal of Applied Psychology, 76,* 350–366.

Hom, P.W., & Griffeth, R.W. (1995). *Employee turnover.* Cincinnati, OH: Southwestern Publishing Company.

Hom, P.W., Griffeth, R.W., & Sellaro, L. (1984). The validity of Mobley's (1977) model of employee turnover. *Organizational Behavior and Human Performance, 34,* 141–174.

Hom, P.W., & Kinicki, A.J. (2001). Toward a greater understanding of how dissatisfaction drives employee turnover. *Academy of Management Journal, 44,* 975–987.

Hulin, C.L., Roznowski, M., & Hachiya, D. (1985). Alternative opportunities and withdrawal decisions: Empirical and theoretical discrepancies and an integration. *Psychological Bulletin, 97,* 233–250.

Hunt, S.D., & Morgan, R.M. (1994). Organizational commitment: One of many commitments or key mediating construct? *Academy of Management Journal, 37,* 1568–1587.

Jaros, S.J., Jermier, J.M., Koehler, J.W., & Sincich, T. (1993). Effects of continuance, affective, and moral commitment on the withdrawal process: An evaluation of eight structural equation models. *Academy of Management Journal, 36,* 951–995.

Kras, E.S. (1989). *Management in two cultures: Bridging the gap between U.S. and Mexican managers.* Yarmouth, ME: Intercultural Press Inc.

Kras, E.S., & Whatley, A. (1990). Using organizational development technology in Mexico: Issues and problems. *International Journal of Management, 7,* 196–204.

Lawrence, J.J., & Yeh, R. (1994). The influence of Mexican culture on the use of Japanese manufacturing techniques in Mexico. *Management International Review, 34,* 49–66.

Lee, T.W., & Mitchell, T.R. (1994). An alternative approach: The unfolding model of voluntary employee turnover. *Academy of Management Review, 19,* 51–89.

Lee, T.W., Mitchell, T.R., Holtom, B.C., McDaniel, L.S., & Hill, J.W. (1999). The unfolding model of voluntary turnover: A replication and extension. *Academy of Management Journal, 42,* 450–462.

Lee, T.W., Mitchell, T.R., Wise, L., Fireman, S. (1996). An unfolding model of voluntary employee turnover. *Academy of Management Journal, 39,* 5–36.

Lucker. G.W. (1987). The hidden cost of worker turnover: A case study in the in-bond industry in Mexico. *Journal of Borderlands Studies, 2,* 93–98.

Maertz, C.P. (1999). Biographical predictors of turnover among Mexican workers: An empirical study. *International Journal of Management, 16,* 112–119.

Maertz, C.P., Stevens, M.J., Campion, M.A., & Fernandez, A. (1996, August). *Worker turnover in Mexican factories: A qualitative investigation and model development.* Paper presented at the annual meeting of the Academy of Management, Cincinnati, OH.

March, J.G., & Simon, H.A. (1958). *Organizations.* New York: John Wiley.

Mathieu, J.E., & Zajac, D.M. (1990). A review and meta-analysis of the antecedents, correlates, and consequences of organizational commitment. *Psychological Bulletin, 108,* 171–194.

Meyer, J.P., & Allen, N.J. (1991). A three-component conceptualization of organizational commitment. *Human Resource Management Review, 1,* 61–98.

Meyer, J.P., & Allen, N.J. (1997). *Commitment in the workplace: Theory, research, and application.* Thousand Oaks, CA: Sage Publications.

Miller, J.S., Hom, P.W., & Gomez-Mejia, L.R. (2001). The high costs of low wages: Does maquiladora compensation reduce turnover? *Journal of International Business Studies 32*, 585–595.

Mitchell, O.S. (1982). Fringe benefits and labor mobility. *The Journal of Human Resources, 17*, 286–298.

Mitchell, T.R., Holtom, B.C., Lee, T.W., Sablynski, C.J., & Erez, M. (2001). Why people stay: Using job embeddedness to predict voluntary turnover. *Academy of Management Journal, 44*, 1102–1121.

Mitchell, T.R., & Lee, T.W. (2001). The unfolding model of voluntary turnover and job embeddedness: Foundations for a comprehensive theory of attachment. *Research in Organizational Behavior, 23*, 189–246.

Mobley, W.H. (1977). Intermediate linkages in the relationship between job satisfaction and employee turnover. *Journal of Applied Psychology, 62*, 237–240.

Mobley, W.H., Horner, S.O., & Hollingsworth, A.T. (1978). An evaluation of precursors of hospital employee turnover. *Journal of Applied Psychology, 63*, 408–414.

Moffett, M. (1984, July 17). U.S. companies with factories in Mexico are having difficulty in retaining workers. *The Wall Street Journal*, p. A33.

Netemeyer, R.G., Boles, J.S., & McMurrian, R. (1996). Development and validation of work-family conflict and family-work conflict scales. *Journal of Applied Psychology, 78*, 538–551.

Paik, Y., & Teagarden. M.B. (1995). Strategic international human resource management approaches in the maquiladora industry: A comparison of Japanese, Korean and U.S. firms. *International Journal of Human Resource Management, 6*, 568–587.

Price, J.L. (1977). *The study of turnover.* Ames: Iowa State University Press.

Price, J.L., & Mueller, C.W. (1981). *Professional turnover: The case of nurses.* New York: SP Medical and Scientific Books.

Price, J.L., & Mueller, C.W. (1986). *Absenteeism and turnover of hospital employees.* Greenwich, CT: JAI Press.

Randall, D.M., & Cote, J.A. (1991). Interrelationships of work commitment constructs. *Work and Occupations, 18*, 194–211.

Reichers, A.E. (1985). A review and reconceptualization of organizational commitment. *Academy of Management Review, 10*, 465–476.

Sager, J.K., Griffeth, R.W., & Hom, P.W. (1998). A comparison of structural models representing turnover cognitions. *Journal of Vocational Behavior, 53*, 254–273.

Selby, H.A., & Murphy, A.D. (1982). *The Mexican urban household and the decision to migrate to the United States.* Philadelphia: Institute for the Study of Human Issues.

Shaffer, M.A., & Harrison, D.A. (1998). Expatriates' psychological withdrawal from international assignments: Work, nonwork, and family influence. *Personnel Psychology, 51*, 86–118.

Silvers, A., & Lara Valencia, F. (1990). Labor absorption and turnover in the maquila industry. *Arizona Review, 38*, 17–23.

Sklair, L. (1989). *Assembling for development: The maquila industry in Mexico and the United States.* Boston: Unwin Hyman.

Steers, R.M., & Mowday, R.T. (1981). Employee turnover and post-decision accommodation processes. In L. Cummings & B. Staw (Eds.), *Research in organizational behavior* (Vol. 3, pp. 235–281). Greenwich, CT: JAI Press.

Stoddard, E.R. (1987). *Maquila: Assembly plants in northern Mexico.* El Paso, TX: Texas Western.

Teagarden, M.B., Butler, M.C., & Von Glinow, M.A. (1992). Mexico's maquiladora industry: Where strategic human resource management makes a difference. *Organizational Dynamics, Winter, 20*(3), 34–47.

Teagarden, M.B., & Von Glinow, M.A. (1990). Contextual determinants of HRM effectiveness in cooperative alliances: Mexican evidence. *Management International Review, 30, Special Issue,* 23–36.

Tepper, B. (2000). Consequences of abusive supervision. *Academy of Management Journal, 43,* 178–190.

Tett, R.P., & Meyer, J.P. (1993). Job satisfaction, organizational commitment, turnover intention, and turnover: Path analyses based on meta-analytic findings. *Personnel Psychology, 46,* 259–293.

Thomas, L.T., & Ganster, D.C. (1995). Impact of family-supportive work variables on work-family conflict and strain: A control perspective. *Journal of Applied Psychology, 80,* 6–15.

Tiano, S. (1994). *Patriarchy on the line: Labor gender and ideology in the Mexican maquila industry.* Philadelphia: Temple University Press.

Ting, Y. (1997). Determinants of job satisfaction of federal government employees. *Public Personnel Management, 26,* 313–334.

Triandis, H.C. (1989). The self and social behavior in differing cultural contexts. *Psychological Review, 96,* 506–520.

Vargas, L. (1998). The maquiladora industry in historical perspective (Part 2). *Business Frontiers, 4,* 1–6.

Wallace, J.E. (1997). Becker's side-bet theory of commitment revisited: Is it time for a moratorium or a resurrection? *Human Relations, 50,* 727–749.

West, M.S. (2000). *Employee turnover in Mexico: A cultural investigation of causes.* Unpublished doctoral dissertation, Arizona State University, Tempe.

Williams, E.J., & Passé-Smith, J.T. (1989). *Turnover and recruitment in the maquiladora industry: Causes and solutions* (Borderlands Research Monograph Series No. 5). Las Cruces: New Mexico State University, Joint Border Research Institute.

Young, G., & Fort, L. (1994). Household responses to economic change: Migration and maquiladora work in Ciudad Juárez, Mexico. *Social Science Quarterly, 75,* 656–669.